Dartmouth and the World

Dartmouth and the World

Religion and Political Economy circa 1769

Edited by

Henry C. Clark

FAIRLEIGH DICKINSON UNIVERSITY PRESS
Vancouver • Madison • Teaneck • Wroxton

Published by Fairleigh Dickinson University Press
Copublished by The Rowman & Littlefield Publishing Group, Inc.
4501 Forbes Boulevard, Suite 200, Lanham, Maryland 20706
www.rowman.com

86-90 Paul Street, London EC2A 4NE, United Kingdom

Copyright © 2022 by The Rowman & Littlefield Publishing Group, Inc.

All rights reserved. No part of this book may be reproduced in any form or by any electronic or mechanical means, including information storage and retrieval systems, without written permission from the publisher, except by a reviewer who may quote passages in a review.

Fairleigh Dickinson University Press gratefully acknowledges the support received for scholarly publishing from the Friends of FDU Press.

British Library Cataloguing in Publication Information Available

Library of Congress Cataloging-in-Publication Data

Names: Clark, Henry C., editor.
Title: Dartmouth and the world : religion and political economy circa 1769 / edited by Henry C. Clark.
Description: Teaneck, New Jersey : Fairleigh Dickinson University Press ; Lanham, Maryland : Rowman & Littlefield Publishing Group, Inc., 2022. | Includes bibliographical references and index. | Summary: "What are the best ways of thinking about the founding of Dartmouth College in 1769-in the context of the religious, political, and economic history of Britain, colonial America, and even the world? In Dartmouth and the World, a distinguished panel of scholars approaches the issue in a rich variety of ways"—Provided by publisher.
Identifiers: LCCN 2021046091 (print) | LCCN 2021046092 (ebook) | ISBN 9781683933175 (cloth) | ISBN 9781683933199 (paper) | ISBN 9781683933182 (epub)
Subjects: LCSH: Dartmouth College—History. | United States—History—Colonial period, ca. 1600–1775.
Classification: LCC LD1438.3 .D37 2022 (print) | LCC LD1438.3 (ebook) | DDC 378.742/3—dc23/eng/20211018
LC record available at https://lccn.loc.gov/2021046091
LC ebook record available at https://lccn.loc.gov/2021046092

Contents

Acknowledgments	vii
Introduction	1
Chapter 1: 1769: Dartmouth, Machines, and Modernity *Jack A. Goldstone (George Mason University)*	17
Chapter 2: Dartmouth College and Patriot State Building *Steve Pincus (The University of Chicago)*	39
Chapter 3: Life and Living Standards in Britain's Industrial Revolution *Emma Griffin (University of East Anglia)*	65
Chapter 4: George Whitefield's Changing Commercial Theology *Kristen Beales (Warren Center, Harvard University)*	85
Chapter 5: Religious Conversion, the Stamp Act, and Revolution in New England *Mark Valeri (Vanderbilt University)*	109
Chapter 6: The Making of a "Rebel Lady": Gender, Virtue, and Bloodshed in Mercy Otis Warren's Radicalization, 1769–1772 *J. Patrick Mullins, PhD (Marquette University)*	129
Chapter 7: Recovering the Native Origins of Dartmouth College through *The Occom Circle* *Ivy Schweitzer (Dartmouth College)*	153
Index	173
About the Authors	187

Acknowledgments

On behalf of the Political Economy Project, I extend my sincerest thanks to the Academic Planning Committee for Dartmouth's sestercentennial and its co-chairs, Professors Donald Pease (English), Silvia Spitta (Spanish and Comparative Literature) and Dean Wilcox (Chemistry), for their moral and financial support of the scholarly conference that took place on the weekend of Sept. 27–28, 2019, out of which the present volume emerged. Professor Paul Musselwhite of the Department of History was instrumental in the organization and logistics of this conference, and has been a fount of wise and generous counsel in the volume preparation as well. Graziella Parati, then-director of the Leslie Center for the Humanities, also supplied exceedingly useful and timely advice. Finally, I thank the PEP co-directors, Professors Doug Irwin and Russ Muirhead, for their unstinting encouragement of this initiative from the outset.

On June 11, 2019, the Alumni Relations Office at Dartmouth collaborated with the Political Economy Project in hosting a public event at which four Dartmouth students presented their own research on the founding of Dartmouth College. College archivist Peter Carini took time to help these students prepare their research. Warmest thanks go to Christianne Hardy of the President's Office, and to Angela Stafford and Patrick J. Bedard of the Alumni Relations Office, for all of their kindness and assistance in making that event possible. Attended by over one hundred people, including members of the Classes of '59 and '64, the event featured the following presentations: Margaret Cross ('19), "Dartmouth's 'Religious Politician': Eleazar Wheelock's Views on Church and State, Revolution and the Gift Economy"; Brian A. Morrison ('21), "Finance and Politics in the Founding of Dartmouth College: Eleazar Wheelock in English Perspective"; Dominic Carrese ('19), "Wilderness Subjugation in American Political Thought: Eleazar Wheelock in Context"; and Madison Wilson, "The Trip to Europe: A Reconstruction and Commentary on Samson Occom and Nathaniel Whitaker's Fundraising Tour." These four estimable recent graduates had also been invitees to a Templeton-sponsored dinner on May 8, 2019, at which the present editor offered some reflections on "Eleazar Wheelock and the Ethics of Commemoration." Kent Dahlberg was kind enough to arrange that memorable occasion.

Special thanks must go to William Legge, the tenth Earl of Dartmouth. Invited to visit the College in September of 2019 by his friend Kathy Rines, a Dartmouth student in 1971 and classmate of his at the Harvard Business School, William Dartmouth presented a lecture, co-sponsored by the Political Economy Project and the Masters in Liberal Studies (MALS) program, entitled "Thoughts on Brexit" on September 24, graciously agreeing to join a number of PEP students to dinner afterward.

The present volume, then, is the culmination of quite a varied array of sestercentennial events in which the Political Economy Project was privileged to take part.

Introduction

Henry C. Clark (Dartmouth College)

To commemorate the sestercentennial of the founding of Dartmouth College, the Political Economy Project organized and hosted a weekend scholarly conference on September 27–28, 2019 entitled "Dartmouth and the World: Religion and Political Economy @1769." In addition to the seven authors represented in this volume, the conference featured a number of other participants. Shannon Stimson, the Thomas and Dorothy Leavey Chair in the Foundations of American Freedom, professor of government, and faculty fellow of the Berkley Center for Religion, Peace and World Affairs at Georgetown University, delivered a paper on "Heterodoxy and Wealth: Sir William Petty and the Ends of Political Economy." Philip J. Stern, the Gilhuly Family Associate Professor in the History Department at Duke University, spoke on "Charters, Contracts, and Corporations: The Legacies of the Eighteenth-Century British Empire in *Dartmouth College v. Woodward* (1819)." T. H. Breen, the William Smith Mason Professor of American History Emeritus at Northwestern University, and now James Marsh Professor-at-Large at the University of Vermont, gave a talk on "Reconciliation and Revenge: The Refugee Crisis that Ended the American Revolution." Kate Carté, associate professor of history at Southern Methodist University, concluded the conference with her paper "Wheelock to Dartmouth: The Apotheosis of British Protestantism." All of the authors present addressed themes that were in one way or another relevant to the task of placing the founding of Dartmouth College in its broader context.

The world was a different place in 1769. With conspicuous exceptions, everyone in it was "poor" by modern standards. Per capita income seems to have been roughly three dollars a day (current measures), and life expectancy at birth was roughly thirty.[1] Even to achieve this modest sustenance required heroic efforts. Ninety percent or more of the world's people were illiterate, partly because roughly 75,000 times as much of their labor was needed to acquire an hour's worth of artificial light as for us.[2]

Beneath the surface of these broad generalizations lay a tenor of life difficult for those born into a world of mass abundance to fathom. Women had six to eight children on average, spending about 70 percent of their adult years bearing and rearing them; over half their progeny failed to reach adulthood—victims of disease, starvation, or violence.[3] Nor were they likely to have much choice of partner: In fact, the more we learn about the past weight of family authority, the starker the contrast seems between their world and ours.[4] The caste system in India, which some revisionists had begun to imagine was a mostly recent contrivance imposed by British colonialists to divide and conquer, has been revealed by ancient DNA studies to have been "overwhelmingly important for millenia."[5] Footbinding in China, sometimes seen as an elite sexual or aesthetic indulgence, now looks to have been integral to the labor discipline of ordinary households—only disappearing with the adoption of modern textile production.[6] Rigid control was the order of the day, from hut to kingly court: autocracies were dominant, democracies absent.[7] Slavery was legal and customary, virtually everywhere—rarely in harsher form than in the very places where its abolition would first become thinkable.

Precious few of the eight hundred million or so humans alive in 1769 (about a tenth our current complement) might have imagined that these grim parameters would ever change, or even what it might mean to do so. Most were acculturated in religious, moral, and family traditions tracing their legitimacy back centuries, and teaching patience, humility, and forbearance toward the inscrutable ways of heaven. The number of those who could truly visualize a different way was meager indeed.

Jack A. Goldstone ("1769—Dartmouth, Machines and Modernity"), one of our leading comparative historians, tells a story of striking resemblance and even synchronicity connecting China, the Middle East and Europe before 1769. They seemed to resonate to the same rhythms of climate, demography, popular subsistence, even social rebellion and political stabilization. The very modes of legitimacy show remarkable affinities over the centuries, based as they were on religious and philosophical texts harking back millennia. Paradoxically, one of the signal features of these eternal, tradition-bound authorities was to be *"changeable and arbitrary."*

Where, then, did visions of a different way come from? Goldstone finds key stirrings in science, religion and politics. It was after Columbus that traditional authority began to yield ground in science, and after Luther in religion. New standards brought a crisis of confidence in inherited truth, raising the status of experimental and mathematical approaches to the world. Though states faced a rash of fearsome threats in the seventeenth century in India, China and the Middle East as well as in Europe, they mostly achieved restoration after mid-century, largely by teaming up with elites. The major exception was England, an island on the Eurasian periphery where continued ferment in religion and politics survived its 1660 Restoration, accompanied by new scientific approaches whose appeal had only grown by the early eighteenth century, now also bringing society and politics under its purview.

It was especially in the Scottish Enlightenment universities that this yeasty combination was most active. The absence of a real established church in the English colonies made it easier for Scotch Presbyterians and Dissenters to broadcast new religious ideas that would be relatively independent of inherited authority, while reaching a new and wider audience that included women, blacks, Indians, and others of the unenfranchised. Goldstone links them to a wave of new academic institutions in the American colonies. These were built, however, not only on religious foundations but on a certain commitment to the new scientific knowledge itself, the Great Awakening finding its analogue in figures like the traveling popularizer John Desaguliers (1683–1744). It is no accident, Goldstone argues, that 1769 saw not only Dartmouth's founding, but Watt and Arkwright's patents and Franklin's election as president of the Philosophical Society. The patents were epochal breakthroughs in the age-old quest to harness nature for the "relief of man's estate,"[8] doing much to launch the Industrial Revolution. Nor is it an accident, he concludes, that Dartmouth, founded ostensibly for religious reasons, was soon producing distinguished graduates in science and engineering as well as literature, the law, and politics.

In a way, Steve Pincus's boldly revisionist essay ("Dartmouth College and Patriot State Building") goes even further: Far from being a religious school that evolved into a secular one, Dartmouth College was founded primarily for worldly improvement from the start. A graduate of Dartmouth himself (History and Classical Archeology, '84) and now one of our leading British historians, Pincus places more emphasis on political than religious modernization, while agreeing that a "political economy of improvement" was increasingly on the agenda: Science, secular culture, and state interests were not only prominent in the decision to found the "college on a hill," they were central to it.

He thus takes issue with a long-standing view of Dartmouth as a private venture. This was the view canonized during an 1819 Supreme Court case when Daniel Webster (Class of 1801) famously declaimed, "It is, sir, as I have said, a small college, and yet there are those who love it." Taking the side of the half-forgotten Ichabod Bartlett (Class of 1808), Pincus argues that the college was conceived to be separate from Eleazar Wheelock's other educational venture, Moor's Charity School, and was designed precisely as an agent of political, cultural, and economic development in the New England colonies.

The generation before 1769, Pincus finds, saw a significant shift—especially among a party he calls the patriots—toward a focus on development rather than mere mercantilist extraction, one that favored consumption over production, and free labor over slavery. The key figure in his Dartmouth story is not so much Eleazar Wheelock as John Wentworth. Provincial governor of New Hampshire at the College's founding, Wentworth embodied the new agenda to a tee. Part of a patriot circle back in England, the youthful administrator (he had barely turned thirty) brought a reformer's zeal to his task as colonial governor. Even the name of the new college, it seems, may have been a way of announcing the patriot designs of the founding.

Like Goldstone, Pincus remarks on the flurry of new schools set up during this period. Noting the absence of a religious test among Dartmouth students in the Royal Charter, he nonetheless lays emphasis upon the role of the state. Part of an abortive idea of a "confederal" union with strong and well-integrated colonies, a vision that was largely forgotten after the colonial rebellion of the 1770s, the founding of Dartmouth took its place amid a whole wave of improvement ultimately seeking nothing less than "the welfare of mankind."

If this lofty language of universal betterment was mostly that of religious, scientific, and political elites, Emma Griffin's essay ("Life and Living Standards in Britain's Industrial Revolution") turns our attention to the mundane condition of the masses. In it, she addresses one of the knottiest questions of modern historical research: what effect did the Industrial Revolution have on those who lived through it? As president of the Royal Historical Society, Griffin is well placed to address this question. Her book *Liberty's Dawn: A People's History of the Industrial Revolution* had challenged what she calls the "social catastrophe" school of interpretation. That is the one we are mostly familiar with: namely, that the first generation of industrial workers suffered enough in the way of alienation, exploitation, and immiseration to provide the breeding ground for durable threats of systemic revolution. Drawing instead on the written accounts of workers who lived through the process, Griffin paints a quite different picture, finding that these accounts "offer little support for the pessimistic interpretation of living standards." It was thus the humble autobiographers themselves, not naïve economists or closeted Whig historians, who "spoke in remarkably consistent terms of improvements and progress."

Partly, this is because the world they left behind, the late eighteenth-century Anglo-American world—Wheelock's world—was anything but idyllic. Despite the well-known indignities on the shop floor, status and a sense of worth were more accessible *after* the factory turn than before, both at work and in the community. Men were no longer at such risk of arbitrary dismissal, but were instead more able to exercise a right of exit. The "balance of power between master and servant," lopsided even in the household of a man of the cloth such as Eleazar Wheelock, was upended by the advent of industrial capitalism. Partly, this bespeaks the constricted supply of employment in the earlier period, when "servants' need for work outstripped the masters' ability to provide it." The new industrial laborers appreciated the higher wages, greater variety of employment and more regular demand for their services (for men, at least) than in the days before industry, when workers were far more beholden to the "vagaries of the seasons." The technologies of the late eighteenth century—including those key patents of 1769—became the private wealth of the nineteenth century, some of it reaching even the commonest of laborers, and in historically unprecedented fashion.

Though many specialists trace this great escape from the long Malthusian straitjacket to science, technology, and industry, a few highlight changes in commercial and business practices, which supposedly brought a rationalizing focus to profit-making enterprises. As early as the Renaissance, as one put it, "symbolic algebra functioned together with double-entry bookkeeping as the main instruments for the determination of objective value, the basic idea of the mercantile society."[9] This algebraic objectivity is not exactly the kind of "accounting" that is meant by the next author in our collection, Kristen Beales. In "George Whitefield's Changing Commercial Theology," Beales, a Warren Center Fellow at Harvard, takes us behind the scenes of Great Awakening luminary George Whitefield's founding of an orphanage, an enterprise certainly more philanthropic than commercial in nature. On the other hand, the very fact that the accounting practices of an Evangelical preacher reached public attention is perhaps noteworthy. The expanding post-Gutenberg print culture of Atlantic-oriented Europe has been plausibly linked to the birth of modernity in multiple ways, not least for its self-corrective effects (Eisenstein 1979, McCusker 2005, Buringh and van Zanden 2009, Marks 2016, ch 4, Rubin 2017, chs. 5–6, though note Van Zanden 2013 and Mokyr 2016, 293). Whitefield's career is worthy of attention, among other reasons, for featuring just such a mid-course correction.

In a famous episode, Ben Franklin grudgingly softened his perennial hostility long enough to donate to the fiery preacher's collection plate, "gold and all." Beales cites the anecdote as an entrée into the fascinating changes this leading Evangelical minister, patron and counselor to Eleazar Wheelock underwent in developing what she calls his "commercial theology"—his method of combining accounting practices, mercantile thinking and theological precepts. At first, inspired by a German Pietist of the 1680s, Whitefield stressed the direct dependence of his proposed orphanage upon God, by taking only the spontaneous offerings of auditors like Franklin. He also utilized every possible occasion, including controversy over his own sermonizing, to drum up donors to the new institution. Indeed, the accounts themselves became part of this early strategy to promote a kind of "experimental Christianity."

Once the setbacks started around 1741, he rethought his financial approach, placing much more emphasis on longer-term planning. Even his increased reliance upon slave labor, Beales argues, is a function of this new emphasis on steady private subscriptions. Thus, by the time he began to advise Occom and Wheelock in the late 1750s, Beales finds Whitefield to be "a different man" from the firebrand of the Great Awakening. He now advised they settle in populous Connecticut and publicly audit all accounts, rather than relying on spontaneous donations of the Ben Franklin sort. The "tremendous spiritual power that he attributed to money" is often seen as an early version of the Prosperity Gospel—the Methodist idea by which the poor were encouraged to seek out signs of God's election through visible worldly success. By focusing on his new commercial theology, Beales shows that the Great Awakening had its accounting side.

Religion was part of a more directly political "awakening" at this time as well. In "Religious Conversion, the Stamp Act, and Revolution in New England," Mark Valeri highlights the conflicted loyalties that Wheelock and his peers felt upon the onset of revolution. Evangelical merchants and preachers alike had long promoted the Protestant British Atlantic against that of Catholic Spain, Portugal and France. Even in the 1760s, Wheelock and others worked closely with leading British political figures in preparing the new college's Royal Charter in 1769, as we have seen. But a combination of fiscal, constitutional, and religious factors drew them away from that same establishment as well.

One thing that made it easier to pull away was the new form this religious orientation was now taking. Originally, Evangelicals had emphasized depravity of will and the centrality of divine grace in salvation. But a new generation in the 1750s and 1760s, sometimes influenced by Francis Hutcheson and the Scottish Enlightenment's more optimistic idea of an innate "moral sense," now celebrated the voluntarist agency they saw at the heart of spiritual rebirth. Under this approach, "conversion rested on moral freedom and competence," and its ready availability helps explain why people so invested in the British Empire might nonetheless conceive of turning against it. Valeri highlights a clear association in many minds between embracing the new religious light and re-evaluating one's loyalty to the British empire at its time of crisis. Enslavement to sin had become conflated with enslavement to corrupt politics; conversely, religious conversion and political renewal had virtually merged. The place of individual conscience and personal witness in recent religious developments turned out to be highly congenial to a remarkably flexible approach to political authority as well. In Hanover, Wheelock noted a nearly "universal" concern for conversion at the very moment of the political upheavals, even if he remained circumspect in his own dealings with the authorities.

J. Patrick Mullins ("The Making of a 'Rebel Lady': Gender, Virtue, and Bloodshed in Mercy Otis Warren's Radicalization, 1769–1772") also gives us a ground-level view of the advent of revolution, though from a quite different point of view. By focusing on two women historians, he evokes one of those ambient features of the age of Wheelock that has very deep roots indeed. For if there was one aspect of pre-industrial life that really did distinguish Europe (or at least Northwest Europe) from the rest of Eurasia for a very long time, it was the state of male-female relations. In recent decades, historians have discovered a distinctive "European Marriage Pattern" going back not just to the Enlightenment but much further. This pattern is usually defined as a combination of late age-at-first-marriage, nuclear households, close age of partners, frequent celibacy in both sexes, correspondingly high degrees of personal autonomy in the selection of partners, and widespread practice of paid domestic servanthood rather than strictly endogamous household economy (Hajnal 1965). So pervasive, and so striking, was this pattern in certain parts of Europe—including the Low Countries, the British Isles, northern sections of France and Germany—that some have wondered whether a truly "patriarchal" order ever emerged there at all (Van Zanden et al. 2019, 5), though many contemporaries of course aspired to one.

Although historians are still divided over the larger implications of this striking phenomenon, one implication stands out: if "equality" first became a burning preoccupation in northwest Europe (and its offshoots), was this partly because something approaching equality in the household had already prevailed there for centuries (Hartman 2004, 3–4, 7–8; de Moor and Van Zanden, 3)? Whether this pattern is owing to changes in marriage law going back as far as the sixth century, when the Catholic Church waged war against cousin marriage and clan-based kinship on behalf of the Biblical injunction to strict monogamy (Henrich 2020), or whether it is instead more related to differences in property arrangements and land markets (Macfarlane 1986, ch 6, Macfarlane 1987, Hartman 2004, 75, 125) is of secondary concern here. What matters is that it was not so "progressive" for contemporary women to thrust their heads above a veil and claim some share of public attention; it was part of a low-grade drumbeat of Western life for centuries (Lougee 1976, Schwoerer 1986, King and Rabil 1996, Stuurman 1997, Hanley 2003). What the growth of an eighteenth-century reading public did was merely to further massify, marketize, and highlight this process, bringing women—with all their residual cultural and legal incapacities, to be sure—somewhat more to the fore. Female authors like Emilie du Chatelet and Françoise de Graffigny had already distinguished themselves in fields like science and literature (Brading 2019, Showalter 2004). It could scarcely have been a great shock if women took part in the public debate over the American Revolution—as they had done during the English Revolution over a century before (Feroli 2006, Hughes 2012) and would soon do during the French Revolution (Hunt 1996, 58–60, 109–30, Applewhite and Levy, 1991).

Eleazar Wheelock can be seen in this light as well. Sharing the Great Awakening desire to broaden the circle of testimonies to include hitherto marginalized figures (Caldwell 2017, 22–24), Wheelock made an open attitude to the instruction of women, and of Indian women in particular, a signal feature of his educational enterprises. By the time of Mercy Otis Warren's plays, Wheelock had been admitting girls to his school for over a decade. Though his own agenda was to promote Christianity, in the hope these girls would become "missionaries to the tribes, or at least the wives and helpmates of missionaries" (Calloway 2010, 7), the fifteen or so female students who enrolled in Moor's Charity School enjoyed "more autonomy" to shape their missionary education than did their male counterparts (Criales 2017, 283).

Likewise, the transatlantic community of restless radical reformers such as Warren, her ill-fated brother James Otis, and the English historian Catherine Macauley that Mullins introduces shared a strong belief in the competence and near-equality of women: Thus, in July of 1769, just months before Dartmouth's founding, James told Macauley of how "God and Nature have 'been equally kind to both Sexes,' 'at least in point of genius.'"

The use of this "genius" did not exclude the most astringent public criticism. Likening Thomas Hutchinson's Massachusetts to "Upper Servia" under the Ottomans, Warren employed a trope of Western liberty versus Eastern despotism going back to Herodotus, and made popular again by Montesquieu's *Persian Letters* half a century before. Just as the Frenchman had evoked the domestic condition of women as a convenient metaphor for broaching the delicate topic of political liberty, so does Mullins find similar affinities between the domestic and the public in Warren. Legitimizing revolutionary violence well before most of her peers, she savaged the Crown by indirection for the Boston Massacre of 1770 (death toll: 5) in her popular 1772 play *The Adulateur*, in which she evoked a supposed conspiracy to proceed to the massacre of all Boston. It is hard not to see elements of Valeri's sanctification of politics in this account.

If book culture and legal pluralism, available for centuries in the Western world, broadened the menu of options open to many women, they did not have a similar effect on the mostly dismal fate of American Indians. Subject to imported diseases to which they had little immunity, and facing the fearsome firepower of Western guns fueled by religious self-certainty and unabating mercantilist rivalry, native Americans tended to experience books and laws mostly as further instruments of dispossession. Goldstone had already noted the "brutal" dimension of European merchant interlopers in the East, and Pincus had remarked on the "crudely racist" undercurrent percolating through Dartmouth's historical self-commemorations. Ivy Schweitzer's essay "Recovering the Native Origins of Dartmouth College Through *The Occom Circle*" expands upon these themes. Initiator and project coordinator of an ambitious cross-disciplinary, NEH-funded digital edition of writings by, to, and about the remarkable Mohegan Samson Occom, Schweitzer looks at the founding of Dartmouth College primarily through the lens of its original mission as a school for American Indians, and the different ways that mission came to be perceived by its immediate constituencies.

All members of the extended Dartmouth community are at least dimly aware of the falling out that its two principal progenitors went through. Wheelock's original aspiration had been to provide a peaceful alternative to exactly the dreary cycle of atrocity and reprisal that had so marked Anglo-Indian relations for generations. Missionaries and school teachers, he felt, were the best alternatives to fortresses and firearms (Calloway 2010, 3). Schweitzer acknowledges that the Indians within his orbit could manage to carve out spaces for "adapting the imperial technologies of knowledge, rhetoric, law, religion and politics to their own purposes." On balance, however, the story she tells is one of rejection and tragic loss.

Half a century ago, as part of the College Bicentennial of 1969, Dartmouth historian Jere Daniell detailed the complex ins and outs of Wheelock's negotiations over the Charter, depicting him as a politically wily maneuverer (Daniell 1969). Likewise, while Occom emerges in Schweitzer's account as a lifelong Mohegan patriot with at best a secondary interest in religious education, Wheelock appears as a shiftless operator who sent his protégé off to England to distract from land disputes at home, altered the terms of the 1769 Charter to avoid offending his English donors, and ultimately left his Indian collaborator in the lurch, despite one of the most impressive religious fund-raising campaigns in memory. Her essay culminates in a close, fine-grained reading of the "breakup letter" in which Occom vented his sense of betrayal over the new college's abrupt—and, as it turned out, permanent—change in mission.

Wheelock's enterprise had certainly always rested upon confident assumptions about the willingness of native peoples to trade in their own customs for the more "enlightened" practices of Christian Englishmen. Everything from the use of corporal punishment on Indian children to the hope that Iroquois women would abandon farming for domestic work—not to mention the larger expectation that nomadic hunting would give way to the civilized life of settled agriculture—marks out his project as promoting not only religious conversion but wholesale cultural transformation. It seems to have included "unquestioning obedience, subordination, and even expressions of self-loathing" on the part of his Indian charges (Calloway 2010, 3, 11–12). Perhaps when he lost faith that this transformation was imminent, the very idea of an Indian college lost some of its attraction. On the other hand, his commitment to Indian education remained strong. He had brought Moor's Charity School up from Connecticut when he founded the college, and for several generations, there were actually more Indian students there than at Dartmouth. Wheelock, we do well to recall, "displayed concern for the fate and future of Indians, at a time when few did." (Calloway 2010, xv, 3) The precise relationship between the charity school and the college remains an intriguing, if painful, conundrum of Dartmouth history to this day.

As the seven essays in this volume attest, the anxious drive for improvement that brought forth Dartmouth College was, in global terms, a polyglot affair, including religion and political economy (broadly conceived) on both sides of the Atlantic. It is a curious fact that two of the Scottish pioneers of the forward-looking new discipline of political economy, David Hume and Adam Smith, were exact contemporaries of the two Dartmouth pioneers—Hume being born the same year as Wheelock, Smith the same year as Occom. Each in his own way participated in arenas of public dispute that were unique to this part of the world. At the very time Wheelock was consciously expanding his radius of auditors, preaching ever more to African-Americans, offering instruction to women, doggedly mounting a school seeking fellowship with Indians, a period when Occom was breaking all manner of precedents in his astonishing grand tour of the British Isles, Smith and Hume were imagining unheard-of ways to validate the humble aspirations of producers, traders and consumers alike by transforming relations amongst them, as well as between the states and markets that mediated them.

All four of these figures suffered insult and indignity for their efforts. Smith, who once called *Wealth of Nations* his "very violent attack . . . upon the whole commercial system of Great Britain" (Smith 1977, 251; also Smith 2018), offered a withering denunciation of slavery that met with indignation from colonists such as the Virginian Arthur Lee (Smith 1976, V.2.9.206–7; Lee 1764). Hume was barred from an academic post for his outspoken religious skepticism and undisguised hostility toward fifteen hundred years of Christian history (Mossner 1980, ch, 12). Wheelock, on his grand preaching tour, was called "anti-christ" among other choice epithets. (Kidd 2009, 113–14) And Occom suffered all of the expected abuses of the outsider—hypocrisy, condescension, betrayal—not a few of them at the hands of Wheelock himself.

By bringing their controversial commitments into the public square, all four of these men were also enacting a distinctly Western drama that was already centuries old. The very word "Renaissance," as used in the fourteenth and fifteenth centuries, carried with it a polemical connotation grounded in genuine revulsion at the "Gothic" past, now defined as a mere "middle age" of darkness and barbarism between two eras of supposed light (Ferguson 1948). The Reformation likewise was a convulsion spurning the previous thousand years of Christian history not only as wrong, but as desecration and defilement. This kind of wholesale disgust at large portions of history, one's own history, was an integral part of the enterprises of all four of these "cultural entrepreneurs" (Mokyr 2016, 59).

There are sestercentennial angles worth noting as well. Wheelock, looking back exactly two hundred fifty years from the College Charter, could find perfect targets for his own ample powers of moral denunciation. For 1519 was the year of the fatal rift between the Papacy and Martin Luther, whose supporters quickly responded to his eventual excommunication by christening the Pope the Whore of Babylon (Scribner 1981, Hendel 2018). That was also the year when the Spanish adventurer Hernan Cortez set in motion his campaign against the ill-fated Aztec Empire, unleashing generations of upheaval that gave birth to the famed "black legend" (Maltby 1971) of Spanish colonialism, which included rampant "Papist" missionizing of local peoples and a vigorous Protestant counter-missionizing in its turn.

If the passage of time telescopes Wheelock's allegiances, making his Anglo-Protestant expansionism seem far more of a piece with that of his Catholic rivals than it did to him, how confident can we be that a similar phenomenon may not be in store for us? If there is an "ethics of commemoration," might it include scrutinizing not only the vices of the past through the virtues of the present, but the deficiencies of the present through the expediencies of the past? Might some future historian, a quarter-millenium hence, detect in the Dartmouth of 2019 an institution bearing unacknowledged marks of its founding—a small, isolated rural school not only improbably successful at attracting rare talent across countless fields from afar, infused with a legendary sense of warmly welcoming community, but at the same time restless for further improvement, pulsating with impatient commitments to ever greater inclusion, desperate to put the stamp of its irrepressible idealism on nothing less than "the world," not without a hint of the ambient moral narcissism, even brutal dogmatism of its postmodern generation, descended from (if no longer tethered to) the religious energies that created it? From this longer perspective, might Wheelock himself appear—as indeed he may already appear—not only as an avatar of perennial Western self-condemnation, but as that most fascinating and exasperating of creatures on the global stage: the perpetually self-renewing and self-fashioning American?

NOTES

1. Maddison 2010 and 2018; World Bank 2020a; World Bank 2019; Bourguignon and Morrisson 2002; Maddison 2006, 33, Tab. 1–5; in Bailey and Tupy, trends 1, 2, 13, and 24.

2. See World Bank 2020b and Nordhaus 1996, 52, Tab. 1.6. Since some used tallow candle and others sperm whale candlelight, which had differential levels of efficiency, I split the difference between them to reach this figure. See also Bailey and Tupy 2020, trends 18 and 61.

3. See Lee, 2003, esp. 168, Tab. 1; cited in Bailey and Tupy 2020, trend 17.

4. A marriage, as the Confucian sage Mencius famously put it, was an arrangement between two surnames. See Eastman 1988, 24; cited in de Moor and van Zanden 2010, 6.

5. Reich 2018, 144–45.

6. See Bossen and Gates 2017, Appendix A.2, A.3, A.5, A.6, and A.8, 178, 180–81. See also Gates 2015, esp. Fig. 1.1, 17, which traces the data to 1854, and 1.4, 21, which shows the vast majority of footbinding to have begun before the age of eight.

7. Marshall and Elzinga-Marshall 2017; cited in Bailey and Tupy 2020, trend 8.

8. Bacon 1893 [1605], I,v.11.

9. Heeffer 2011, 109.

REFERENCES

Applewhite, Harriet, and Darline G. Levy, editors. 1991. *Women and Politics in the Age of the Democratic Revolution.* Ann Arbor: University of Michigan Press.

Bacon, Francis. 1893 [1605]. *The Advancement of Learning.* Edited by David Price. London: Cassell.

Bailey, Ronald, and Marian L. Tupy. 2020. *Ten Global Trends Every Smart Person Should Know.* Washington, DC: Cato.

Bossen, Laurel, and Hill Gates. 2017. *Bound Feet, Young Hands: Tracking the Demise of Footbinding in Village China.* Stanford, CA: Stanford University Press.

Brading, Katherine. 2019. *Emilie de Châtelet and the Foundations of Physical Science.* London: Routledge.

Bourguignon, François, and Christian Morrisson. 2002. "Inequality among World Citizens: 1820-1992." Pp. 727–44 in *American Economic Review*, 92, no. 4.

Buringh, Eltjo and Jan Luiten van Zanden. 2009. "Charting the 'Rise of the West': Manuscripts and Printed Books in Europe, A Long-Term Perspective from the Sixth through Eighteenth Centuries." Pp. 409–45 in *The Journal of Economic History*, 69, no. 2.

Caldwell, Robert W., III. 2017. *Theologies of the American Revivalists: From Whitefield to Finney.* Westmont, IL: InterVarsity Press.

Calloway, Colin. 2010. *The Indian History of an American Institution: Native Americans and Dartmouth.* Hanover, NH: Dartmouth College Press.

Criales, Jessica Lauren. 2017. "'My Obligation to the Doctor for his Paternal Care': Eleazar Wheelock and the Female Students at Moor's Indian Charity School, 1761-69." Pp. 279–97 in *Social Sciences and Missions*, 30, nos. 3-4.

Daniell, Jere. 1969. "Eleazar Wheelock and the Dartmouth College Charter." Pp. 3–44 in *Historical New Hampshire*, 24, Winter.

Eastman, Lloyd E. 1988. *Family, Fields, and Ancestors: Constancy and Change in China's Social and Economic History, 1550-1949*. Oxford, UK: Oxford University Press.

Eisenstein, Elisabeth L. 1979. *The Printing Press as an Agent of Change: Communications and Cultural Transformations in Early Modern Europe*. Cambridge, UK: Cambridge University Press.

Feroli, Teresa. 2006. *Political Speaking Justified: Women Prophets and the English Revolution*. Newark: University of Delaware Press.

Ferguson, Wallace K. 1948. *The Renaissance in Historical Thought: Five Centuries of Interpretation*. Boston: Houghton-Mifflin.

Gates, Hill. 2015. *Footbinding and Women's Labor in Sichuan*. London: Routledge.

Hajnal, John. 1965. "European Marriage Patterns in Perspective." Pp. 101–47 in *Population in History: Essays in Historical Demography*. Edited by D.V. Glass and D.E.C. Eversley. Chicago: Aldine.

Idem. 1982. "Two Kinds of Preindustrial Household Formation System." Pp. 449–94 in *Population and Development Review*, 8, no. 3.

Hanley, Sarah. 2003. "'The Jurisprudence of the Arrêts': Marital Union, Civil Society, and State Formation in France, 1550-1650." Pp. 1–40 in *Law and History Review*, 21, no. 1.

Hartman, Mary S. 2004. *The Household and the Making of History: A Subversive View of the Western Past*. Cambridge, UK: Cambridge University Press.

Heeffer, Albrecht. 2011. "On the curious coincidence of algebra and double-entry bookkeeping." Pp. 109–30 in *Foundations of the Formal Sciences*, 7.

Hendel, Kurt K. 2018. "Another Quincentennial: The 1519 Leipzig Debate." Pp. 446–54 in *Lutheran Quarterly*, 32, no. 4.

Henrich, Joseph. 2020. *The WEIRDest People in the World: How the West Became Psychologically Peculiar and Particularly Prosperous*. New York: Farrar, Straus, and Giroux.

Hughes, Ann. 2012. *Gender and the English Revolution*. London: Routledge.

Kidd, Thomas S. 2009. *The Great Awakening: The Roots of Evangelical Christianity in Colonial America*. New Haven, CT: Yale University Press.

King, Margaret L. and Albert Rabil Jr., series editors. 1996-. *The Other Voice in Early Modern Europe*. 60 vols. Chicago: The University of Chicago Press.

[Lee, Arthur]. 1764. *An Essay in Vindication of the Continental Colonies of America, from a Censure of Mr. Adam Smith, in his* Theory of Moral Sentiments. London: Becket and De Hondt.

Lee, Ronald. 2003. "The Demographic Transition: Three Centuries of Fundamental Change." Pp. 167–90 in *Journal of Economic Perspectives*, 17, no. 4.

Lougee, Carolyn. 1976. *"Le Paradis des Femmes": Women, Salons, and Social Stratification in Seventeenth-Century France*. Princeton, NJ: Princeton University Press.

Macfarlane, Alan. 1986. *Marriage and Love in England, 1300-1840: Modes of Reproduction*. New York: Blackwell.

Idem. 1987. *The Culture of Capitalism*. Oxford: Basil Blackwell.

Maddison, Angus. 2006. *The World Economy, Volume One.* Paris: OECD Development Centre, 2006.

"Maddison Project Database 2010." https://www.rug.nl/ggdc/historicaldevelopment/maddison/releases/maddison-database-2010 Groningen Growth and Development Centre.

"Maddison Project Database 2018." https://www.rug.nl/ggdc/historicaldevelopment/maddison/releases/maddison-project-database-2018 Groningen Growth and Development Centre.

Maltby, William S. 1971. *The Black Legend in England: The Development of Anti-Spanish Sentiment, 1558-1660.* Durham, NC: Duke University Press.

Marks, Steven. 2016. *The Information Nexus: Global Capitalism from the Renaissance to the Present.* Cambridge, UK: Cambridge University Press.

Marshall, Monty G., and Gabrielle Elzinga-Marshall. 2017. "Global Report 2017: Conflict, Governance, and State Fragility." Vienna, VA: Center for Systemic Peace.

McCusker, John J. 2005. "The Demise of Distance: The Business Press and the Origins of the Information Revolution in the Early Modern Atlantic World." Pp. 295–321 in *American Historical Review*, 110, no. 2.

Mokyr, Joel. 2016. *A Culture of Growth: The Origins of the Modern Economy.* Princeton, NJ: Princeton University Press.

De Moor, Tine, and Jan Luiten van Zanden. 2010. "Girl power: the European marriage pattern and labour markets in the North Sea region in the late medieval and early modern period." Pp. 1–33 in *The Economic History Review*, 63, no. 1.

Mossner, E.C. 1980. *The Life of David Hume.* Second edition. Oxford, UK: Oxford University Press.

Nordhaus, William D. 1996. "Do Real-Output and Real-Wage Measures Capture Reality? The History of Lighting Suggests Not." Pp. 27–70 in *The Economics of New Goods.* Edited by Timothy F. Breshahan and Robert J. Gordon. Chicago: University of Chicago Press.

Reich, David. 2018. *Who We Are and How We Got Here: Ancient DNA and the New Science of the Human Past.* New York: Vintage Books.

Rubin, Jared. 2017. *Rulers, Religion, and Riches: Why the West Got Rich and the Middle East Did Not.* Cambridge, UK: Cambridge University Press.

Schwoerer, Lois G. 1986. "Women and the Glorious Revolution." Pp. 195–218 in *Albion*, 18, no. 2.

Scribner, Robert W. 1981. *For the Sake of Simple Folk: Popular Propaganda for the German Reformation.* Oxford, UK: Clarendon Press.

Showalter, English. 2004. *Françoise de Graffigny: Her Life and Works.* Oxford, UK: Voltaire Foundation.

Smith, Adam. 1976 [1759]. *The Theory of Moral Sentiments.* Edited by D.D. Raphael and A.L. Macfie. Oxford, UK: Oxford University Press.

Idem. 1977. *The Correspondence of Adam Smith.* Edited by Ernest Campbell Mossner and Ian Simpson Ross. Oxford, UK: Oxford University Press.

Idem. 2018. *Adam Smith and the Death of David Hume: The Letter to Strahan and Related Texts.* Edited by Dennis C. Rasmussen. Lanham, MD: Lexington Books.

Stuurman, Siep. 1997. "Social Cartesianism: François Poulain de la Barre and the Origins of the Enlightenment." Pp. 617–40 in *Journal of the History of Ideas*, 58, no. 4.

World Bank. 2019. "Poverty Head Count Ratio" chart, https://data.worldbank.org/topic/poverty

World Bank. 2020a. "Global Gross Domestic Product, Purchasing Power Parity" chart, https://data.worldbank.org/indicator/NY.GDP.MKTP.PP.KD

World Bank. 2020b. "Literacy Rate, Adult Total" chart, https://data.worldbank.org/indicator/SE.ADT.LITR.ZS

Zanden, Jan Luiten van. 2013. "Explaining the Global Distribution of Book Production before 1800." Pp. 323–40 in *Technology, Skills and the Pre-Modern Economy in the East and the West*. Edited by Maarten Prak and Jan Luiten van Zanden. Leiden: Brill.

Zanden, Jan Luiten van, Tine de Moor, and Sarah G. Carmichael. 2019. *Capital Women: The European Marriage Pattern, Female Empowerment and Economic Development in Western Europe, 1300-1800*. Oxford, UK: Oxford University Press.

Chapter 1

1769

Dartmouth, Machines, and Modernity

Jack A. Goldstone (George Mason University)

Dartmouth College was created in 1769. Its founding was led by a congregational minister, Eleazer Wheelock, who in his earlier endeavors sought to Christianize the "pagan" Native Americans by providing them with a liberal arts education. Named for the 2nd Earl of Dartmouth (an early backer of Wheelock), the land for the college was provided by the Royal Governor of New Hampshire, under a royal charter in the name of King George III. Even more than most American colleges and universities, Dartmouth was thus very much a colonial enterprise. For much of its early history, the majority of its graduates became Christian ministers.

Yet the timing of Dartmouth's founding also forced it to look forward. In fact, its future drew more from the Scottish and English Enlightenment than traditional religious impulses. Less than thirty years after its founding, Dartmouth added the country's fourth School of Medicine, and by the nineteenth century, Dartmouth was producing famous politicians, judges, college presidents, writers, and entrepreneurs. These included early presidents of Vassar, Middlebury, Bowdoin, Kenyon, Williams, and Amherst Colleges; U.S. senators from New Hampshire, Maine, Massachusetts, and Vermont, including Daniel Webster; America's first great environmental writer George Perkins March; U.S Supreme Court Chief Justice Salmon Chase; and America's first oil baron, George Bissell (1845).

This essay examines the radical changes ongoing in the intellectual world at the time of Dartmouth's founding, changes that shaped Dartmouth's milieu and direction. The year 1769 was in many ways the year the Enlightenment ideal took wing, as that year produced two of the breakthrough achievements of rational thought that would reshape the global economy: James Watt patented his far more efficient (and thus more practicably usable) steam engine, and Richard Arkwright patented the first machine for spinning cotton into thread.

Yet the idea that the rational design of machines could create breakthroughs extended to far more than machines to pump water, pound metal or spin yarn. It soon reached to the creation of a new design for government, embodied in the movement for independence and then the U.S. Constitution. It even extended to the idea of God's rational design of the universe, guided by universal laws of nature, a belief immensely strengthened by the researches in the preceding century of Isaac Newton and Robert Boyle, and disseminated through the work of the Royal Society and its provincial counterparts, including the Birmingham Lunar Society (founded in 1765, which included Watt in its membership) and the American Philosophical Society—which also in 1769 elected Benjamin Franklin as its president. A pivotal year indeed.

A WORLD OF TRADITIONAL AUTHORITY

Virtually throughout human history, mankind's view of the universe was dominated by traditional authority. By this I do not simply mean kings and bishops, sultans and caliphs, ancestor worship and emperors. Such figures derived their power from traditional authority, and in some ways embodied it, but they did not create it; at best they maintained it. Rather, by "traditional authority" I mean the venerated precepts drawn from three sources: historical precedent and custom; the collected observations of the unaided senses over millennia; and revered foundational texts that characterized the origins of all major civilizations.

To be sure, such traditional authority has on several occasions been challenged. In classical Greece, the philosophical schools of Aristotle, Plato, Diogenes, Epicurus, and others, and the mathematical advances of Euclid and the Alexandrians, used rational thought and argument to challenge the cosmology of the pagan Homeric world, developing new ideas of how earthly and heavenly bodies behaved that were based on natural characteristics, not the actions of "the gods." The Greeks also applied rational thought to politics, mapping out the major types of government (democracy, oligarchy, aristocracy, monarchy, tyranny) and the reasons why societies transitioned among them. Yet even Greek (and Persian, Indian, and Chinese) studies of nature relied entirely on what could be observed with the naked eye and measured with limited methods of marking time, weight, and distance (measurement of heat, pressure, work, and force had to wait until those concepts were developed with precision in the seventeenth and eighteenth centuries). The discoveries of reason also wrestled, often unsuccessfully (as depicted in the tragedy of *Antigone*), with the inheritance of local customs.

Once Christianity spread across the Roman Empire, however, the authority of the Greek philosophers was overshadowed by the word of God as revealed in the Old and New Testaments. Then with the collapse of the Roman Empire, much of the heritage of classical texts was lost altogether in Europe; the writings of the early Church fathers, along with the Bible, became the dominant traditional texts. When the works of Aristotle and other classical scholars were recovered in the Middle Ages, St. Thomas and other scholars sought to reconcile the classics with Christian thought, producing a commanding synthesis that assumed the character of the ultimate authority in Europe on matters of life, nature, government, and morals. Even in the Renaissance, despite novel advances in art, architecture, and observation, the accomplishments of the ancients (now corrected by advances in philology and textual scholarship) remained the target of emulation.

Further east, another charismatic challenge to older traditional authority had developed in Arabia, where the prophet Muhammad offered his own hearing of the Word of God in the Quran.

For believers, the Quran and the Prophet's sayings displaced Christian texts or Persian Zoroastrian precepts as the ultimate authority on all that mattered. Despite this, Arab scholars, especially during height of the "Golden Age" of Islamic science (ninth through twelfth centuries), made extensive advances in optics, chemistry, mathematics, and astronomy, seeking to correct and surpass the classical Greek corpus, from Aristotle to Ptolemy. In the eleventh century, Arab libraries and translators brought together the knowledge of the Chinese, Indians, and Greeks (borrowing "Arabic" numerals from India, among other advances). Yet this challenge also was turned back; in the twelfth century, Islamist scholars such as al-Ghazali argued that the diverse and often contradictory schools of Greek, Chinese, and Indian thought promoted illusory knowledge and that the only true wisdom was to be found in faithfully following the Quran. These scholars urged rulers to treat departures from the orthodoxy of Sunni Islam as apostasy and blasphemy (Kuru 2019). Then in the thirteenth century, Mongol invaders destroyed the great libraries of the Arab world, further hindering any intellectual advance beyond the confines of Muslim orthodoxy.

In India, China, and Southeastern and Eastern Asia, a mélange of customary and local religions and beliefs melded. These included the sacred Sanskrit texts of Hinduism (the Veda including the Upanishads [philosophical texts], and the later epics), the Buddhist Sutras, and the Confucian classics (not just the Analects of Confucius, but also earlier books such as the *I Ching* said to be compiled by Confucius, the writings of Mencius, and other works collected into the canonical "Four Books and Five Classics.") These were challenged at various times by Legalism or Daoism among others, and supplemented by local folk-religion (ancestor worship), traditional medicine, Chinese astrology and alchemy, but the Confucian classics emerged as the dominant sacred texts of the Chinese state and elites after the Song, while the Hindu classics remained dominant in most of India, and Buddhist beliefs spread everywhere in Asia, but became dominant only in a few regions (Thailand, Myanmar, Sri Lanka, Bhutan, and Tibet).

Thus, by about 1300, the great philosophical and religious texts of what historians call the "Axial age" (Eisenstadt 1986)—when transcendent morality religions emerged—had fought off or absorbed various challenges, and become firmly entrenched in all the great civilizations of the Old World. Wherever one looked, any challenges to the world views embodied in the Vedas, Analects, the Quran, or the Bible were vilified, their proponents condemned.

This was all the more true because temporal rulers—kings and emperors—had formed unions with religious authorities. Where in earlier centuries these groups had often been at odds, with prophets, popes, Confucian scholars, and Islamic mystics and preachers chastising and challenging rulers, by the late Middle Ages most rulers and religious masters and leaders had entered into a bargain: rulers would use the power of the state to enforce the national religion and punish heretics; religious authorities would then use their religious doctrines to legitimate the power of the rulers. Thus Indian monarchs were sanctified by elite Brahmins; Christian Kings were crowned by their bishops; Islamic kings and sultans were supported by the ulama (Islamic scholars), and the Chinese emperor's rule was not possible without the Confucian mandarins and gentry.

What was the nature of this traditional authority? Though it promulgated laws to reduce social conflict and protect property, the essence of traditional authority was that it was *changeable and arbitrary.* Sacred texts promoted belief in miracles; nature did not operate by laws but was whatever God chose to do. If there were regularities, it was in nature's impact on man and society, to be discerned through astrology or the study of omens. Kings, sultans, and emperors gave laws but in the main were not bound by them; the ruler's authority was divinely given and justified, so almost anything the ruler did was also divinely justified and not to be challenged (Kilkullen and Robinson 2019).

The world of appearances was held to be often deceptive and misleading (as indeed naked-eye judgements of distance and timing often were). Obvious properties of nature were well known: the planets moved in cycles across the heavens, but earthly objects fell to the ground; heat melted things and cold froze them; fire and smoke rose and water was wet, capable of supporting, soaking, or dissolving solids. But explanations of these facts had to correspond to what could be seen or assessed from common-sense experience, or to what could be found in the sacred texts.

To be sure, architects, military engineers, road and bridge and canal builders, as well as merchants and state administrators, had to have systems of counting, measuring, and rules of thumb for forces and construction to make sure that things worked! And astrologers had to keep track of the movements of the planets through the constellations of the zodiac. But such "practical" knowledge and calculations were demeaned as akin to merely skilled craftsmanship; "real" understanding of philosophy and theology which dealt in "ultimate truths" was esteemed far more highly (Galileo, in his early career, chafed mightily that his skills in mathematics and military ballistics did not earn him the esteem of professors of theology [Wootton 2010]).

Of course, one can identify individuals who sought to depart from the strictures of traditional knowledge, even in medieval times. In England, William of Ockham advocated ideas of natural law and liberty; the Oxford calculators sought to measure a wide variety of properties to improve upon and resolve the paradoxes of classical (Aristotelean) physics, and Roger Bacon sought to promote an experimental, empirical approach to building knowledge. But the great forces of authority remained traditional. At the outset of the sixteenth century, European universities entertained no serious alternatives to the science and philosophy of the ancient Greeks and the cosmology and political doctrines of the Bible and Church fathers. And yet, the European world view was about to undergo a drastic change.

FROM TRADITIONAL AUTHORITY TO RATIONAL DESIGN

By the late Middle Ages, traditional authority delivered a very good deal for the secular and spiritual authorities, and the aristocratic and clerical or bureaucratic elites who served them. A high level of inequality was justified as part of the divine order. Rulers might face rebellious nobles, and uprisings by distressed peasants, and every so often there were movements of heretics, but the overall social system of elite domination was largely unchallenged. Those who sought privileges from rulers—guilds, universities, towns—in turn gave recognition and payments to those rulers in exchange for the monopolies or oligopolies that conserved their positions. To a striking degree, unlike at any time since the early first millennium, the same social categories, and the same basic economic and power relationships prevailed in 1500 as in 1200, whether in Europe, the Middle East, South Asia, or China.

Things started to change in the late fifteenth century. The spread of gunpowder weapons, so that artillery and infantry became the critical core of military force instead of cavalry, led to the expansion and centralization of power in states that had the money and skills to produce and utilize these arms. The Mughals conquered most of India; kings gained the upper hand over nobles in Europe; while the Ottomans and Safavid Persians divided the lands of Islam (Hodgson 1977). Europeans were on the move as well, sailing around Africa and into the Indian Ocean, and across the Atlantic to discover the New World.

For Arabs, Indians, and Chinese—all longtime ocean-going seafarers—the arrival of Europeans in their ports and seas was a major headache: the Europeans were new competitors, and ones that were particularly brutal (Goldstone 2009). Yet for Asian societies, the announcement of new lands to the West, beyond the Atlantic Ocean, barely merited a shrug. After all, Chinese, Indian, and Arab navigators had been traveling to new lands all across Eurasia: "new lands" across the Atlantic were no more alarming than discovering the island-continent of Madagascar off the coast of Africa, or hearing about the British Isles off the coast of Europe.

But for the traditional world view of Europeans, the discovery of new plants, animals, and materials from travels to Asia, and the discovery of even stranger plants, animals, and unknown civilizations in Mexico and Peru, was a shock to the system. The Europeans, after all, had struggled to assemble and integrate their classical and sacred texts, many lost after the collapse of the western Roman empire and then slowly recovered in the Crusades into Spain and the Holy Land, into a cohesive system of knowledge. The view of the world in those texts--the geography of Ptolemy, the botany of Dioscorides, the zoology of Aristotle, the medical and anatomical writings of Galen, the cosmology and astronomy of Aristotle, Ptolemy and the Bible—was taken, along with the actual Gospel, as the metaphorical gospel of nature, and remained the core of university teaching throughout the later Middle Ages and early modern period.

However, once it was recognized that the New World was in fact wholly new, and was not (as Columbus never ceased believing) the islands of Indonesia and the Asian mainland reached via a shortcut, European scholars and cartographers realized they had a problem. The new continents, new human societies, new plants and animals, all meant that things *existed* that were not known in the hitherto perfect and authoritative writings of the ancients or the Bible. There were attempts to square the circle, as by identifying Native Americans as the "lost tribes of Israel." But there was just too much new land, new wealth, too many new things, for the reality to be denied. The Europeans of the sixteenth century found themselves in possession of knowledge that no prior generations nor prior authorities had evidenced (the brief settlement of the Vikings in Newfoundland being unknown or forgotten).

The discoveries touched off a sudden passion for novel artifacts and collections of curiosities. Ostrich eggs were given gilded mounts; royal collections of plants and animals from around the world were initiated, and people began to look at the world around them with greater curiosity. Maybe the old bones found in the fields (were they dragons?) or the strange creatures preserved in the rocks of hillsides (marine fossils in sedimentary rocks) had origins or meanings that could now be discovered. If the knowledge of the ancient, traditional authorities was at best incomplete, what else could be learned?

At about the same time as the nature-knowledge of the ancient texts was coming under criticism as faulty, the moral superiority of the authorities came under devastating attack as well.

Martin Luther, a German monk who was also a brilliant writer and devastatingly effective propagandist and critic, had grown outraged that the Papacy had embarked on a massive sale of indulgences to augment its finances. Such indulgences essentially meant that money (which Jesus had described as the root of all evil) could now be traded with the Church for the remission of sins; those who could afford it were now able to use silver rather than virtue to buy an admission ticket to Heaven. While Luther at first intended only to critique a practice he found horrific, not to overthrow the Catholic Church, in the course of his arguments he became more and more convinced that salvation could not be granted to anyone by the Church and its clergy, not through indulgences, nor partaking of communion, nor the intervention of saints. Rather, salvation could only come through the faith of the believer, faith that had to come from the direct experience of the individual with the Word of God by reading and studying the Bible.

Luther's followers later created a variety of local and national Protestant Churches: the Anglican in England, Lutheran in Scandinavia and Germany, Presbyterian in Scotland, and Calvinist in Geneva and the Netherlands. What all had in common was a rejection of the authority of the Pope in both religious and earthly affairs. But while they changed the interpretation, they did not change the authority of the sacred texts. Indeed, in some ways the authority of the biblical text (as opposed to Papal pronouncements) was magnified. In Scotland, heretics were still hanged in the seventeenth century; and in Calvinist Holland, the Dutch Reformed Church forced Descartes to flee and Spinoza not to publish, because their writings on rational understanding and belief challenged the Church's teaching on divine revelation.

It is sometimes argued (most famously by Robert Merton [Cohen 1990]) that Protestantism was more favorable to scientific advance and experimental methods than Catholicism. Yet while some reduction of Papal and Biblical authority was no doubt essential to modern scientific advancement, it did not follow that Protestant doctrine itself was supportive of rational scientific inquiry. In fact, for the first century after the Reformation, the great scientific advances were predominantly in Catholic countries: Copernicus was Catholic, as were Kepler, Galileo, Pascal and Torricelli. And as just noted, rigorous Protestant Churches seeking conformism to their orthodoxy could be just as hostile to rationalist thought as the Catholics. As we will note below, what emerged in late seventeenth Britain that was particularly supportive of rationalist thought was a kind of religious standoff that produced a limited official pluralism and a reduction in the state's efforts to force all citizens into a single religion.

But that did not happen until 1689. In the preceding century, both the authority of the Papacy and Catholic Church and the authority of the classical/Biblical view of nature underwent a steady, and sometimes sharp, erosion. Wars between kings and princes who had adopted Protestantism and those who held to Catholicism wracked Europe. Some territories, such as the United Provinces of the Netherlands, were freed from Catholic control; others, such as Bohemia, were restored to it. The Church itself created a new order, the Jesuits, and a new institution, the Inquisition, to wage a counter-Reformation to reverse the rejection of Papal authority. In many countries, civil wars were fought among contenders for national authority of different religions.

Yet by the late seventeenth century, such wars of religion had the paradoxical effect of *increasing* the rigor with which orthodoxy in religion was sought by the state; whether that religion was Protestant or Catholic, it seemed that having all citizens practice the same faith in the same manner was the only way to assure national harmony. The same conclusion was reached outside of Europe at about the same time: whether in the Ottoman Empire after the *jelali* rebellions of the seventeenth century, or in China after the collapse of the Ming dynasty, or in India under the late Mughal ruler Aurangzeb, governments responded to disorders by strengthening their support for more rigid orthodoxy, elevating the study of sacred texts, and waging war on novelty and heterodox thought (Goldstone 2016).

Before this renewal of orthodoxy, the impetus to discovery and novelty that began in Europe in the sixteenth century spurred a number of hypotheses and new findings about nature. Nicholaus Copernicus, knowing that Ptolemy's earthly geography had wrongly treated the Mediterranean as the center of the world, wondered if his astronomy could also be improved. Viewing the Sun as the most truly heavenly of all bodies, Copernicus developed calculations of planetary positions using a scheme that placed the Sun at the center of the solar system, instead of the earth. This allowed Copernicus to dispense with many (but not all) of the epicycles and other devices that Ptolemy had used to account for the apparent motions of the planets, such as the fact that they appear to sometimes shift backwards in their movements across the sky, then resume their course. This is easy to show in a heliocentric system as a natural consequence of the planets moving around the sun at different speeds, so that the earth sometimes overtakes them in their orbit, making them appear to move backwards, while for Ptolemy it required complex devices. Still, this required that the earth not be stationary, but to be rotating each day and revolving annually around the sun, motions that seemed at odds with common sense as well as Biblical and classical descriptions. Copernicus's *De Revolutionibus* was published in 1543; even half a century later the distinguished astronomer Tycho Brahe wrote that the Copernican system "expertly and completely circumvents all that is superfluous or discordant in the system of Ptolemy. On no point does it offend the principle of mathematics. Yet it ascribes to the Earth, that hulking, lazy body, unfit for motion, a motion as quick as that of the aethereal torches, and a triple motion at that" (Gingerich 1993, p. 181). (Copernicus's system stipulated three motions of the Earth: daily rotation, annual revolution around the sun, and the seasonal precession of the equinoxes.)

While most astronomers thus set aside Copernicus's theory, they continued to make ever more accurate observations and records of planetary motions. One of Brahe's assistants, the gifted mathematician Johannes Kepler, was convinced that the true order of nature would be found in calculating the movements of the planets and finding a numerological pattern in those movements. Seeing that neither Ptolemy's nor Copernicus's calculations fit the exact observations of planetary motions, Kepler decided to experiment with different mathematical forms. Both Ptolemy and Copernicus had followed the same rule in composing their systems, a rule inherited from the Greek belief that as the heavens were perfect and eternal, the only allowed form of motion was movement in perfect circles at uniform velocity (hence the epicycles and other devices to compound uniform circular movements to produce the planets' variable speed and direction actually observed in the night skies.) Kepler decided to try using ellipses, instead of circles, for the planetary orbits. This led to an extraordinary "aha" moment: the elliptical orbits fit the observations almost perfectly. What is more, a different form of "uniform motion" could be preserved: if the planets moved faster as they grew closer to the sun, and more slowly as they moved away, such that the radius from the planet to the sun *swept out equal areas in the ellipse in equal times*, that motion then matched the observed motion of the planets. Kepler announced these laws to the world in 1609 in his treatise whose title declared *A New Astronomy*.

As Kepler worked further on his calculations, he made a third discovery: Behind the motion of *all* the planets lay a simple rule: if one took the square of the time it took for a planet to complete one orbit, and the cube of the long radius of the elliptical orbit, the ratio of these two values was always the same. While this may seem just an oddity to us, to Kepler it was a revelation. Instead of the tangle of complex cycles, epicycles, and other artifices, the motion of the planets was now revealed to have a simple harmony of arithmetic proportions. The distances of the planets from the sun, their speed of motion, and the size of their orbits were all related by a simple uniform rule. It was as if the motions of the planets were like notes in a musical scale (and to Kepler, who was a numerologist and mystic, that is exactly what he concluded and claimed in his 1619 book presenting this law, *Harmonices Mundi*). Or, one could say the motions of the planets were like the hands of a watch, moving regularly in response to the rules set by the watchmaker. One could hardly think of a more radical departure from the arbitrary and changeable world of divine intervention, or from the perfectly uniform motions by planets that, as denizens of heaven, are completely different in nature and obey different rules than the heavy, unmovable earth.

Of course, hardly any astronomers or theologians were numerical mystics, so were not convinced by his "harmony" of the spheres. Yet the idea of a clockwork universe, ruled by laws that applied equally to the Earth and the heavenly bodies, gained increasing traction as irrefutable evidence began to pile up that the Earth and the rest of the solar system did not have wholly different natures. In the early seventeenth century, when Galileo assembled a series of lenses to make the first telescope designed to study the heavens, he discovered that the moon, though a heavenly body, had rugged features, such as mountains and valleys, like Earth. He also discovered four moons circling around Jupiter, meaning that this planet, like the earth, had its own satellites. Galileo even found that the sun was not a perfect body, but had dark spots transiting its surface. In short, the motion of Earth around the sun could no longer be denied on the basis of Earth having a wholly different nature from the bodies in the heavens. Galileo also demonstrated that Aristotle had been wrong not only about the nature of the heavens, but even about the mechanics of motion on earth; for Galileo's experiments showed that bodies of different weights fall with exactly the same uniform acceleration, rather than heavy bodies falling faster than light ones.

Calculations, instrument-aided observations, and experiment were thus revealing to Europeans features of nature that were simply unknown to those who depended on common sense, naked-eye observations, and "rules" drawn from classical and sacred texts to understand the world. Additional observations about anatomy (from precise dissection and recording), astronomy (from the study of comets and supernovae), and magnetism (from empirical study of magnetic and electrostatic attraction) further created a crisis of knowledge: it was abundantly clear that the statements of Galen, Aristotle, the Bible, and other classical authorities were either ignorant of, or flat out wrong about, the phenomena now being observed. Thus, by the early seventeenth century, the leading thinkers of Europe, notably Francis Bacon in England and Rene Descartes in France, sought new ways to find knowledge that could be trusted.

Both argued that Aristotle had to be abandoned as an authority on nature. Both argued that the only way to understand God and his works was to look closely at nature with measurement, systemic observation, and calculations, and to reason with logic rather than intuition or faith alone. In this, they were followed by more and more European philosophers and students of nature and man. Major advances in measurement and calculation were made, from the use of logarithms (developed by the Scot John Napier) to the development of calculus (the use of infinitesimals) by Leibniz and Newton.

Experiments and mathematical formulae thus began their mission to displace traditional authority as the basis for understanding nature and organizing society. Of course, that would entail radical innovations that would threaten the authority of the Church and the power of Kings. How could such things be permitted in a world where the Church and Kings still ruled?

FROM REASON VS. RULERS TO REASON AS THE FRAMEWORK FOR GOVERNMENT AND LIFE

One answer is that by the early to mid-seventeenth century, many rulers were losing their grip on society. A combination of rising population since 1500 with a sharp deterioration of the weather in the early to mid-1600s meant that rulers were having trouble collecting tax revenues, real wages were dropping, and elite competition for revenues and positions intensified (Parker 2013; Goldstone 2016). Revolutions shook monarchs all across Europe: the Puritan Revolution in Great Britain; the *Frondes* in France; and revolts and revolutions in Portugal, Catalonia, and Sicily against the Spanish monarchy all occurred in the 1640s. The same period saw recurrent religious wars in Europe, from the Netherlands to Bohemia and all across the German lands. There was famine and civil war in India, a series of military and provincial rebellions in the Ottoman Empire, the Ming dynasty in China collapsed and was conquered by the Manchus, eastern Europe was wracked by the massive Khmelnitsky Cossack uprising, and Russia was torn by nobles' revolts that ended the Rurik dynasty and led to the reign of the Romanovs. Altogether Geoffrey Parker (2013, p. 668) identified "50 or so revolutions and rebellions that occurred around the world between 1618 and 1688."

This period of collapsing royal authority was also a period of dynamic religious and political heterodoxies. In Europe, the remaining Parliaments and Estates asserted their rights against Kings; Protestants opposed the authority of Catholic rulers; in China scholars in independent academies criticized the moral failings of the late Ming rulers; in the Ottoman Empire Sufi orders spread, their leaders often championing the common man against the government; and in India the Mughal rulers debated whether pluralism or rigid orthodoxy should guide their rule.

After the 1660s, the wave of disorders subsided. Population stabilized or declined in the wake of the crisis, food prices came down, and elites sought to work with rulers to restore order. In order to manage the transition and avoid the recurrence of rebellions and civil wars, rulers strengthened their bureaucracies and militaries. They also sought to stamp out heterodox beliefs and philosophies that challenged their rule, by means ranging from the Inquisition in Catholic Europe to the burning of non-Confucian books in China. In Europe, rulers agreed that each monarch should be free to fix the religion in their country, such that France in 1685 revoked the right of Protestants to worship. In the Ottoman Empire, the ulema promoted the "Circle of Justice," a principle similar to the "Chain of Being" in Christian thought: a view of the universe in which order depended on obedience to the God-given authority of rulers. In China, the new Manchu dynasty sought to keep the Chinese mandarins occupied and loyal by sponsoring huge projects to collect and perfect Confucian literature and doctrine—which demanded filial obedience to the Emperor from all. In India, the Mughal ruler Aurangzeb was not only a pious Sunni Muslim; he insisted that a rigid Sunni orthodoxy be followed by all Muslims in India, forced Hindus to convert to Islam, destroyed their temples, and imposed harsh taxes on non-Muslims

While monarchs around the world enjoyed greater authority, higher revenues, and enforced greater conformity to the state religion, the kingdoms of Great Britain were a modest exception. Due to vagaries of history and conquest, the King of Anglican England was also the king of fiercely Presbyterian Scotland and of passionately Catholic Ireland. An earlier effort to impress Anglican religious practice on Scotland and Ireland had been one of the chief causes of the mid-century civil wars. Thus after the 1660s, when the radical Protestant Commonwealth of Oliver Cromwell had fallen and the Stuart monarchy was restored, it did not seek to impose religious conformity across its domains. Instead, it settled for keeping the vast majority of elite position in the hands of Anglicans, with a minority of Catholic gentry and Lords, and separate rules for Scotland, reserving its hostility mainly for the radical egalitarian Protestant sects (Congregationalists, Quakers, Baptists and others collectively known as "Dissenters" from the Anglican orthodoxy).

But a religious crisis arose in the kingdoms in the 1680s. In 1685, the Anglican King Charles II died without an heir, and the throne passed to his brother, James II, a practicing Catholic who admired the absolute monarchy of his cousin Louis XIV in France. A Protestant rebellion arose almost at once, led by Charles's Protestant but illegitimate son, the Duke of Monmouth.

Poorly organized and worse led, the rebellion was quickly put down. Its significance lay in James II now being able to point to the threat to his authority to justify installing loyal Catholic officers in the army, maintaining a standing military force, and implementing more absolutist judicial and bureaucratic procedures. James appointed Catholics to high offices of state and important positions at Oxford Colleges; when Parliament objected, James prorogued and then dissolved Parliament, got into a dispute with Anglican bishops, and sought to control the composition of future Parliaments.

From the 1660s to the 1680s, empirical and mathematical science had made rapid progress in Britain. In 1660, Charles II granted a charter to the Royal Society, and these decades saw the publication of pivotal works by Fellows of the Society: on air pressure and gases by Robert Boyle, on research with microscopes by Richard Hooke, on climate and astronomy by Edmund Halley, and on mechanics and gravity by Isaac Newton. But this progress was threatened by James's efforts to restore Catholic teachings and install Catholic leadership at Oxford and Cambridge—efforts to which Newton was particularly hostile.

James was also active in reshaping the government of the American colonies to increase royal authority (Lovejoy 1987). He amalgamated all the colonies of New England with New York and New Jersey into a single Royal Dominion, withdrew their charters, abolished their local governments, and placed them under the control of a royal governor on a model similar to that used by Spain for its vice-royalties in the Americas. In Virginia, James told the governor to dissolve the House of Burgesses and remove any disloyal officials.

We do not know where all these efforts to create a continental-style, divine Catholic monarchy in Britain and America would have led, because they were cut short in 1688. In that year, the birth of a male heir to James, which held the promise of a permanent Catholic succession, galvanized the British elites into action. Correspondence with the Protestant leader of Holland, William of Orange, who was married to James's daughter Mary, had begun earlier and now turned to a direct invitation to William to come to England and assert his right to the Crown.

In autumn of 1688, braving risky weather in the English Channel, William landed a substantial army in the south of England. James, largely abandoned by the British elites, fled to France. In subsequent years, William, ruling as William III of Britain and stadtholder of Holland, would lead Protestant armies to defend his throne and his territories against opponents in Ireland and France. Without his success, it is entirely plausible that James would have remained in power, and working with his cousin Louis XIV would have defeated Holland and created a Catholic domination over the kingdoms of

Scotland, Ireland, England, and Wales and the United Provinces, ending the Protestant dominion in northwestern Europe (Goldstone 2006).

But that did not happen. Instead, William's success put the British Isles on a unique trajectory among all the monarchies of Europe and the empires of the Old World (Pincus 2009). For in the process of assuming the British throne, William had to assent to the conditions set by Britain's Anglican leadership: Parliament was to meet regularly and have sole power to raise revenues; religious toleration was institutionalized for all Protestants, and a bill of rights was enacted, spelling out limitations to royal power and the rights of citizens to fair treatment under the law. In the American colonies, the deposition of James was followed by revolts against his royal governors, dissolution of the Dominion, and the recovery of charters and local representative government.

While the "Glorious Revolution," as it was called, succeeded, it was justified not as a radical move, but as a restoration of the old balance of power between king and Parliament. Yet the Act of Settlement that gave the Crown to William and his Protestant heirs clearly implied that Parliament, not God and divine right, was the arbiter of who would exercise royal authority. Not everyone accepted that radical alteration of traditional authority: Jacobite rebellions seeking to restore the heirs of James II to the throne as the true and rightful Kings "by grace of God" recurred in 1715, 1719, and 1745. However, the events of 1640–1688, which included two revolutions, several rebellions, two civil wars, one king (Charles I) executed for treason, and another (James II) forced from power, had severely undermined the theory of divine monarchy.

Instead, influenced by the success of empiricism and rational analysis in reforming the understanding of nature, political thinkers looked to use similar methods to justify and design political authority. As early as 1651, in the wake of the civil wars and just two years after Charles I's execution by a radicalized Parliament, Thomas Hobbes produced his *Leviathan: Or the Matter, Forme and Power of a Commonwealth, Ecclesiasticall and Civil*. Instead of attributing the authority of Kings to divine right from God, Hobbes argued from observation and rational analysis that, starting from consideration of the condition of man in a state of nature, only a powerful state could keep men from using violence against each other in a war of all against all. Hobbes proceeded to derive all the necessary conditions of government, and its relation to religious authority, from what he constructed as natural laws of society.

In the later seventeenth century, debates continued in Britain on whether society was best served by a commonwealth with representation in Parliament, or by kingship with absolute or even divine authority. In 1680 Robert Filmer published a full-throated defense of the traditional authority and divine right of Kings. However, his arguments were effectively opposed and dismantled by John Locke, who in his *Two Treatises on Government* showed how the natural laws of society, uncovered by reason, dictate that the purpose of government is to protect the property, and improvements thereto, created by men. That being the purpose of government, a ruler who instead of protecting the property of his subjects, attacks that property and seeks to undermine their rights to control their property, can rightly be deposed by those subjects.

Locke's views were dangerous in Britain when James II was seeking to build up his absolute authority, so Locke had to flee to Holland. But he returned after James was deposed, traveling to England with the future Queen Mary, and the *Two Treatises* were published in 1689.

Both Hobbes and Locke were deeply influenced by, and engaged in, the scientific debates of their day when writing on government and natural law. Hobbes engaged in extended debates on experimental methods, the vacuum, and the mechanics of gases with Boyle (Shapin and Schaffer 1985), while Locke wrote extensively on human perception, scientific experiment, and the basis for scientific knowledge. The development of new notions of natural rights, civil society, and government by contract and design thus occurred in tandem with the attack on the traditional authority of sacred texts, and the religious and monarchical powers that relied on them to legitimate their authority.

As noted above, elsewhere across the world the desire for peace and order in the wake of rebellions and civil wars had led to conservative restorations or new dynasties that affirmed and enforced orthodoxy in religious beliefs. Those religions and their sacred texts also had systems for understanding the natural world, which were also affirmed with the same intensity. Novelty of all kinds, including foreign knowledge, was dismissed and impugned. It was only with the expansion of European power in Asia after 1800 that the Asian empires sought to avail themselves of Western science and technology, and then only in areas of necessity, from armaments to finance, while eschewing broader shifts in epistemology or principles of government.

Even in much of Europe, the substitution of rational and empirical scientific thought for traditional authority was resisted. The Jesuits adopted a model of the solar system developed by Tycho Brahe that allowed the other planets (of a different, divine substance) to revolve around the sun, while the sun and all the planets moved around a stationary, heavy earth. Throughout Catholic Europe, innovation and ideas that clashed with the teachings of the Church were discouraged. In most of the continent, while Newton's mechanics were respected, his idea of gravity as a universal force that acted across enormous distances was widely dismissed. Instead, Rene Descartes's version of non-Aristotelian mechanics and planetary movement, in which the planets were swirled around by vortices in the ether, was favored. Some of Aristotle's views—such as the belief that nature abhors a vacuum, so no vacuum could be observed in nature, continued to hold sway (both Hobbes and Descartes, despite being anti-Aristotelian in so many ways, could not accept the idea of "empty space" and rejected the possibility of creating a vacuum in a jar.) To be sure, all across Europe there was increasing acceptance of the "mechanical philosophy," where in contrast to Aristotle's view that matter acted according to "its nature," all actions were seen to be the result of the movements and collisions among bodies in motion. Nonetheless, this belief was not allowed to spread to ideas about Church or royal authority, which were zealously guarded by both Protestant and Catholic monarchs and Churches.

Britain, however, had rejected the idea of divine royal authority, and by the end of the seventeenth century was the home of the leading proponents of new scientific methods. William III's ascension to the throne, along with the new regime of toleration for Dissenting Protestants and the limits on royal authority, helped pave the way for a nationwide embrace of the new sciences in place of the traditional authorities. But Britain also needed a belief system to help restore order and avoid the passionate conflicts that had fueled two generations of violent conflicts. So British elites and the Anglican Church took a different turn. They embraced Newton's view of the solar system and mechanical forces as displaying an eternal order, as perfect as mathematical symmetries and discernible by careful observation and reason. God was seen as the great Legislator, who had established laws of the Universe that all matter obeyed. Embracing Newton allowed the Anglican authorities to place themselves separate from, and superior to, the Papist superstitions about an unmoving Earth and a world of recurring miracles and saintly interventions (Jacob 1997).

By the 1700s, there was a virtual craze for the new science sweeping Great Britain. Lecturers like John Desaguliers, who had been an assistant to Newton, and was an important scientist in his own right (his work on electricity coined the terms conductor and insulator), gave lectures promoting the Newtonian world view. Desaguliers started advertising his public lectures on "the Experimental Philosophy" in 1712, and over his life gave some 140 courses of some twenty lectures each on mechanics, hydrostatics, pneumatics, optics and astronomy, designing his own apparatus for scientific demonstrations, and playing to audiences ranging from London craftsmen to King George I and his family (Carpenter 2011).

Though Desaguliers was perhaps the most successful of those educating the public on the new science, he was not alone. Gentlemen vied to show their sophistication by their collection and use of scientific instruments (for which London became the world's premiere market), and provincial scientific clubs and academies flourished. In the course of the eighteenth century, Anglican preachers invoked and public schools taught the basics of the Newtonian world view—in marked contrast to France, where Newton's mechanics were displaced by Descartes, and not taught in schools until after the French Revolution.

By the mid-eighteenth century, the Scottish universities in Edinburgh, Glasgow, St. Andrews, and Aberdeen had eagerly grasped the new experimental science, making it the basis for their curriculum. At the University of Glasgow, William Cullen gave advanced lectures on chemistry and became mentor to Joseph Black, who first isolated carbon dioxide and developed the idea of latent heat. Black engaged with a young scientific instrument maker at the university, James Watt, whose insights on heat and energy greatly advanced the steam engine by separating the condenser (where hot steam was cooled) from the pressure cylinder, thus saving heat energy, and thereby fuel, increasing efficiency several fold.

But chemistry was just one area where the Scottish universities shined; they also excelled in history, moral philosophy, and economics, producing, among others, David Hume and Adam Smith. The Scots also became proponents of teaching the new sciences and natural law as the basis for higher education, and their principles became the guiding light of eighteenth-century American colleges. Many of the founding fathers had their educations shaped by Scottish teachers, or studied at universities shaped by Scottish immigrants.

In the eighteenth century, Great Britain became the wonder and workshop of the world.

The society where science advanced by machines and instrumental experiments—vacuum pumps, telescopes, microscopes, barometers, calorimeters—consequently became the nation of industry advanced by machines—spinning and weaving machines, puddling and rolling machines, steam engines (alone or driving water wheels), boring tools, pumping machines, and factories.

The approach of using experiment and empirical study to develop fundamental ideas and new designs extended to the science of government as well. The derivation of natural laws, and the argument that government institutions could be designed by *reason*, using empirical knowledge gained from past experience, became the dominant view among the highly educated in Britain and America, seconded by European critics of monarchy from Montesquieu to Voltaire. These ideas were transplanted to the New World in part in the great wave of university foundations of the eighteenth century.

THE GREAT AWAKENING AND THE WAVE OF AMERICAN UNIVERSITY FOUNDATIONS

Prior to the Glorious Revolution, America had only one significant college: Harvard College, founded by the Puritans of the Massachusetts Bay Colony in 1636. Its curriculum was focused on rote learning of the Bible to prepare preachers. However, after 1689, new universities were founded to teach the new approach to religion, science, mathematics and the liberal arts.

The first to obtain a royal charter was Virginia's College of William and Mary, named after the new rulers of Britain and founded in 1693 by James Blair, a Scotsman who had been educated at Aberdeen and Edinburgh. Under Blair's leadership, the university's curriculum included natural and moral philosophy on the Scottish university model, as well as divinity and grammar. It was thus the first college in America to have a full faculty, not merely one in divinity and theology. Among its graduates were Thomas Jefferson, James Monroe, John Marshall, sixteen members of the Continental Congress and four signers of the Declaration of Independence. The college also provided George Washington's only formal education—he earned his surveyor's license there.

This was soon followed by the foundation of St. John's University in Annapolis, Maryland, in 1696. The college's original charter, reflecting the Masonic value of religious tolerance as well as the religious diversity of the founders (which included Presbyterians, Episcopalians, and Roman Catholics) stated that "youth of all religious denominations shall be freely and liberally admitted" and also adopted a combined divinity and liberal arts curriculum. A few years later, in 1701, Yale College was founded by the government of Connecticut, which chartered it to teach the arts and sciences to prepare graduates "for Publick employment both in Church and Civil State."

While Anglicans dominated religious life in England, religion in America was more diverse, as shown in the founders of St. John's. Unlike England, there was no official state religion in America, although many of the elites identified with the Anglican Church, and joined Episcopal churches. In both countries, however, after 1700, religion was increasingly seen as a personal choice of conscience, and not a matter to be dictated by the state. And with the rise of interest in the new experimental science and the declining power of traditional authority, formal religious practice lost much of its attraction.

Yet this process, like most social changes, also produced a counter-reaction. Starting in Scotland in the 1710s, then brought by Scottish immigrants to the American colonies in the 1740s, a "Great Awakening" of religious passion arose. This movement did not take the form of reviving clerical authority over everyday life, or rebuilding a hierarchy of any sort. Rather, it consisted of popular preachers who whipped up enthusiasm for salvation and denounced sin. The movement's leaders drew on the Calvinist theology of Scottish Presbyterianism, but preached to everyone, especially Dissenters but also Anglicans and Catholics, in the open air and vast meeting halls. They provided a simple message: All people can be saved if they seek forgiveness and accept God's grace, entering a direct and emotional connection with God. They argued that religion shouldn't be formal and institutionalized, but rather casual and personal. They were the direct precursors of today's evangelical "super Churches" in the United States.

The leaders of the Great Awakening led a movement in which religion was deeply personal and moral; therefore religion could be kept separate from government and did not require powerful religious authorities, and religious belief could be kept separate from natural science. The leaders of the Great Awakening also had a great zeal for education, desiring to train new generations of preachers and leaders of strong morality. They thus set out to found institutions of higher education that, like William and Mary, would combine instruction in theology with the liberal arts and sciences.

In 1726 the Scottish Presbyterian minister William Tennent and his son, who had migrated to America, founded a school that would become the College of New Jersey and then Princeton University. In the 1750s and 1760s, other figures in the Great Awakening would also start educational institutions that became major universities: Columbia in 1754, Brown in 1764, Rutgers in 1766, and Dartmouth in 1769.

Despite their clerical origins, America's eighteenth-century universities remained strongly shaped by their roots in the Scottish Enlightenment and their dedication to teaching the new experimental science. This was reinforced by Benjamin Franklin's foundation of the University of Pennsylvania 1751 with the aim of teaching practical skills. It was further strengthened by the appointment of an exceptional Scottish scholar, John Witherspoon, as the sixth President of Princeton in 1768.

Witherspoon was a product of the University of Edinburgh, a prominent Presbyterian minister in Scotland who believed in natural law and was an advocate of republicanism when he was recruited to lead Princeton. He saw no contradiction between reason and religion, and reformed the Princeton curriculum to place greater emphasis on moral philosophy and natural science on the latest Scottish models. He likely had a greater influence on the generation of the Founding Fathers than any other educational leader: indeed he was the only minister and only college president to sign the Declaration of Independence. He had students at Princeton study "modern" philosophers such as Machiavelli, Locke, Hume, and Montesquieu—an influence that was clear on his greatest student, James Madison. Witherspoon's model for teaching Enlightenment philosophy was influential across American universities, as well as in his students, which included ten future cabinet officers, six members of the Continental Congress, thirty-nine congressmen, twenty-one senators, and twelve state governors.

Witherspoon was deeply hostile to royal interference in the colonies, and was a fervent advocate of limited government. He manifested a deep suspicion of all traditional authorities in favor of free thought and original inquiry—a movement that had been building up in Europe since the early 1500s but only came to bloom into a dominant world view in eighteenth-century England and, even more so, in its colonies.

DARTMOUTH AND THE DAWN OF THE MODERN AGE

When less than a decade after Dartmouth's founding, America's leaders signed the Declaration of Independence and set out to create a new nation with a new form of government, whose legitimacy and design were grounded wholly on natural law and rational design, they were continuing a trajectory that had begun with Copernicus's challenge to the Bible and Ptolemy, and continued through two centuries of discoveries and inventions that demonstrated how original thought and rational design could transcend the inherited limitations of traditional religious and political world views (Ferris 2010). The U.S. Constitution adopted the idea of managing social conflict through government that worked not because of the power of divine authority (exercised through Church and Crown) but like a machine, with checks and balances preventing great deviations from rational authority.

The fact that 1769 marked not only the founding of Dartmouth College, but also the patenting of Watt's steam engine and Arkwright's mechanical spinning machine, and Benjamin Franklin's election to lead the Philosophical Society of America was thus no coincidence; nor was America's revolution against royal authority seven years later and its creation of a novel constitution eleven years after that. Dartmouth's founding, like Britain's early industrial advances and America's original-design government, was part of the sweeping, irresistible movement that created the modern world, and changed the position of Western Civilization within world history. The world of instrument-driven science, machine-based industry, and government based on rational design and checks and balances gave us the three revolutions—Scientific, Industrial, and Democratic—that created modernity. The eighteenth-century founding of new universities in America to teach the Enlightenment ideals was an essential part of that process.

REFERENCES

Carpenter, A. T. 2011. *John Theophilus Desaguliers: A Natural Philosopher, Engineer and Freemason in Newtonian England*. London: Continuum/Bloomsbury.

Cohen, I. Bernard, ed. 1990. Puritanism and the rise of modern science: the Merton thesis. New Brunswick, NJ: Rutgers University Press.

Eisenstadt, S.N., ed. 1986. *The Origins and Diversity of Axial Age Civilizations* (SUNY Series in Near Eastern Studies). Albany, NY: SUNY Press.

Ferris, Timothy. 2010. *The Science of Liberty: Democracy, Reason, and the Laws of Nature*. New York: Harper.

Gingerich, Owen. 1993. *The eye of heaven: Ptolemy, Copernicus, Kepler*. New York: American Institute of Physics.

Goldstone, Jack A. 2006. "Europe's Peculiar Path: Would the World be 'Modern' if William III's Invasion of England in 1688 had Failed?" Pp. 168–196 in *Unmaking the West: What-if? Scenarios that Rewrite World History*, Philip E. Tetlock, Ned Lebow, and Geoffrey Parker, eds. Ann Arbor, MI: University of Michigan Press.

Goldstone, Jack A. 2009. *Why Europe? The Rise of the West in World History*. Boston: McGraw-Hill.

Goldstone, Jack A. 2016. *Revolution and Rebellion in the Early Modern World, 25th anniversary edition*. New York: Routledge.

Hodgson, Marshall. 1977. *The Venture of Islam, vol. 3: The Gunpowder Empires*. Chicago: University of Chicago Press.

Jacob, Margaret C. 1997. *Scientific Culture and the Making of the Industrial West*. New York: Oxford University Press.

Kilcullen, John and Jonathan Robinson. 2019. "Medieval Political Philosophy", The Stanford Encyclopedia of Philosophy. Edward N. Zalta (ed.), URL = https://plato.stanford.edu/archives/win2019/entries/medieval-political/.

Kuru, Ahmet. 2019. *Islam, Authoritarianism, and Underdevelopment: A Global and Historical Comparison*. Cambridge, UK: Cambridge University Press.

Lovejoy, David. 1987. *The Glorious Revolution in America*. Middletown, CT: Wesleyan University Press.

Parker, Geoffrey. 2013. *Global Crisis: War, Climate Change, & Catastrophe in the Seventeenth Century*. New Haven, CT: Yale University Press.

Pincus, Steve. 2009. *1688: The First Modern Revolution*. New Haven, CT: Yale University Press.

Shapin, Steven and Simon Schaffer. 1985. *Leviathan and the Air Pump: Hobbes, Boyle and the Experimental Life, Including a Translation of Thomas Hobbes, Dialogus Physicus De Natura Aeris*. Princeton, NJ: Princeton University Press.

Wootton, David. 2010. *Galileo: Watcher of the Skies*. New Haven, CT: Yale University Press.

Chapter 2

Dartmouth College and Patriot State Building

Steve Pincus (The University of Chicago)

"Let colleges be erected, youth educated, literature promoted and encouraged," enthused the author of an essay printed in the *New Hampshire Gazette* celebrating the founding of Dartmouth College. This new institution will "instill noble, generous and virtuous sentiments, into young and tender minds which will grow up, flourish, and bear fruit, like the beauteous olive." These college alumni will in turn fill "the desk and courts of justice." Their "wise and virtuous practice will lead the unthinking into peaceful ways."[1] This essayist predicted that the alumni of Dartmouth College would staff the newly proliferating institutions of the provincial state and diffuse their learning among the new settlers in western New Hampshire.

This narrative of Dartmouth's founding as a state institution meant to educate lawyers, magistrates, judges, and bureaucrats in the rapidly growing Province of New Hampshire sits in uneasy contrast to the received narrative. In that narrative, summarized in the crudely racist college song "Eleazar Wheelock was a very pious man / he went into the wilderness to teach the Indian"—the college was a private charity founded by a pious New England minister to educate Indian youth.[2] The college's own website proclaims that "Dartmouth's founder, Eleazar Wheelock, a Congregational minister from Connecticut, established the college as an institution to educate Native Americans."[3] This story has often been repackaged and retold. "The germ of Dartmouth College," writes Baxter Perry Smith in his *History of Dartmouth College*, "was a deep-seated and long-cherished desire, of the foremost of its founders [Eleazar Wheelock], to elevate the Indian race in America." That Wheelock's college was a private institution was made clear by the charter's insistence that the clergy were the "best depositories of educational trusts."[4] Daniel Webster famously narrated this story for the Supreme Court of the United States. Dr. Wheelock, he said, "had founded a charity on funds owned and procured by himself; and that he was at that time sole dispenser and sole administrator, as well as the legal owner of these funds; that he had made his will, devising this property in trust, to continue the existence and uses of the school, and appointed trustees." It is true that when the college moved from Lebanon, Connecticut, to Hanover, New Hampshire, Wheelock decided "to extend the design of it to the education of the youth of that province," but he retained full control and named the trustees of the college in his will. It was, Webster insisted, "a private charity, originally founded and endowed by an individual, with a charter obtained for it at his request, for the better administration of his charity."[5] It was in this sense, in the sense of a private institution, that Webster concluded that "it is, sir, as I have said, a small college. And yet there are those who love it."[6] The lesson we have been taught, Robert Bonner neatly concludes, is that Dartmouth was and always has been a purveyor of "private liberal arts education" rather than a "large scale public university."[7]

Against this narrative, I argue that there were two separate institutions founded by Eleazar Wheelock: one, an Indian Charity School that relied on private donations; and a second, Dartmouth College, that was in effect organized and established by Governor John Wentworth. Wentworth's contribution has been systematically underplayed in part because Wheelock published a widely distributed narrative of his projects geared toward appeasing English and Scottish donors who were furious at his abandonment of the charity school.[8] Wentworth's college needs to be understood as part of a broad cross-imperial partisan project of state formation. Patriots right across the Empire, from the 1720s onward, sought to promote colonial development rather than colonial extraction as the best means to promote the good of the Empire as a whole. John Wentworth returned from Britain to serve as governor of New Hampshire to implement those ideals. Wentworth collaborated with Wheelock to found an institution that would educate New Hampshire settlers and North Americans more broadly in the tools of good government. Dartmouth College was founded as a public institution dedicated to promoting the Patriot party's political economy of improvement.

I

Those who have told and retold the story that Dartmouth College was founded as a private institution insist that the college established in 1769 was merely an expansion of the charity school Eleazar Wheelock had founded in Lebanon, Connecticut. In that story, Wheelock "adopted a plan, which was new and till then never attempted" to remove Indian children from their families and "all connection with their countrymen" in order "to instruct them in the principles of learning the Christian religion, and the arts of civilized life." At the same school, Wheelock proposed to educate "a number of promising English youth, who would devote themselves to the service of the Redeemer in the capacity of missionaries." That project proved so successful that "the number of students, missionaries, and school masters" outstripped Wheelock's financial capacity. Wheelock therefore sent Nathaniel Whitaker and his former Indian pupil Samson Occom to Britain to raise money. They raised over £10,000. In England, a trust was created to manage the money, led by William Legge, second earl of Dartmouth. Wheelock soon decided that "the school" did not have "the endowments and privileges sufficient to afford the students such a course of studies as was thought necessary for preachers of the gospel." Wheelock, therefore, thought "that a college, in connection with" the Indian school "should be founded that the extended design of the institution might be more perfectly accomplished." Unfortunately, there was not enough land to build such an institution in Connecticut, so Wheelock sought to remove "to some remote part of the new forming settlements."[9] The success of Dr. Wheelock's Indian charity school in Connecticut led ineluctably to the establishment of the expanded college on the banks of the Connecticut River in New Hampshire. The institution remained private and primarily devoted to the education of Indians and missionaries to evangelize among the Indians.

Was this the case? Did Wheelock remain committed primarily to the education of Indians? Was the college merely the upper school to be attached to the Indian charity lower school?

In fact, the evidence suggests otherwise. Eleazar Wheelock's experimental school did prosper at first. As late as July 1768, Wheelock claimed that "the number in my Indian charity school is now . . . become so large, as that it is necessary" to find a new site "to erect suitable buildings" to accommodate the students.[10] But the numbers were dwindling. Wheelock had achieved a reputation for treating his Indian students harshly.[11] Sir William Johnson, superintendent for Indian Affairs and close ally of the Six Nations, turned against Wheelock and his charity school because he thought it disguised a design to seize Iroquois lands.[12] Johnson's opposition had an almost immediate effect. "I heard your Mohawk and Oneida boys don't intend to come back to school again," reported Samson Occom, Wheelock's Mohican former student.[13]

Second, the money raised by the English Trust was insufficient to fund a college with permanent buildings and a generous annual operating budget. Alan Taylor may be right to claim that the £12,000 raised by Nathaniel Whitaker and Samson Occom in their two-year tour of Britain was "a fortune for that era."[14] But it was still not nearly enough. Even as he received news of the donations in England and Scotland, Wheelock worried that he did not have enough to meet "the expenses of the school."[15] After the funding drive had concluded, George Whitefield, who had ample experience in raising funds for American projects, warned that "I do not see how an annual disbursement of six or seven hundred pounds per annum"—the amount he thought a minimum to cover yearly operating expenses—"can possibly be supported by the present fund."[16] Indeed, within a decade, the sums raised by Occom and Whitaker were all "expended."[17] Certainly this sum was dwarfed by the large financial grants and 40,000 acres, which by 1770 had been granted to and deemed essential for the endowment and support of Dartmouth College.[18]

Third, the choice of settling the college in Hanover, New Hampshire was less than ideal if the goal was to attract and educate Indians. Governor John Penn had suggested placing the college in southwestern Pennsylvania, which was "excellently situated for the Indians."[19] The Stockbridge Mohicans had also bid to have the college situated on their lands.[20] Eliphalet Dyer and Jedediah Elderkin offered 38,000 acres in the Susquehanna Valley to educate "aboriginal natives in those parts."[21] Western New Hampshire, by contrast, was a less than ideal location from which to recruit Indian students. Hanover "is so remote from the Six Nations (which probably will send most children to the school)," noted Timothy Woodbridge and Oliver Partridge, "that they will never be willing to send them there."[22] The new college in New Hampshire was something very different from the Indian charity school. Samson Occom was convinced that in Wheelock's new plan "the Indian was converted into an English school and that the English had crowded out the Indian youths."[23] George Whitefield, too, was sure "the college will finally become a seat of learning only for the English people."[24] "Doctor Wheelock has got bestowed upon him 3000 acres of land on which he is building an academy for whites and blacks," heard the Anglican minister Matthew Graves, "the latter will have little share [and] less profit there. 'Tis all a farce."[25] Wheelock's claim that Indians would come because they had used the area as "hunting ground" in previous generations proved incorrect. In the first list of students enrolled in Hanover at the college and Moor's Charity School, only four of the thirty-four were Indians.[26] In 1779, Ezra Stiles reported that "though this was primarily designed for Indians, yet the only Indian that has graduated there (Daniel Simons) was obliged to beg elsewhere towards supporting him the last year of his College Residence."[27]

Indeed, it was clear to all who commented that Moor's Charity School for Indians and Dartmouth College were separate institutions. Dartmouth College was a new foundation with a very different purpose than Wheelock's earlier Indian school. When they heard of the charter creating Dartmouth College, the English trustees for the Indian charity school were furious. "We cannot but look upon the Charter you have obtained and your intention of building a College and educating English youths, as going beyond the line by which both you and we are circumscribed," they wrote. The college bore no relationship to the project of educating Indian youths. They therefore demanded "that you keep a regular and distinct account of the monies laid out in erecting the School, educating Indian youths, and equipping and maintaining missionaries agreeable to the design of our institution, and that you do not blend them with your College."[28] When asked to join the English Trust, which he refused to do, Richard Terrick, Bishop of London, clearly understood there were two separate designs. One, he told the earl of Dartmouth, was "for establishing the Indian school, which seems to have been the object of your Lordship and the Trustees at home." The other project was "for erecting and endowing a College which is the present plan of Governor Wentworth and the Trustees in America."[29]

The contemporary evidence overwhelmingly suggests that when Eleazar Wheelock chose to move his family from Lebanon, Connecticut, to Hanover, New Hampshire, he did so because he was beginning a new institution, a college to educate English youth. That Wheelock continued to head an Indian school, Moor's Charity School, also located in Hanover, New Hampshire, has confused many commentators. But these were separate institutions with distinct aims. Daniel Webster had confounded Dartmouth College with "Moor's Indian Charity School," insisted Webster's lifelong antagonist Ichabod Bartlett '08, before the New Hampshire Supreme Court. "Now no fact on record is more clearly stated than that this institution," Dartmouth College, "and Moor's Indian Charity School were entirely distinct and independent of each other in their origin and establishment; were ever governed separately, without the least connection," Bartlett correctly maintained.[30]

II

If Wheelock's Indian Charity School and Dartmouth College were not a single institution with a single history, why was Dartmouth College founded? What was "the present plan of Governor [John] Wentworth" of which the Bishop of London spoke?

In order to answer these questions, it is essential to shift the focus away from Eleazar Wheelock and toward the ideological commitments of the new Governor of New Hampshire. And, to unpack those ideological commitments requires a reorientation away from the local context of New England and onto the broader stage of the British Empire.

When John Wentworth returned to England in December 1763, he immediately made a set of connections with a Patriot ideological tinge. Wentworth's first contact was the North American merchant and Patriot politician Barlow

Trecothick. Trecothick, who had lived in Boston for over a decade and married a daughter of a Boston merchant, was the business partner of the New Hampshire agent John Tomlinson. Trecothick was about to launch his career in Patriot politics. In 1764 he was elected alderman of London, becoming Lord Mayor in 1770. While he did not enter the Commons until 1768, he had already established connections with those opposed to the ministries of John Stuart, third earl of Bute, and George Grenville. In 1765, he presented evidence that proved decisive in promoting the repeal of the Stamp Act.[31]

Wentworth soon befriended a range of Trecothick's Patriot associates. Significantly, Wentworth soon called John Huske, formerly a New Hampshire merchant and longtime critic of his uncle Benning Wentworth, "my friend" whose political activities in London had "great merit."[32] Perhaps most importantly, Wentworth soon became an intimate friend of his distant cousin, Charles Watson-Wentworth, second Marquess of Rockingham. The two apparently met at a racetrack and became fast friends, with John Wentworth spending months with Rockingham at his Yorkshire estate, Wentworth-Woodhouse. At this key moment, Rockingham had become the leader of the Patriot opposition in Parliament. He supported John Wilkes's campaign against General Warrants, opposed Grenville's Cider Tax in 1763, and in February 1764 supported the creation of the radical Wildman's opposition Club. On July 13, 1765, he replaced George Grenville as first Lord of the Treasury. On March 18, 1766, Rockingham's administration successfully repealed George Grenville's despised Stamp Act. In New Hampshire, Rockingham's achievement "was thrice welcome to our country." Readers of the *New Hampshire Gazette* understood well that it was to "Patriot" politicians in Britain that the empire owed the return "to halcyon days." John Wentworth had cemented a new set of connections that tied him intimately to British Patriot politics.[33]

On what was to prove the last day of the first Rockingham ministry, July 22, 1766, Charles Lennox, third Duke of Richmond, secretary of state and Patriot politician extraordinaire, informed the Board of Trade that John Wentworth had been appointed governor of New Hampshire.[34] When Wentworth arrived in Portsmouth to take up his new post in June 1767, the Governor's Council, the clergy, "officers of the militia and most of the gentlemen" of Portsmouth interpreted his appointment as Patriot partisan triumph. They offered toasts to their new governor along with the Patriot heroes William Pitt, earl of Chatham, Charles Pratt, Lord Camden, and the Marquis of Rockingham. The following month, the New Hampshire House of Representatives thanked John Wentworth for his "eminent service" in working with the Rockingham government to repeal the Stamp Act.[35]

If John Wentworth sought to present himself as a Patriot politician, what did Patriots want? What did the Patriots, as opposed to establishment Whigs or Neo-Tories, think the British government should be doing? What was the Patriot imperial vision?

Readers of the *New Hampshire Gazette* in the 1760s and 1770s would have been well aware, as were most across the British Empire, that "party animosities run high" in Britain.[36] While there were certainly moments of political dominance by establishment Whigs under the leadership of Robert Walpole, and profound moments of party realignment in the 1740s and 1750s, few could doubt the intensity of party political conflict in the 1760s and 1770s.[37]

The Patriot grouping with which John Wentworth aligned himself upon his arrival in London in 1763 had begun to develop in the second decade of the eighteenth century. By the late 1720s and 1730s, the Patriots began to develop a coherent and powerful ideological critique of the Walpolean political program. That critique they disseminated throughout the Empire in pamphlets, newspapers, and evocative songs and ballads.

Sir Robert Walpole and his supporters had developed a coherent imperial program in the 1720s and 1730s. Walpole, following a Whig tradition that emerged in the 1670s and 1680s, placed heavy emphasis on the importance of labor and colonial production as being the key to promoting imperial prosperity. Unsurprisingly, then, the Walpoleians believed that the most valuable British possessions were the West Indian Sugar Islands, followed by the tobacco-producing middle colonies, and rice-producing South Carolina. In Walpoleian political economy the chief value of New England was in producing wheat to feed slaves in the sugar and tobacco colonies and timber for ships and vital buildings. Since all of the productive colonies depended on slave labor, Walpoleian political economists were at one in defending the vital importance of slavery and the slave trade. The Walpoleian, or establishment Whig, imperial vision was profoundly Anglocentric. The empire, they believed, was valuable insofar as it relieved the tax burden on English landed gentlemen and promoted the prosperity of English men and women more generally.

In the 1720s and 1730s, a range of radical Whigs and former Tories coalesced to form a new political alignment: the Patriots. Whereas the establishment Whigs highlighted the importance of colonial production, Patriots thought that colonies were valuable for what they consumed. Since European markets were increasingly shut to British manufactures by ever increasing tariff barriers and outright prohibitions, Patriots argued that the ever-growing demand for British manufactures from colonial consumers provided the best hope for long-term British economic growth. Since the Patriots placed the heaviest emphasis on colonial consumption rather than colonial consumption they were understandably less enthusiastic about the sugar, tobacco, and rice colonies. Indeed they developed a political economic critique of slavery. Slaves, some Patriots maintained, were unlikely to be robust consumers.

Slave societies tended to create oligarchies, with a very few consumers purchasing luxury goods. Whereas the establishment Whigs were profoundly Anglocentric in outlook, the Patriots argued that the British government should seek to promote imperial prosperity. They therefore insisted that the British government do all it could to promote imperial consumption and development. Patriots consistently pushed for imperial spending on colonial infrastructure.[38]

John Wentworth actively endorsed the Patriot program. In 1765, as Wentworth later recalled, he drew up "some sheets" for the Marquis of Rockingham on the general topic of "revenue" in "Europe and America," a subject which had long been the object of his "particular attention."[39] Wentworth began his argument with a full-throated rejection of establishment Whig orthodoxy. "Trade" rather than "their present ability considerably to increase or rather create a revenue" was the primary value of the American colonies. It was therefore "the true interest" of the British government "to promote population and to direct and encourage them to the most proper employments." Wentworth highlighted the great value to Great Britain, "where all their profit centers," of the "extensive demand of manufactures" in the colonies. The "present advantage" of the American colonies to Great Britain, Wentworth reiterated, "must arise from their trade which requires manufactures" from Britain. When he came to summarize the advantages which Britain had gained from its colonies, Wentworth unsurprisingly listed first "securing and augmenting a vent for their trade and manufactures." "This cannot be a proper time to form a revenue in America," Wentworth pithily remarked. On the contrary, he recommended the Patriot program to augment colonial consumption of manufactures and consequently colonial development. He advised "repealing the Stamp Act," "reducing the duty on foreign molasses," and offering "a bounty" to support New England lumber production "as it will be paid for in manufactures and save a large exportation of money to foreigners." Wentworth also bemoaned the "late restrictions" imposed by the Grenville government on trade with Spanish America, which had the effect of restricting colonial money supply. Crucially Wentworth argued that the imperial government's support for development should be supplemented by an activist provincial government. Provincial government should provide a "variety of essential service." Wentworth, tellingly, maintained that "provincial laws may be improved, internal regularity and order promoted, a speedy and direct administration of justice ascertained, and a regulation of their militia attended to." Finally, good provincial government should "promote population by proper encouragement."[40]

Wentworth's commitment to promoting provincial development only increased upon being appointed Governor. He argued that the Board of Trade should support him "in clearing roads" and giving "small rewards to agriculture" because the result would be "that the number of [the King's] faithful subjects in New Hampshire would be doubled in ten years." The benefit of such colonial development, Wentworth made clear, was that colonial "demand and payment for British goods would be five times increased and exceedingly facilitate the desires of government."[41]

The printer of the *New Hampshire Gazette*, Daniel Fowle, echoed and reinforced John Wentworth's commitment to Patriot political economy. Fowle reprinted an essay emphasizing that colonial development benefited the entire British Empire. "The trade of the nation has hitherto increased with the trade of the colonies," he averred. "If these flourish more, in the same proportion will the trade, the riches and the strength of the nation also increase." But since the accession of George III imperial prosperity had been put at risk by the misguided policies of those who had a "misguided jealousy" of colonial wealth and the prospect of colonial independence.[42] Because the population of British North America doubled every twenty years, opined the author of one essay printed by Fowle that echoed comments from Benjamin Franklin, "the consumption of British manufactures" in North America must also grow "in proportion."[43] This essayist therefore condemned the political economic principles guiding the Grenville ministry. "These wise gentlemen," he sarcastically noted, "took it into their heads that the riches of North America was a loss to this country, and therefore sent ships of war to prevent their getting any" money through trade with Spanish America "to send to their Mother Country in exchange for what they wanted." If this wasn't enough, this essayist continued, "they have very wisely imposed taxes upon them which they were unable to pay, and by a method contrary to their Charters." In essence, the Grenville ministry had treated the colonies "in the way the Children of Israel were by the Egyptians."[44] Like Wentworth, Fowle praised "the patriotic spirit" of those, on both sides of the Atlantic, who opposed the Stamp Act.[45] While Fowle himself owned slaves, in print he followed the Patriot lead in condemning "the infamous traffic in slaves" for infringing on "divine and human law."[46] This sentiment almost certainly followed from Fowle's embrace of the Patriot political economy that privileged colonial consumption rather than colonial production. Slave societies, most Patriots accepted, were societies in which consumption was limited. In general, Fowle endorsed the proposition adopted in "all civilized countries" that those "individuals who enjoy most of the blessings of a government, and whose properties thereby become intrinsically enriched" should "contribute most to the contingent expenses and support of that government."[47] The *New Hampshire Gazette* drummed into its readers the basic principles of Patriot political economy. Fowle called for an imperial and provincial government committed to colonial development on the basis of taxing the wealthiest beneficiaries of imperial prosperity rather than by extracting revenue from the most dynamic elements of the imperial economy.

John Wentworth, who became governor of New Hampshire in July 1766, just three years prior to the founding of Dartmouth College, had, unlike his uncle and predecessor, embraced the ideology of the Patriots. He was committed to an ideology of colonial development rather than colonial extraction. He, like the Patriot editor of the *New Hampshire Gazette*, not only condemned the extractive policies of the Bute and Grenville ministries, but he embraced a program calling for colonial development with the support of both the imperial and provincial government. In essence John Wentworth embraced the notion that the best possibility for imperial prosperity lay in the creation of a confederal empire.

III

What did Patriot governments actually do? Is there evidence that British Patriot politicians actually carried out their ideology into action? In particular, is there evidence that John Wentworth implemented his own calls for provincial governmental activism?

From the moment that Patriot politicians forced Robert Walpole, against his own preferences, to begin the War of Jenkins Ear against the Spanish in 1739, Patriots had played a significant role in shaping British imperial policy. In recent years scholars have shown that far from being an unusually weak state, the British state in Europe managed to develop a remarkably powerful and efficient government without being dirigiste.[48]

The British imperial state was even stronger outside Europe. Whereas most European polities spent between 80 and 93 percent of their revenues on warfare, the British state in the long eighteenth century spent between 61 and 74 percent of its revenue on warfare, averaging around 65 percent for the entire period. On what then did Britain spend the additional 15 percent of disposable revenue? The British state, it turns out, was at its most financially active not in England, but in the empire: in Scotland, Ireland, and in the overseas colonies. Parliament mostly passed enabling acts in England—such as the Turnpike Acts that gave local magistrates the authority but not the resources to build roads. In Scotland, Ireland, and overseas, the British government directly financed infrastructural improvements. The imperial Parliament subsidized immigration to a range of colonies, supporting the settlement of Georgia in the 1730s and Nova Scotia in the 1750s. The imperial state directly financed road construction in New Jersey, New York, and New England. The state helped subsidize the reconstruction of Charleston, South Carolina, after the devastating fire of 1740. In 1781, despite fighting the expensive American Revolutionary War, the imperial government provided disaster relief in the Caribbean after a devastating hurricane. This imperial spending was not limited to the Western Hemisphere. In South Asia the British state spent lavishly on buildings, ships and developing port facilities. Just as the British state subsidized the immigration of Palatine Germans to North America in the early eighteenth century, so it devoted similar resources to settling Palatines in Sumatra. Just as the British state increasingly invested in infrastructural improvements to penetrate the American interior beginning in the 1750s, the government similarly devoted resources towards building roads into the South Asian interior from Calcutta and Madras.[49]

Governor Wentworth continued to voice his Patriot opposition to the extractive policies pursued by the ministers who succeeded his cousin Rockingham.[50] Nevertheless, once in New Hampshire, Wentworth turned the bulk of his attention to the other plank of the Patriot program: provincial state-building.[51] Indeed he insisted that priority be given to provincial rather than central development schemes. He urged that imperial "officers" be made "more independent," that they should be entrusted to "dispense the benefits" of state activity, and that the metropolitan authorities should "consider candidly their advice and information."[52] Wentworth pursued three developmental projects in New Hampshire. First, he sought to divide the province into counties, so that each resident of New Hampshire would have easy access to county courts and British justice. Second, he was determined to build roads into the New Hampshire interior in order to facilitate commercial communications and economic development. Finally, Wentworth devoted his energies to create a provincial educational institution that could train judges, magistrates, and bureaucrats.

Almost from the moment of his return to New Hampshire, Wentworth was fixated on the difficulty of securing access to justice for those who lived far from Portsmouth. He lamented that for those living in distant parts "to record a conveyance, to administer on an estate, to prove a will, to recover a debt in the courts of law" was "in truth insupportable and consumes small estates" because of the "expense of time, travel and delay." Not only did it harm individual inhabitants of New Hampshire, Wentworth complained to his old friend Barlow Trecothick, the absence of locally administered justice risked allowing new settlements to descend into "ungovernable disorder, licentiousness, and disregard of government."[53]

For all of John Wentworth's enthusiasm for the establishment of counties, he was by no means the first person in New Hampshire to propose such an administrative expansion. Members of the assembly had proposed the division of New Hampshire into counties at least since 1760. But Governor Benning Wentworth had opposed the plan.[54] Not two months after John Wentworth's return to New Hampshire as governor, the assembly returned to its plan to create counties so as to obviate "the great expense and charge to the inhabitants" who lived far from Portsmouth.[55] Within two years, John Wentworth's endorsement of the proposal convinced the British Board of Trade to "consent" to an act creating five counties.[56] John Wentworth's support soon compelled the Council to withdraw their objections to the plan.[57] On April 27, 1769, the New Hampshire Assembly passed the act dividing the province for the first time into counties with courts of justice in each county.[58] Significantly, several of the counties were named after Patriot heroes. One was called Rockingham, for the minister who had led the repeal of the Stamp Act. Another received the name of Strafford after William Wentworth the 2nd earl, who had formed part of John Wentworth's social set in London and was closely allied with Horace Walpole and his group of Patriot sympathizers in the 1760s. A third county, Grafton, was named after Rockingham's secretary of state.[59]

John Wentworth was just as enthusiastic in his support of road-building. After all, road construction appealed both to establishment Whigs who wanted to facilitate the exports of colonial products and Patriots who valued colonial consumption of British manufactured goods. But while John Wentworth's uncle had supported road construction in principle, he had been reticent about committing imperial resources to the project. John Wentworth, by contrast, successfully lobbied the imperial government to allow him to devote quitrents to these vital economic infrastructure projects. John Wentworth called on the General Assembly to consider "the important necessity of making roads through the Province whereby the labor of the increasing Province may be advantageous here." Such infrastructural improvements, he was sure, would "increase the circulation of money,"[60] and was "essential to the public good."[61] More importantly, John Wentworth took action. In 1768, he began the development of the Province Road connecting Durham, New Hampshire, to Haverhill in the West. In 1769, the governor and assembly worked together to begin work on other roads connecting the Atlantic coast to new communities on the Connecticut and Merrimack rivers. In 1771, the assembly passed an act, urged by John Wentworth, to connect the eastern districts of the province to the newly founded Dartmouth College.[62]

John Wentworth argued passionately that founding an institution for higher learning would be the crown jewel of his provincial development program. From the first, Wentworth expressed his support for Eleazar Wheelock's plans for his charity school, on the grounds that it afforded prestige to the province.[63] From the first, Wentworth made clear that provincial support for Wheelock was contingent on some measure of state control. He told Wheelock that he expected "that His Majesty's Governor and Commander in Chief for the time being for the Province of New Hampshire shall always be a Trustee."[64] But as Wheelock's financial problems became more apparent and as his focus on Indian education dwindled, Wentworth's interest in and ambition for the educational project grew by leaps and bounds. By early 1769, Wheelock reported to the charismatic preacher and Patriot politician George Whitefield that "the township proposed to be given in New Hampshire" was on "choice land, abounding with great plenty of choice white pines; a river running through the middle affording the best conveniences for mills." Crucially, "the government," no doubt at Wentworth's urging, would "grant an annual allowance at least for a number of years."[65]

In the event, Wentworth's support proved pivotal to the founding of the college. Wentworth, as Eleazar Wheelock acknowledged, played a central role in securing the royal charter for the new institution in December 1769. He praised Governor Wentworth, "whom God has raised up and commissioned for this purpose."[66] Wheelock even promised the governor to name one of the college's new buildings "after your own name."[67] Tellingly, the college was built on 3,300 acres of donated Wentworth family land.[68]

Once the charter was secured, Governor Wentworth and his allies made it clear that the new college would prove crucial to the development of the province. The cause of Dartmouth College, Wentworth told the assembly, was "the cause of education and religion; it is therefore your peculiar care."[69] The new institution would attract "many hundred respectable families from other colonies" who would be induced "to settle in and cultivate the remotest district of this government."[70] "The people" of New Hampshire "will be essentially benefitted" through the foundation of the college, Wentworth insisted.[71] The foundation of the college, he elaborated, was essential because "no people can ever remain smothered in ignorance, the parent of slavery and bane of liberal improvement."[72] Though the members of the assembly were always more reserved in their assessment of the college, no doubt concerned about the taxes that would be necessary to support the new institution, the house concurred that the "settlement of Dartmouth College" was an "event which in time will be a great advantage to the Province."[73]

Wentworth ultimately made clear the intimate ties between the province and Dartmouth College by two acts. First, he made Eleazar Wheelock, the president of the college, a justice of the peace. The intent was clear. By endowing Wheelock with state-sanctioned powers, the college president could advance the good of "the country but more especially the College" by ensuring that "all internal regulations may be duly effected, and every pernicious intrusion suppressed upon its appearance."[74] Second, Wentworth worked with the assembly to facilitate travel to the new college. He urged the assembly to lay out a new road from Portsmouth to the college in order that the new institution would "attract the interest of many."[75] By April 1771, the assembly duly passed an act creating the road that "will greatly promote the design of that valuable institution" funded by a new tax to be levied for the purpose.[76]

Why, given the centrality of provincial support for the new college to be situated in New Hampshire, did Wheelock and Wentworth decide to name the institution Dartmouth College? Most have assumed that naming the college after the head of the English Trust for the Indian school was a means to soften the double blow that the institution would not be narrowly an Indian charity school and that the New Hampshire-based Board of Trustees would assume the primary role in administering the institution.[77] While these concerns no doubt played a role in the calculations of Wheelock and Wentworth, there is good reason to suspect that the name had as much to do with their effort to announce the Patriot nature of their project. Wheelock himself announced that the charter had listed the new institution "under the Patriotic name of Dartmouth College."[78] In the late 1760s and early 1770s, William Legge, second earl of Dartmouth, had indeed a well-established and well-earned reputation as a Patriot partisan. Dartmouth had presented the merchants' petition for the repeal of the Stamp Act in 1766.[79] The Sons of Liberty proposed a toast to Dartmouth in Boston on the anniversary celebration of the Repeal.[80] In New Hampshire, Dartmouth was widely praised for being a member "of the Rockingham party."[81] If Dartmouth College was to be an institution for the education of "Patriot" students as its defenders claimed it was, then few could have proposed a more appropriate name.[82]

Dartmouth College was founded as part of Governor John Wentworth's Patriot state-building project. John Wentworth had established a different set of partisan connections in Britain than those who had supported the administration of his uncle Benning Wentworth. Benning's connections and policies were impeccably Old Guard Whig. John Wentworth instead embraced the ideology of the Patriot members of Wildman's Club. In particular, John Wentworth advanced a state-building agenda geared toward increasing colonial consumption of British manufactured goods. This project depended on connecting the provincial interior commercially, ideologically and administratively through new infrastructure projects. Wentworth's founding of Dartmouth was merely one of the most lasting and visible consequences of that ambitious plan for colonial development.

IV

What of the Royal Charter founding the college promulgated in December 1769? Did the charter of incorporation create a private charity school or a public institution?

In fact, the charter made clear that two different types of institutions were envisaged. One part was intended "to encourage the laudable and charitable design of spreading Christian knowledge among the Savages of our American Wilderness." The second element was for "the best means of education" to "be established in our Province of New Hampshire for the benefit of said province."[83]

The charter provided for a governing body that made clear the priority that was to be given to the interests of the province over Christianizing mission. Half of the initial body of twelve Trustees were selected from among the Governor's Council. The trustees were to recruit their own replacements, with two provisos. First, that "eight of the aforesaid whole number of the body of the trustees shall be resident and respectable freeholders of our said Province of New Hampshire." Second, the royal charter specified that at least "seven" of the twelve Trustees "shall be laymen." The charter specified that in perpetuity, the Board of Trustees would be dominated by those committed to the secular interests of the Province of New Hampshire.

Whereas Wheelock's Indian Charity School had been created to promote Christian faith in the Congregational Way among Indians, the Royal Charter establishing Dartmouth College was remarkable in that it imposed no religious test for its students. The college was specifically prohibited from "excluding any person of any religious denomination whatsoever from free and equal liberty and advantage of education or from any of the liberties and privileges or immunities of the said College on account of his or their speculative sentiments in religion or his or their being of a religious profession different from the said Trustees of the said Dartmouth College." While the Charter did, of course, indicate that one of the goals of the new institution was the "civilizing and Christianizing children of pagans," this was clearly not the top priority.

From the beginning, Dartmouth College's existence depended on public support. The initial lands granted to the college for its maintenance and support were delivered by John Wentworth and those "animated and excited thereto by the generous example of His Excellency the Governor." "The source whence this institution has derived its support" ever since, Ichabod Bartlett pointed out in the middle of the nineteenth century, "is of a nature so public that no difficulty occurs in pointing to it." Chief among these, Bartlett detailed from the public record, were "public grants" of land "for its establishment and support."[84]

One of the most powerful arguments advanced by Daniel Webster in defense of his claim that Dartmouth College was in fact a private institution was that in English law, a college was private and only a university was public. Since the royal charter clearly announced the creation of "Dartmouth College," there could be little doubt of the institution's status. This claim assumed that English legal distinctions held true in British America. In fact, the true legal test should be "the design" rather than the name of the institution.[85] That Dartmouth College was created to provide instruction rather than merely housing and was specifically granted the power to confer degrees, as universities were in England, demonstrated that the design was always to be a university. Indeed, Eleazar Wheelock himself made exactly this point. Governor John Wentworth, he recalled, had granted "a generous charter by the name of Dartmouth College, endowed with all the powers and privileges of a university."[86]

Governor Wentworth's royal charter for Dartmouth College made clear that he had created a state institution of higher learning. It is true that appending Moor's Charity School, the rump of Eleazar Wheelock's old Indian Charity School, onto the College gave the Governor some room for later confusion. Nevertheless, Wentworth's 1769 Charter created an institution in which the interests of the province of New Hampshire were to take priority over the education of Indian youth, that secular education was to be more important than spiritual improvement, and that the institution was to depend on grants from the American province rather than from the benevolence of English private donors.

V

Why should we care that Dartmouth College was founded as a state institution? Why does it matter that Dartmouth College and Eleazar Wheelock's Indian charity school project had two separate histories? What is the significance that John Wentworth supported the creation of Dartmouth College as part of his Patriot state-building project?

The fact that Dartmouth College and Moor's Charity School to educate Indian youth were two separate institutions demonstrates the limited commitment of both the provincial state and Eleazar Wheelock himself toward integrating Indians into British American society. Wheelock, it is true, had founded an Indian school in Lebanon, Connecticut. But as that school ran into pedagogical and financial difficulties, Wheelock grew less attached to his earlier assimilationist ideals. That both Governor Wentworth and President Wheelock were far more committed to creating an institution for the education of white youth goes a long way to explain why so few Native Americans were graduated from Dartmouth prior to the presidency of John Kemeny in 1970.[87]

That Dartmouth College was in fact founded as part of a provincial state-building project reveals a hitherto little-noticed trend toward state-supported education in the British Empire in the eighteenth century. In British

America in particular—though there is evidence for similar developments in British India, Ireland, Scotland, and the West Indies—provincial governments increasingly supported educational institutions as part of their program of economic development. Harvard College, whatever its origins, became a state institution in 1673, when "an addition was made to the members of the corporation of Harvard College, against the will of the corporation."[88] Similarly, Yale, for all of its own foundational myths, was really founded at the behest of Governor Fitzjohn Winthrop. The initial "collegiate school" was created by legislative Act in 1701. By the 1720s, the province took unequivocal control with the passage of an act in the Connecticut state legislature that expanded the number of trustees, created "new offices," and devised new rules for convening the Trustees. In 1745, the Connecticut legislature committed to paying the annual salaries of the "president and fellows of the college."[89] King's College (the original name of the institution that would become Columbia) was incorporated by charter by Governor James DeLancey in October 1754. A group of "creole improvers" had promoted the project with the explicit aim of "improving" the province.[90] The month after Governor John Wentworth secured the royal charter for Dartmouth College, Governor William Bull urged the founding of what would become the College of Charleston on remarkably similar grounds. Bull called on the South Carolina Commons House of Assembly to finance "the establishing in this province seminaries of liberal education" so that "our youth, the future hopes and support of their country will be rendered more capable of serving themselves and the community of which they are members." The goal, he said, was to be able to complete the education of those destined for "the learned professions" and "those to be placed in the foremost rank of public servants."[91]

By the late colonial era, British American institutions of higher learning were becoming state institutions. While we tend to imagine a radical distinction between the venerable private foundations of the pre-revolutionary era and the land-grant institutions of the late nineteenth century, there was in fact a far larger degree of continuity. Patriot politicians right across the British Empire had come to believe that support of education was vital to continued imperial development.

Finally, the Patriot commitment to promoting provincial development projects suggests that the assumed conflict between American and imperial conceptions of sovereignty was illusory. Patriots right across the empire increasingly argued for a confederal model of empire. In the 1750s, the most widely read, discussed, and cited Patriot political economist, Malachy Postlethwayt, argued that the key to imperial posterity lay in creating a confederal empire overseen by an information-gathering imperial council. Such a constitutional model, he believed, would make it possible for provincial governments to pursue development schemes appropriate to their local circumstances, calling on the imperial state for support where needed. "Our great aim tends towards such a union amongst all His Majesty's dominions, as will promote the strength and vigor, as well as mutual prosperity of them all." "For the happy general union that we would cement," Postlethwayt explained, "is no less constitutional than commercial, and such also as may the least interfere with the particular interest of each other, but advance that of the whole." This was the only way to "strengthen the whole British Empire."[92] Early defenders of Dartmouth College placed their cherished institution in this broader context of provincial state formation. "As the colleges in New England are almost all universally patronized and endowed by the legislative body of the province where they are situate," argued one essayist in the *New Hampshire Gazette*, "may we not with eager expectation look for the desired effects; especially may we in New Hampshire look for them from young Dartmouth College."[93]

Daniel Webster and his fellow jurists in *Dartmouth College v. Woodward* had fundamentally misunderstood the British constitutional issues surrounding the foundation of the college. The issue in the end was not whether Dartmouth College was a public or private institution, but what role the provincial government should play in promoting development. Patriot politicians in Britain and America were moving toward adopting a confederal constitutional model for the empire. That the Patriots ultimately lost out in Britain to the more authoritarian commitment to unitary sovereignty preferred by the government of Lord North should not obscure the particular confederal context of the founding of Dartmouth College.

Dartmouth College, then, was founded not as an Indian school, but as part of a pan-imperial Patriot project of state development. "A splendid object which now catches our attention in this part of the continent is Dartmouth College in New Hamsphire," wrote one early commentator. The new college presented "a pleasing prospect to every lover of his country, who knows the connection between literature and liberty" and "that learning is, under Providence, the great fountain of human happiness." The "Patriot" educated at New Hampshire's new institution of higher learning would undoubtedly promote "with unremitting ardor the welfare of mankind, guarding against the inroads of evils and laying foundations for public and universal happiness."[94]

NOTES

1. *New Hampshire Gazette*, February 5, 1773, p. [1].
2. Grover 1898, 76.
3. https://admissions.dartmouth.edu/about/history-traditions. Accessed September 25, 2019.

4. Smith 1878, 1, 48.
5. Daniel Webster, in *Report* [1819], 239–40, 248.
6. Whipple 1906, xxi.
7. Bonner 2019.
8. Wheelock 1773. A similar narrative is reproduced in McClure and Parish 1811.
9. McClure and Parish 1811, 19–20, 44–47.
10. Commission for Ebenezer Cleaveland of Gloucester Mass. and Ralph Wheelock, July 20, 1768, Dartmouth College, Wheelock Papers, 768420.3 (Reel 6).
11. Silverman 2010, 83–86; Edward Deake (Charlestown, Mass.) to Eleazar Wheelock, June 21, 1768, Dartmouth College, Wheelock Papers, 768371.2 (Reel 6).
12. Taylor 2006, 61–62; Robert Keen (London) to Eleazar Wheelock, April 12, 1769, Dartmouth College, Wheelock Papers, 769262 (Reel 6).
13. Samson Occom (Mohegan) to Eleazar Wheelock, July 1, 1769, Dartmouth College, Wheelock Papers, 769401 (Reel 6); Solomon Williams (Lebanon, CT) to Eleazar Wheelock, November 24, 1770, Dartmouth College, Wheelock Papers 770624 (Reel 7).
14. Taylor 2006, 62.
15. Eleazar Wheelock (Lebanon, CT) to Robert Keen, May 31, 1768, Dartmouth College, Wheelock Papers, 768331.1 (Reel 6).
16. George Whitefield (London) to Eleazar Wheelock, November 3, 1768, Dartmouth College, Wheelock Papers, 768603 (Reel 6).
17. Ezra Stiles, May 24, 1779, in Dexter 1901, 2:338.
18. Wheelock 1771, 13; Eleazar Wheelock (Lebanon, CT) to George Whitefield, February 10, 1769, Dartmouth College, Wheelock Papers, 769160.1 (Reel 6); Eleazar Wheelock (Lebanon, CT) to John Erskine, December 7, 1770, Dartmouth College, Wheelock Papers, 770657.1 (Reel 7).
19. Nathaniel Whitaker (Woodbridge) to Eleazar Wheelock, September 15, 1768, Dartmouth College, Wheelock Papers, 768515.1 (Reel 6).
20. Silverman 2010, 82.
21. Eliphalet Dyer and Jedediah Elderkin (Hartford) to Eleazar Wheelock, December 30, 1768, Dartmouth College, Wheelock Papers, 768680.1 (Reel 6). This may well have been related to the plans for economic improvement of the Susquehanna Company: Mancall 1991, 111–24.
22. Timothy Woodbridge and Oliver Partridge (Hatfield, Mass.) to Eleazar Wheelock, September 24, 1768, Dartmouth College, Wheelock Papers, 768524.3 (Reel 6); and December 12, 1768, Dartmouth College, Wheelock Papers, 768662 (Reel 6).
23. David MacCluer (Lebanon, CT) to Eleazar Wheelock, May 21, 1770, Dartmouth College, Wheelock Papers, 770321 (Reel 7).
24. Nathaniel Whitaker (Salem, Mass.) to Eleazar Wheelock, September 8, 1770, Dartmouth College, Wheelock Papers, 77058 (Reel 7).
25. Matthew Graves (London) to Samuel Lloyd, August 5, 1770, Dartmouth College, Wheelock Papers, 770455 (Reel 7).
26. Eleazar Wheelock (Lebanon, CT) to English Trustees, July 29, 1770, Dartmouth College, Wheelock Papers, 770429 (Reel 7); Eleazar Wheelock, *A Catalogue of the*

Members of Dartmouth College and More's School, February 1771, Dartmouth College, Wheelock Papers, 771190 (Reel 7).

27. Stiles, May 24, 1779, in Dexter 1901, 2:338.

28. Robert Keen (London) to Eleazar Wheelock, July 30, 1770, Dartmouth College, Wheelock Papers, 770430 (Reel 7); English Trustees (London) to Eleazar Wheelock, April 25, 1771, Dartmouth College, Wheelock Papers, 771275 (Reel 7).

29. Richard Terrick, Bishop of London (Fulham) to William Legge 2nd earl of Dartmouth, July 9, 1771, Dartmouth College, Wheelock Papers, 771409 (Reel 7).

30. Ichabod Bartlett, in Report [1819], 180; Shirley 1895, 154.

31. Wilderson 1994, 52; Jervey 1931, 157–58; Daniell 1970, 39; Pincus 2016, 77.

32. Sir John Wentworth (Portsmouth) to Dr. Anthony Relhan, August 9, 1768, Nova Scotia Archives, RG 1/55; Wilderson 1994, 289; Pincus 2016, 79–80. On Huske's opposition to Benning Wentworth, see Daniell 1970, 37. It is worth noting that Huske's own political connections took a radical turn in 1764. He abandoned his earlier associations with Grenville in favor of Patriot Whig connections.

33. Wilderson 1994, 56–59; Daniell 1970, 39; Cuthbertson 1983, 7–10; *New Hampshire Gazette*, 2 January 1767, p. [1]. On the importance of principle to Rockinghamite politics, see Bourke 2015, 224. On the radical nature of Wildman's Club, see Watson 1968, 194–237.

34. Wilderson 1994, 82; Daniell 1970, 40.

35. *New Hampshire Gazette*, June 19, 1767, p. [1]; *New Hampshire Gazette*, July 10, 1767, p. [1].

36. *New Hampshire Gazette*, May 29, 1767, p. [3].

37. For a long time, early American historiography has been influenced by a reading of eighteenth-century British history that minimized the importance of ideology and party divisions. Those who held that view were deeply influenced by the work of Lewis Namier. See Morgan 1957. Tim Breen noticed some time ago that the Namierite understanding had come under attack: see Breen 1997. The evidence for the importance of partisanship is now strong: see Brewer 1976, Sjonsberg 2021, and Vaughn 2019.

38. These two paragraphs summarize the findings of an increasingly robust literature on Patriot political economy. See Pincus 2016, 25–88; Pincus and Watson 2019, 155–174; Watson, 2018, 57–84; Watson 2020; Pincus 2018; Kinkel 2018.

39. Sir John Wentworth (Portsmouth) to William Parker, September 10, 1767, Nova Scotia Archives, RG 1/55.

40. John Wentworth (London) to Charles Watson-Wentworth 2nd Marquess of Rockingham, September 1, 1765, printed in Watson 1972.

41. Sir John Wentworth (Portsmouth) to earl of Shelburne and Board of Trade, March 25, 1768, Nova Scotia Archives, RG 1/55. See the similar arguments in Sir John Wentworth (Portsmouth) to earl of Shelburne and Board of Trade, March 5, 1768, Nova Scotia Archives, RG 1/55.

42. *New Hampshire Gazette*, January 3, 1766, p. [2]. Reprinted from Lloyd's Evening Post, 11 September 1765.

43. *New Hampshire Gazette*, February 7, 1766, p. [1]. From *Public Advertiser*, November 15, 1765.

44. Ibid.

45. *New Hampshire Gazette*, January 3, 1766, [2]; *New Hampshire Gazette*, January 10, 1766, [1]; *New Hampshire Gazette*, January 31, 1766, [1]; *New Hampshire Gazette*, February 14, 1766, [4]; *New Hampshire Gazette*, February 21, 1766, [2]; *New Hampshire Gazette*, March 7, 1766, [1–2].

46. *New Hampshire Gazette*, April 10, 1767, [1].

47. *New Hampshire Gazette*, September 25, 1767, [1].

48. Brewer 1989; Braddick 2000; Harling 2001.

49. The previous two paragraphs draw on data presented in Pincus and Robinson 2016; and Pincus, Bains and Reichardt 2019.

50. Sir John Wentworth (Portsmouth) to Robert Temple (Charlestown), January 29, 1768, Nova Scotia Archives, RG 1/55; Sir John Wentworth (Portsmouth) to Dr. Anthony Relhan, August 9, 1768, Nova Scotia Archives, RG 1/55; Sir John Wentworth (Portsmouth) to Charles Watson-Wentworth 2nd Marquess of Rockingham, November 13, 1768, Nova Scotia Archives, RG 1/55; Sir John Wentworth (Portsmouth) to Paul Wentworth, November 15, 1768, Nova Scotia Archives, RG 1/55.

51. Wilderson 1994, 115.

52. Sir John Wentworth (Portsmouth) to Dr. Anthony Relhan, August 9, 1768, Nova Scotia Archives, RG 1/55.

53. Sir John Wentworth (Portsmouth) to Barlow Trecothick and Stephen Apthorp, May 23, 1768, Nova Scotia Archives, RG 1/55.

54. Daniell 1970, 20; Wilderson 1994, 115.

55. "Journal of the House," August 22, 1767, in Bouton 1873, 7:130.

56. "Journal of the House," March 9, 1769, in Bouton 1873, 7:203.

57. "Journal of the House," March 15, 1769, in Bouton 1873, 7:208.

58. "Journal of the House," April 27, 1769, in Bouton 1873, 7:228.

59. Wilderson 1994, 122.

60. Speech of John Wentworth, January 10, 1770, "Journal of the House," in Bouton 1873, 7:232.

61. Speech of John Wentworth, December 13, 1770, "Journal of the House," in Bouton 1873, 7:260.

62. "Journal of the House," October 26, 1768, in Bouton 1873, 7:195; John Wentworth (Portsmouth) to Eleazar Wheelock, February 6, 1771, Dartmouth College, Wheelock Papers, 771156.1 (Reel 7); Act of New Hampshire Assembly, April 13, 1771, TNA, CO 5/958/41; Daniell 1970, 49; Wilderson 1994, 110–114.

63. Sir John Wentworth (Portsmouth) to Eleazar Wheelock, March 21, 1768, Nova Scotia Archives, RG 1/55; John Wentworth (Portsmouth) to Eleazar Wheelock, August 16, 1768, Dartmouth College, Wheelock Papers, 768466.1 (Reel 6); Ebenezer Cleaveland and John Wright, Report of their Journey to Survey Sites, December 17, 1768, Dartmouth College, Wheelock Papers, 768667.1 (Reel 6).

64. Sir John Wentworth (Portsmouth) to Eleazar Wheelock, March 21, 1768, Nova Scotia Archives, RG 1/55.

65. Eleazar Wheelock (Lebanon, CT) to George Whitefield, February 10, 1769, Dartmouth College, Wheelock Papers, 769160.1 (Reel 6).

66. *New Hampshire Gazette*, September 28, 1770, [4].

67. Eleazar Wheelock (Lebanon, CT) to John Wentworth, October 25, 1769, Dartmouth College, Wheelock Papers, 769575.1 (Reel 6); Eleazar Wheelock (Lebanon, CT) to Alexander Phelps, October 25, 1769, Dartmouth College, Wheelock Papers, 769575.3 (Reel 6).

68. Eleazar Wheelock (Lebanon, CT) to English Trustees, July 29, 1770, Dartmouth College, Wheelock Papers, 770429 (Reel 7); *New Hampshire Gazette*, September 28, 1770, [4].

69. Speech of John Wentworth, December 13, 1770, "Journal of the House," in Bouton 1873, 7:260.

70. Speech of John Wentworth, January 10, 1770, "Journal of the House," in Bouton 1873, 7:232.

71. John Wentworth (Wentworth House) to Eleazar Wheelock, September 7, 1770, Dartmouth College, Wheelock Papers, 770507 (Reel 7).

72. John Wentworth (Portsmouth) to Eleazar Wheelock, February 6, 1771, Dartmouth College, Wheelock Papers, 771156.1 (Reel 7).

73. Response of the Assembly, January 13, 1770, "Journal of the House," in Bouton 1873, 7:234.

74. John Wentworth (Portsmouth) to Eleazar Wheelock, January 31, 1771, Dartmouth College, Wheelock Papers, 771131.1 (Reel 7).

75. John Wentworth (Portsmouth) to Eleazar Wheelock, February 6, 1771, Dartmouth College, Wheelock Papers, 771156.1 (Reel 7).

76. "An Act for Establishing and Making Possible a Road," April 12, 1771, "Journal of the House," in Bouton 1873, 7:283–84.

77. Wilderson 1994, 131–32; Smith 1878, 47–48; Chase 1891, 1:116–17.

78. Eleazar Wheelock (Lebanon, CT) to Hugh Wallace, January 26, 1770, Dartmouth College, Wheelock Papers, 770126 (Reel 7). Wheelock was deeply aware in a way that many scholars have not been of the "disunited" and partisan nature of British imperial politics. He himself expressed his support for the non-importation agreements: Eleazar Wheelock (Lebanon, CT) to Jonathan Mason, March 7, 1770, Dartmouth College, Wheelock Papers, 770207 (Reel 7); Hugh Wallace (New York) to Eleazar Wheelock, May 10, 1770, Dartmouth College, Wheelock Papers, 770310 (Reel 7).

79. *New Hampshire Gazette*, May 1, 1766, [3].

80. *New Hampshire Gazette*, August 26, 1768, [2].

81. *New Hampshire Gazette*, November 13, 1772, [3].

82. *New Hampshire Gazette*, September 13, 1771, [2].

83. Charter of Dartmouth College, December 13, 1769, Dartmouth College, Wheelock Papers, 769663.2 (Reel 7). The Charter is easily accessible at https://www.dartmouth.edu/trustees/docs/charter-2010.pdf. The following paragraphs, unless otherwise specified, rely on that document.

84. Bartlett in *Report* [1819], 181.

85. Bartlett in *Report* [1819], 182.

86. Wheelock 1771, 26.

87. https://students.dartmouth.edu/nap/about/history. It should be noted that even the Native American program at Dartmouth confuses Moor's Charity School and Dartmouth College.
88. Bartlett in *Report* [1819], 177–78.
89. Bartlett in *Report* [1819], 177; the relevant statutes are available at https://www.yale.edu/sites/default/files/files/University-Charter.pdf
90. Hulsebosch 2005, 88–90.
91. Speech of William Bull, January 30, 1770, *Journal of the Commons House of Assembly of South Carolina*, January 9-April 11, 1770, 238–239, http://llmc.com.proxy.uchicago.edu/docDisplay5.aspx?set=21118&volume=1770&part=013
92. Postlethwayt 1757, 1:461, 469–70.
93. *New Hampshire Gazette*, February 5, 1773, [1].
94. *New Hampshire Gazette*, September 13, 1771, [2]

REFERENCES

Bonner, Robert. 2019. "How Dartmouth College Commemorated the Bicentennial of the Dartmouth College Case," https://histphil.org/2019/07/16/how-dartmouth-college-commemorated-the-bicentennial-of-the-dartmouth-college-case/

Bourke, Richard. 2015. *Empire and Revolution: The Political Life of Edmund Burke*. Princeton, NJ: Princeton University Press.

Bouton, Nathaniel, editor. 1873. *Documents and Records Relating to the Province of New Hampshire,* Vol. VII. Nashua, NH: Orren C. Moore.

Braddick, Michael J. 2000. *State Formation in Early Modern England*. Cambridge, UK: Cambridge University Press.

Breen, T. H. 1997. "Ideology and Nationalism on the Eve of the American Revolution: Revisions Once More in Need of Revising." Pp. 13–39 in *Journal of American History*. Vol. 84, No. 1 (June).

Brewer, John. 1976. *Party Ideology and Popular Politics at the Accession of George III*. Cambridge, UK: Cambridge University Press.

Brewer, John. 1989. *Sinews of Power*. London: Unwin Hyman.

Chase, Frederick. 1891. *A History of Dartmouth College*. Cambridge, UK: John Wilson and Son. Vol. I.

Cuthbertson, Brian C. 1983. *The Loyalist Governor*. Halifax: Petheric Press.

Daniell, Jere R. 1970. *Experiment in Republicanism: New Hampshire Politics and the American Revolution, 1741-1794*. Cambridge, MA: Harvard University Press.

Dexter, Franklin Bowditch, editor. 1901. *The Literary Diary of Ezra Stiles*. New York: Charles Scribner's Sons.

Grover, Edwin Osgood, editor. 1898. *Dartmouth College Songs: A New Collection of College Songs*. Hanover, NH: Grover and Graham.

Harling, Philip. 2001. *The Modern British State*. Cambridge, UK: Polity Press.

Hulsebosch, Daniel J. 2005. *Constituting Empire: New York and the Transformation of Constitutionalism in the Atlantic World, 1664-1830*. Chapel Hill: University of North Carolina Press.

Jervey, Theodore D. 1931. "Barlow Trecothick," *South Carolina Historical and Genealogical Magazine*. Vol. XXXII, No. 3 (July).

Journal of the Commons House of Assembly of South Carolina. January 9-April 11, 1770.

Kinkel, Sarah. 2018. *Disciplining the Empire*. Cambridge, MA: Harvard University Press.

Lloyd's Evening Post

Mancall, Peter C. 1991. *Valley of Opportunity*. Ithaca, NY: Cornell University Press.

McClure, David and Elijah Parish. 1811. *Memoirs of the Reverend Eleazar Wheelock*. Newburyport, MA: Edward Little & Co.

Morgan, Edmund S. 1957. "The American Revolution: Revisions in Need of Revising." Pp. 3–15 in *William and Mary Quarterly*. Vol. 14 (January).

New Hampshire Gazette

Pincus, Steve. 2018. "Gulliver's Travels, Party Politics, and Empire." In Robert Fredona and Sophus Reinert, editors. Pp. 131–69 in *New Perspectives on the History of Political Economy*. London: Palgrave Macmillan.

Pincus, Steve. 2016. *Heart of the Declaration*. New Haven, CT: Yale University Press.

Pincus, Steve, Tiraana Bains and A. Zuercher Reichardt. 2019. "Thinking the Empire Whole," Pp. 610–37 in *History Australia*. Vol. 14, No. 4 (December).

Pincus, Steve and James Robinson. 2016. "Faire la Guerre et faire l'etat." Pp. 5–35 in *Annales HSS*. Vol 71, No. 1.

Pincus, Steve and Amy Watson. 2019. "Patriotism after the Hanoverian Succession." In Brent S. Sirota and Allan I. MacInnes, editors. *The Hanoverian Succession in Great Britain and Its Empire*. Woodbridge, UK: Boydell Press.

Postlethwayt, Malachy. 1757. *Britain's Commercial Interest Explained and Improved*. London: D. Browne, J. Whiston and B. White, and W. Sandby. Vol. I.

Public Advertiser

Report of the case of the Trustees of Dartmouth College against William H. Woodward. 1819. Portsmouth, NH: John W. Foster.

Shirley, John M. 1895. *The Dartmouth College Causes and the Supreme Court of the United States*. Chicago: G. I. Jones.

Silverman, David J. 2010. *Red Brethren: The Brothertown and Stockbridge Indians and the Problem of Race in Early America*. Ithaca, NY: Cornell University Press.

Sjonsberg, Max. 2021. *The Persistence of Party: Ideas of Harmonious Discord in Eighteenth-Century Britain*. Cambridge, UK: Cambridge University Press.

Smith, Baxter Perry. 1878. *The History of Dartmouth College*. Boston: Houghton, Osgood, and Company.

Taylor, Alan. 2006. *The Divided Ground*. New York: Vintage Books.

Vaughn, James M. 2019. *The Politics of Empire at the Accession of George III*. New Haven, CT: Yale University Press.

Watson, Amy. 2020. "The New York Patriot Movement: Partisanship, the Free Press, and Britain's Imperial Constitution, 1731-1739." Pp. 33–64 in *William and Mary Quarterly*. Vol. 77, No. 1 (January).

Watson, Amy. 2018. "Patriotism and Partisanship in Post-Union Scotland, 1724-1737." Pp. 57–84 in *Scottish Historical Review*. Vol. 98, No. 1 (April).

Watson, Derek Herbert. 1968. *The Duke of Newcastle, the Marquis of Rockingham, and Mercantile Interests in London and the Provinces 1761-68*. PhD thesis, Sheffield University.

Watson, Derek H. 1972. "John Wentworth's Description of the American Colonies in 1765." Pp. 148–65 in *Historical New Hampshire*. Vol. 27, No. 3 (Fall).

Wentworth, Sir John. *Papers*. Nova Scotia Archives, RG 1/55.

Wheelock, Eleazar. 1773. *A Continuation of the Narrative of the Indian Charity School, Begun in Lebanon in Connecticut; now incorporated with Dartmouth College in Hanover*. New Hampshire.

Wheelock, Eleazar. *Papers*. Dartmouth College Library.

Whipple, Edwin P., ed. 1906. *The Speeches and Orations of Daniel Webster*. Boston: Little, Brown, and Company.

Wilderson, Paul W. 1994. *Governor John Wentworth and the American Revolution*. Lebanon, NH: University Press of New England.

Chapter 3

Life and Living Standards in Britain's Industrial Revolution

Emma Griffin (University of East Anglia)

Most historians agree that the Industrial Revolution was a defining moment in modern history, but what were the social consequences of this landmark historical event? What benefits—if any—did industrialization and mechanization bring to the men, women, and children who worked in the factories and made it all happen? These are questions charged with political overtones, and they have polarized historians who have interpreted the disappearance of traditional society and the advent of capitalism in very different ways. My purpose in this essay is to consider these debates and ask what happened to both working people's incomes and their quality of life when Britain transitioned from an agrarian to an industrial economy.

The question is one that has preoccupied commentators and historians for almost two hundred years. In 1839, in response to the rapid social and environmental change occurring around him, the historian Thomas Carlyle coined the expression the "Condition of England,"[1] and Victorian writers and thinkers from Charles Dickens, Elizabeth Gaskill, Benjamin Disraeli, Friedrich Engels, and Karl Marx continued to debate the Condition of England throughout the 1840s and beyond.[2] These writers expressed a complex set of concerns about the ways in which rapid industrial and urban growth were changing the fabric of traditional society, for the most part concluding that life for the laboring poor was worsening as part of this process. Friedrich Engels's highly influential account of the working class in Manchester argued that not only were the workers' living and working conditions worse than ever before, but that their wages were lower too. Like many nineteenth-century commentators, he indulged in a little nostalgia for the old days: pre-industrial workers, he wrote, had lived a "passably comfortable existence . . . and their material position was far better than that of their successors."[3] Of course, such views were never universal. Throughout the mid-Victorian period, there were always a few dissenting voices who believed that the working classes were enjoying new levels of prosperity and contentment, thanks to industrial growth.[4] Yet most were not convinced. For the majority of Victorian commentators, the evidence was reasonably clear: Industrialization was harming, rather than helping, the laboring poor.

With the passage of time, the question of what happened to living standards during the industrial revolution slipped from lived experience to historical event, and as it did so it fell under the purview of historians. It is perhaps significant that Arnold Toynbee, who first popularized the term "Industrial Revolution" in the 1880s, was also the first historian to present a decisive argument about the consequences of this revolution for working-class living standards. Toynbee was emphatic that the effects of industrialization had damaged the well-being of the men, women, and children whose labor had underpinned it: "The steam-engine, the spinning-jenny, the power-loom," he wrote, "had torn up the population by the roots . . . The effects of the Industrial Revolution prove that free competition may produce wealth without producing well-being."[5] It was a hugely influential interpretation of the Industrial Revolution as a social catastrophe that informed writing about working-class living standards throughout the first half of the twentieth century.

By the 1950s, the "Standard of Living Debate" had become established as one of the most important historical problems of its time, and the protagonists had divided themselves into opposing "optimist" and "pessimist" camps.[6] And as the years passed, they found ever more inventive ways to develop their arguments. Scholars have now moved away from the traditional measurements of the male real wage and begun to explore new and innovative ways in which the people's living standards may be measured. Real wages, family incomes, "well-being," life expectancy, child mortality, consumption of tea and coffee, calorie availability and nutrition, heights, work intensity, and child labor have all been exploited to produce a detailed picture of the ways in which working people's lives changed during the Industrial Revolution.[7]

Yet despite the wide and varied points of entry into historical living standards, the methods that underpin this research are far less heterogeneous. In fact, all the recent contributions to the standard of living debate have come from just one of our discipline's subfields—economic history—and all employ a fundamentally similar methodological approach. In each instance, scholars identify one or more variables, which can be quantified, tabulated, and evaluated. In the process, social, cultural, and qualitative historical techniques have lost their currency as a legitimate means of making sense of the human experience of economic modernization. Nor is this all. At the same time as the methodology of the living standards debate has narrowed, so has there been a straightening of historical argument. Economic history has produced a vast literature looking at countless different elements of living standards, yet across this literature we find much the same conclusion repeated over and again: real wages were largely stagnant, while according to all other measures, life actually worsened.

In this essay, I want to provide an alternative account of the impact of industrialization on working people's lives by returning to qualitative material and methods. The source material I shall use—working-class autobiography—is neither new nor unknown to historians. Indeed, autobiographies have been widely used by historians with a range of interests in histories of working-class selfhood, culture, and family.[8] But the personal stories contained in life histories are presumed to belong to the realm of the social and cultural, rather than the economic. It is my contention that we can mine these sources not simply for lively descriptions and personal anecdotes in order to recreate the social history of the period. When exploited systematically, working-class voices can shed light on large economic questions as well and provide an important and illuminating counterpoint to quantitative investigations into the relationship between economic growth and human experience.

This essay draws on a body of work written by working-class people going under such titles as memoirs, life histories, autobiographies, notes, sketches, recollections, and adventures. They have been compiled through a comprehensive survey of the available records as listed in the *Autobiography of the Working Class: An Annotated Critical Bibliography* compiled by John Burnett and his team in the 1980s. This lists almost four hundred autobiographies written by individuals born into impoverished, working-class families in Britain between 1700 and the 1830s, and a close and careful reading of these life-histories forms the basis of the argument that follows.[9]

Though I have sought to obtain and consult all the surviving autobiographies from the period, the writers inevitably constitute no more than a very small subset of those who were alive and potentially able to write, and it is therefore important at the outset to consider how far these writers may be taken to represent working-class experiences more broadly. Autobiographical sources may be rich and illuminating, but they are not, of course, simple portals into past societies. Like all historical documents, they represent the interests and ideas of some social constituencies better than others. Most obviously, they were overwhelmingly written by men, rather than women. Of the four hundred autobiographies that have survived, fewer than thirty were written by women. Girls' educational opportunities were more limited than those of their brothers; women had less money to spend on notebooks, pens, and ink; and women's lives and voices were widely considered to be far less important than those of men. For all these reasons, women struggled to express themselves in the autobiographical form, and we must not lose sight of the fact that the perspective these sources provide is not universal, but rather overwhelmingly that of adult men.

Nor, of course, do autobiographies contain a fully comprehensive account of the lives of their authors. As long lives were condensed into a few written pages, many details were inevitably omitted—sometimes for reasons of space, sometimes owing to judgements about what was considered suitable for a wider audience. Take, for example, the writer and radical, Thomas Frost. Although he did refer to his marriage to his first wife in his *Recollections*, he did not mention that he married a second time, following her death. Nor did he describe how he subsequently left his second wife and cohabited with another woman for many years.[10] Autobiographical accounts involve the reinterpretation of earlier lived events at many years' removal. Complex lived experiences need to be rendered into simple, intelligible narratives, acceptable both to surviving family members and (where published) to the book-buying public. Inevitably, the finished works contain silences, absences, and contradictions.[11]

Yet for all their drawbacks, the autobiographies and memoirs represent a very special set of records in which working people set out to describe their lives in their own words and for their own purposes. Of course, there are other official records gathered by courts, local and national government, and social elites to which we may turn if we want to know something about working-class life. But such documents were always the outcome of an uneven encounter between those who had power and those who did not. And in this respect, life histories and autobiographies are both unusual and unique. Here is a collection of personal stories freely narrated by the ordinary men (and occasionally women) we wish to understand and it is worth emphasizing the rarity of historical testimony of this kind. For all their shortcomings, the autobiographies offer the best way—indeed the only way—to examine how industrialization felt to those who lived through it, and it behooves us to listen to what they say.

Working-class men did not directly address the question of what happened to their living standards with the onset of industrialization. Most were writing before the expression "Industrial Revolution" had entered the English language, and there is no evidence that the concept of industrialization underpinned their understanding of their lives. And yet, as the autobiographical writers entered old age in the 1840s or 1850s, they displayed an unmistakable awareness that the times had changed, that they had lived through a significant historical moment that merited especial consideration.

Their views about the nature of this change were of course not homogeneous, but there is one possibility that can be quickly ruled out: these sources offer little support for the pessimistic interpretation of living standards. In stark contrast to anxieties of modern historians, our writers never lamented that things were getting worse, or regretted the passing of a happier past. "When I hear people talk of the good old days," wrote the railway worker George Mallard, he thought "they must be ignorant of what did happen in those days. I know it was hard times where I was."[12] Instead of nostalgia and regret, the autobiographers spoke in remarkably consistent terms of improvements and progress. Benjamin North, for instance, thought that if his parents and ancestors could "revisit the earth . . . . and see the domestic alterations, commercial improvements, and the wonderful and astonishing activities of life" they would not be able to "believe their own eyes."[13] Robert Dawson Burn wrote that anyone who cared to compare "the state of affairs in Great Britain" in the early nineteenth century with the present (he was talking about the 1850s) would have to admit "that as a nation we have much cause to feel grateful."[14] Moses Horler, a Somerset miner, thought the life of the colliers in the early part of the century "was very different to what it is at the present time." In the 1820s, wages were "so very much lower . . . Life was very hard for the poor then."[15] Such views were not exceptional. They were expressed with remarkable consistency across a large number of writers. In contrast to the claims emerging from so many recent academic treatments of the standard of living debate, these male writers consistently expressed the view that life for working people had changed for the better between the late eighteenth century and the second half of the nineteenth century.

Much of the basis for this assessment was grounded in their belief that the nation's new industrial towns and cities had improved men's prospects in the workplace by providing a wider variety of work, work of greater interest, and perhaps most importantly, work that paid better wages. With industrialization came a raft of new occupations, none of which called for exceptional skills or training that could not be picked up at the workplace. The growth of cottage industry, factories, mills, mining and towns all, in their different ways, helped to increase the demand for male labor, which in turn raised both the wages and the status of the unskilled worker. The result was that the unskilled laborer also had better prospects than at any earlier point in history.

At the pinnacle of Britain's manufacturing sector were the textile districts of Lancashire, Cheshire, and Yorkshire, which offered employment opportunities superior to those available anywhere else. As each of the constituent steps for processing raw cotton into woven textiles was mechanized during the nineteenth century and moved from workshops and cottages into factories, new working patterns were established. It is true the factory owners exhibited an unmistakable preference for employing women and children, regarding them as a cheaper and more submissive source of labor.[16] But adult men, particularly those living in Lancashire, Yorkshire, and the Scottish Lowlands, can also be found moving into new employment in factories, warehouses, and a host of ancillary trades.

For the most part, historians have expressed considerable skepticism that factories provided more favorable employment than the cottage industries they replaced, yet if we attend to the words of the men who made that transition a rather different perspective emerges. For nineteenth-century workers, factory employment was more highly coveted than most other alternatives. Nor is their enthusiasm for the factory system too hard to fathom, for it is clear that there were some very real compensations for adults who worked in the factories. First and foremost were the high wages. Samuel Catton, for example, spent his early years as an agricultural servant, but moved to Stratford in his twenties where he found work at the chemical works for "very good wages."[17] In the Preston cotton mills, Benjamin Shaw found "good work & wages."[18] When John Lincoln was employed at the arsenal at Woolwich he considered that "the pay very good." At one point, his earnings rose as high as 38 shillings a week—a sum significantly higher than the typical agricultural worker's weekly wage of nine to twelve shillings.[19] He also thought "the work was very Light" compared to his earlier work as a farm servant.

Other writers stopped short of describing their pay as good, but nonetheless indicated that their factory wage had enabled them to save fairly considerable sums of money. Recalling his seven-year apprenticeship in a Lancashire factory, one anonymous writer declared that he "was never as happy as I was at that time."[20] As a young married man, he recalled how he and his new wife had enjoyed "plenty of money" and managed to build up a stock of good furniture thanks to his job at the factory: "things went on very smoothly for a long time."[21] Working as a machine grinder and glazer in Heywood, William Marcroft was able to save a sum of £20 in two years and eventually to retire from manual labor altogether.[22] Adam Rushton stashed away enough to contemplate an emigration to Wisconsin, USA.[23] Another writer, William Dodd, whose childhood experiences in the factories were so harrowing that he became a campaigner against child labor, was nonetheless forced to concede that his working conditions and pay both picked up when he reached adulthood.[24] Such examples are not given in order to suggest that the factory districts offered universal gains to all working people, but rather to point out the gulf between historians' gloomy assessments of the rise of the factory and the far more positive accounts provided by the autobiographies. For healthy, adult male workers factories offered well-paid employment, and the attraction of that was self-evident.

Factories and mills were emerging as a major source of employment, particularly in the industrializing north, but these new industrial districts offered more than the promise of employment as a factory operative. After all, mill owners had needs that went beyond the making of goods. One common alternative to working in the factory was working in the warehouse, and with better wages and pleasanter working conditions, most of our writers regarded this as something of a promotion.[25] Thomas Wood found work repairing the machines in the factories of Oldham rather than operating them.[26] And in Preston, Benjamin Shaw made a living fixing spindles and making fly frames, mules, and other parts of the machines that kept the town's cotton industry going.[27] Others kept the books or collected accounts for mill owners.[28] As George Hanby found, goods needed to be weighed as well as made.[29] Then there was work to be done moving raw materials and finished goods around. William Smith minded a turnpike gate.[30] John Hemmingway carried goods on his horse and cart for a fustian manufacturer.[31] James Watson had the charge of a saddle-horse for a Leeds warehouse.[32] Yet others found work on the railways or delivering mail.[33]

The emergence of mills and factories in first half of the nineteenth century offered direct employment opportunities for male workers, but so too did the growing towns within which such industries were located. Urbanization increased demand for a wide range of goods, such as shoes, clothes, bread, buildings, and furniture—items that had traditionally been made by skilled craftsmen. Prior to the onset of industrialization, entry to these skilled trades was typically through a formal seven-year apprenticeship—an agreement by which the worker received nothing, or reduced wages, in return for training in the trade. The costs of entering such a lengthy agreement had effectively closed entry to those without a modest amount of family wealth behind them. Yet rapid population growth and rising demand made it impossible to restrict these trades to the fortunate minority who had served an expensive period of training. As a result, men from more humble backgrounds were beginning to find it possible to enter a wide range of skilled and semi-skilled trades and to enjoy some of the benefits that went with them.

By the early nineteenth century, entry to certain trades became more common outside the confines of an apprenticeship than within it. Tailors and shoemakers, for example, now typically picked up the rudiments of their trade from their workmates while working as an unskilled dogsbody in a workshop, rather than through a formal period of unpaid training.[34] Some perfected their skills by later paying for teaching from a more highly skilled, urban craftsman. A similar route was also taken by many of the bakers, butchers, carpenters, coopers, metalworkers, and shipwrights.[35] Other more unusual trades were also accessible outside the apprenticeship system. Included among those who became skilled laborers without ever mustering the means to pay their master a premium were a coach-trimmer, a chair-maker, a knife-grinder, a shopkeeper, and a maker of pearl ornaments.[36]

In addition to easing entry to the ranks of skilled tradesman, rapid urban growth offered a raft of alternative employment opportunities to adult men in search of work. One option was to set up as a small shopkeeper. George Cooper, for example, was unable to find employment in the Stockport cotton mills following his role in leading the strikes in 1848, so he set up a very small grocers shop instead.[37] One autobiographer gave up manual labor to sell tea. Another sold "cheap cheese" in very small quantities to his neighbors. Yet another sold his own sweets, cakes, and gingerbread.[38] To the dismay of many a polite commentator, the urban workforce had an insatiable appetite for alcohol, so setting up a beer shop provided yet one more alternative for workers seeking a new way to make a living.[39] The urban poor had a taste for entertainment, providing an opening for a handful of singers, ballad writers, sellers of cheap literature, and actors.[40] They also needed policing, or at least so it was thought by those who governed them: just another example of the new opportunities emerging in the towns.[41]

There was, of course, considerable variety in the wages paid by this wide range of modern and traditional employment opportunities—some paid well, others were far less remunerative. Equally, though the opportunities for small businesses were bright, not all were profitable or successful. My argument is not that working men in industrial regions enjoyed easy and universal access to well-paid work. The point, instead, is that these employment opportunities were far brighter than those that existed in the absence of industrialization, where farm-work with perhaps some seasonal opportunities for by-employment was all that was on offer.

The variety of industrial employment and the higher wages it usually offered formed part of the attraction of urban living, but there was one other advantage that was repeatedly stressed by the autobiographical writers: the high level of demand for male workers. The labor requirements of the agricultural calendar were seasonal: large numbers of hands were needed to bring in the harvest, but only a fraction of those workers was required in the dead of winter. Nobody got paid if it rained. As a result, farm-workers' low wages were further depressed by enforced unemployment at some points in the year. Urban and industrial work was not sensitive to the vagaries of the seasons in this way. The wheels of the mill engines continued to turn regardless of the weather, providing steady employment to both millworkers and to many others working in ancillary trades. Workers' demand for goods such as bread, shoes, clothes, furniture, and entertainment was similarly constant across the year. The autobiographical writers frequently commented upon the fact that their employment had been steady and indicated that was an important factor in ensuring their living standards.

Some, particularly those working in factories, not only enjoyed steady employment throughout the year, but also stayed long periods with the one employer. Positions that spanned a decade or more were not unusual and a few men spent almost their entire working life at the one mill. Robert

Collyer's father, for example, worked at one factory "man and boy," for thirty-two years.[42] John Tough spent thirty-seven years with a hosiery manufacturer in Aberdeen.[43] William Wright's father became a weft manager at a mill and held the position for "somewhere about half a century."[44] But even in the absence of long periods of stable employment with one employer, several of the working-class autobiographers indicated that demand for their skills had been high. As a young man, John Bennett had been taught carpentry by his father while living in the sleepy Wiltshire village of South Wraxall, but local incomes were low and demand for carpentry services was also muted, which caused the whole family to live in poverty and sometimes lack sufficient food. As a young man, John made the decision to get away and moved to the nearby large town of Bristol. It was fair time when he arrived and no one was hiring, but within a matter of days the fair had left town and everyone was back at work. As John watched the men going into the shipyard, a workman cried out "Can you saw?" John replied, "Yes . . . top or bottom." The workman shouted, "Come along then," and so began John's life as an urban carpenter.[45] He spent the rest of his adult life working in either Bristol or Bath and appears never to have been out of work. Of course, not all were so lucky, and those working in towns sometimes found themselves in the trough of a trade cycle, experiencing cuts in their wages or even finding themselves out of work altogether. But this should not be permitted to obscure the fact that Britain's growing industrial towns held the promise of steady employment over many years, and that regular employment, alongside wage rates, were a fundamental component of rising living standards.

The same pattern is evident in other areas of the industrializing economy. In mining, for example, wages were generally good and unemployment relatively rare. Almost all of the autobiographers who had worked as miners recorded earning good wages as an adult.[46] Very few of the miners suffered from serious unemployment; indeed, some appear never to have been out of work, though they frequently needed to migrate over short distances in order to remain in full-time employment.[47] As Thomas Oliver summarized, "as a miner I did very well."[48] Demand for construction workers—or "navvies"— was also high, particularly during the mid-century railway building boom, which helped to keep wages buoyant in this industry too. The life of a navvy was summed up by Joseph Arch as "hard work, good wages, rough quarters."[49] One autobiographer noted that his wages doubled overnight when he left the farm and started work as a navvy.[50] When Emanuel Lovekin and his mate went navvying, they found "very good jobs and plenty of money."[51] This is not of course to suggest that mining or navvying was an easy way to earn a living. The work was hard, the conditions unpleasant and often dangerous, and there was an expense and inconvenience involved in moving in search of new work. By the same token, however, our writers did not expect life to be easy. The decision to move a short distance for a full week's work was taken in a heartbeat, too inconsequential to merit much retrospective analysis. It all amounted to one more option for men who had been raised to expect to spend their lives devoted to earning a subsistence wage in agriculture.

The interconnected forces of higher wages and high levels of demand for male workers helped to drive working-class incomes upward and enabled some of the autobiographers to enjoy living standards that were superior to those of their parents. Yet the autobiographers did not simply dwell upon material advantages. Their writing also hints at something else less tangible, but no less important. The combination of good wages and abundant employment was not only enriching, it was also empowering. It helped to improve working men's status and self-worth within the workplace and within his wider community. In a reversal of the traditional pattern of workers being at risk of dismissal for the most trivial of reasons, men working in the most economically vibrant parts of the economy were increasingly able to walk away from employers they did not like. James Powell, for example, gave as his reason for quitting a job at a mill no more than a "trivial act of oppression" that caused him "considerable annoyance."[52] As a young man, Thomas Whittaker left "profitable employment" for what he later described as "a little temper on the part of the master, with too much defiance on the part of the servant."[53] Some industrial workers were prepared to leave work over the frequency of their "drinkings," or breaks. For example, Joshua Dodgson, a dyer in Halifax, left a good position after just two weeks when he realized the drinkings he had been promised were to be discontinued.[54] It is easy for modern readers to miss the significance of these small actions, after all as the writers themselves admitted, they had given up paid employment over matters that did not, with hindsight, appear terribly important. Yet the ability to reject an offer of employment was important, as it was rooted in a fundamental recalibration of the balance of power between master and servant—or, as they were now (in a telling shift in language) more likely to be described, employer and worker.

These kinds of behavior were also evident among the skilled workers. The author John Colin was frequently dismissed for drunkenness, but he was not slow to walk away from positions he disliked either. He quit one master because he was "such a tyrant"; another because he cut his wages for going to a lecture against the Corn Laws; and another simply because he "got sick of the job."[55] William Swan left a good bake shop rather than "beg pardon" from his master after the pair had had some 'high words.'[56] Another London baker handed in his notice rather than waste one more of his precious Sunday mornings at his pious master's family services.[57] There was no doubt some degree of storytelling going on here. Men whose lives had been devoted to serving other men's needs seem to be relishing recounting the moment when the tables had been turned. Yet even allowing for some rhetorical flourish, there is no reason to discount the essential truth at the heart of these accounts. And stories like this remind us that work is about more than pay and hours, important as such things undoubtedly are. All working relationships are defined by a disparity in power, an inequality that is rendered more palatable if we are well remunerated for our services and can leave at will.

It must be emphasized that our writers do not suggest that they found their employment in the mills and towns pleasant and enjoyable or anything else that we might seek from our work today. Many of these jobs were physically demanding. The hours were invariably long and the work was often dangerous. Nor should we neglect the very serious difficulties that many workers experienced when the economy hit the buffers. The first half of the nineteenth century was haunted by trade depressions, with particularly severe downturns in the winter of 1831–1832 and again in 1841–1842.[58] And in addition to these periodic downturns was the constant risk of commercial failures and strikes. Such events could throw the millhands out of work and threaten the livelihoods of those connected to the mills' good fortune. In no time, families that had been enjoying a measure of prosperity were pawning their furniture and living on short rations.[59]

Yet the possibility of hard times should not be allowed to distort our understanding of the impact of industrialization on workers' lives. After all, this was not where the autobiographical writers chose to place their emphasis. Instead, and in contrast to so much academic writing about the subject, they repeatedly suggested that this period saw substantial improvements in men's wages, not in spite of industrialization, but because of it. Of course, much of the reason for this lay simply in the fact that the pre-industrial economy had been so poor at providing for its workers. In most places, there was just not enough to go around, and this left workers with irregular wages that could provide little more than the bare essentials of existence, and too often not even that. Furthermore, these low incomes had cultural, as well as economic consequences. Nothing gave meaning to the words "master" and "servant" more fully than low levels of employment. Deference and submission were part of the natural order of things when the servants' need for work outstripped the masters' ability to provide it.

With industrialization some of the unskilled got to taste good, regular wages and the kind of independence that a reliable earning power could bring. Mills, factories, mines, and quarries needed large numbers of men, not only to produce goods but also to perform a range of ancillary tasks to ensure that raw materials and finished goods were to be found in the places and at the times they were needed. The rise of industry, the growth of towns, and the development of new forms of transportation increased the demand for male workers and improved the amount and variety of work that needed to be done. Industrialization had a remarkable power to raise men's earnings, and for that first generation, that generation which had expected the hunger of their own childhood to be experienced once more by their children and grandchildren, the significance of rising incomes can hardly be overestimated. However much this might jar with our expectations, it is probably worth our while to take these comments seriously.

NOTES

1. Carlyle 1845.
2. See the discussion in Griffin 2013.
3. Engels 1987, p. 51.
4. See for example: Chadwick 1843, p. 88; Ure 1835, pp. 364–70.
5. Toynbee 1884, p.5.
6. A flavor of the interchange between Ashton, Engerman, Gilboy, Hartwell, Hobsbawm, and Thompson can be found in Taylor 1975.
7. Clark 2005; Feinstein 1998; Gazeley and Horrell 2013, pp.781–2; Cinnirella 2008; Floud et al 2011.
8. Vincent 1981; Waters 2000; Strange 2015a.
9. The starting point for anybody interested in looking at working-class autobiography must be Burnett et al 1984. See also Hackett 1985. Many more items have come to light since Burnett et al's work in the 1970s and about 20 percent of the items consulted here are not listed in their bibliography.
10. Frost 1880, p. 42. Contrast with "Thomas Frost," *Oxford Dictionary of National Biography*.
11. The literature on autobiographies as historical source is extensive. See: Rogers and Cuming 2018; Summerfield 2018, pp. 300–402; Strange 2015; Strange 2015b; Doolittle 2009; Steedman 1992; Gagnier 1991; Pennef 1990.
12. Mallard ZA9908/3, X9908/4–15, p. 3.
13. North 1882, p. 95.
14. Burn 1978, p. 133.
15. Horler 1900, p. 14
16. On this, see in particular Berg 1993.
17. Catton 1863, p. 4. See also 1982, p.20.
18. Shaw 1991, p. 45.
19. Lincoln, MC 2669/29, 991X9.
20. *An Exposition of a Coiner*, p. 4.
21. Ibid., pp. 4–5. See also Campbell 1828, p. 23.
22. Marcroft 1886, pp. 39–43. See also "Life of a cotton spinner," 1856; "Life of a journeyman baker," 1856.
23. Rushton 1909, pp. 66, 82–85.
24. Dodd 2007, pp. 200, 202.
25. Gwyer [1877], pp. 8–9; Rushton 1909, p. 54; Teer 1869), p. iv; Townend, 1869, p. 22; Watson 1977, pp. 109–10.

26. Wood 1880, pp. 8–9,14.
27. Shaw 1991, pp. 38, 42.
28. Roberts 2000, pp. 14–15; "Life of handloom weaver" (account collector), *Commonwealth,* April 25, 1857.
29. Hanby 1874, no pagination.
30. Smith 1966, p. 183.
31. Hemmingway, MC 766/1, 795X5 (carrier for "Fustian Cutters of Lymm"), p. 385.
32. Watson 1977, p. 110. See also: Farish 1996, pp. 78–81; Tough 1848, p. 5.
33. Farish 1996, pp. 72–4, 85–6; Langdon 1909, p. 64; Mallard ZA9908/3, X9908/4–15, pp. 11ff.
34. The tailors who learned without serving an apprenticeship are [Cameron] 1888, pp. 12–13; Carter 1845; [Holkinson] 1857; Lowery 1979, pp. 59–61. Robert Crowe served an apprentice though he quit early: Crowe 1986, pp. 4–5. For some examples in shoemaking, see: Askham 1893; Bezer; Bent 1866; Gibbs 1827; Jewell 1964; Spurr 1976, xxvi.
35. Carpenters: uncompleted apprenticeships (Buckley 1897, pp. 78–80, 104–20 and Croll 1896, p. 16); informal arrangements (Bennett, 36907, p. 2; Thomson 1847, pp. 165–7). Bakers: informal arrangements (Innes 1876, pp. 8–9; "Life of Journeyman Baker," December 13, 1856). Whitesmiths: informal arrangements ([Gooch] 1844, p. 16 and [A Self-Reformer] March 2, 1850, 1/9, pp. 284–5). Shipwright: informal arrangement (Thompson [1863], pp. 6–7). Butcher: informal arrangement (Taylor 1893, p. 8).
36. Gammage 1983, p. 37; North 1882, p. 103; Murdoch 1863, pp. 1–17, pp. 8–12; Whetstone 1807, p. 60; Davis 1898, p. 10. Coach-trimming refers to the painting of horse-drawn carriages.
37. Cooper [1974], [p. 20]. See also: Goodliffe DE7196, no pag.; "Life of a cotton spinner," December 27, 1856; Oliver 1914, p. 50.
38. Croll 1896 (tea), p. 20–21; Livesey 1868 ("cheap cheese"), pp. 228–9; Davis 1898 (cakes and gingerbread), p. 13.
39. "Life of Journeyman Baker," December 13 and 20, 1856; "Life of Journeyman Baker," May 2, 1857.
40. See, for example, [Cameron] 1888, pp. 15 ff; Love 1824, pp. 38ff; M'Gonagall, pp. 3–8; [William Wright] 1893.
41. Chadwick 1974, p. 9; Pearman 1988, pp. 188–91.
42. Collyer 1908, p. 2.
43. Tough 1848, p. 6.
44. [Wright] 1893. See also: Bates 1895, thirty years at Paul Speak's mill, p. 2; Catton 1863, 9 years, pp. 4–5; *Exposition of a Coiner,* twelve years, p. 5; Hanson 1884, ten years in Messrs Wards' weaving shop, p. 24; Hemmingway, eleven years at Stirling's Mill in Manchester, p. 385; Lincoln, seven years at Woolwich Arsenal, pp. 26–9.
45. Bennett, "Autobiography," p. 4.
46. Burt 1924, pp. 104, 108, 112; Weaver [1913], p. 73; Wilson 1980, p. 66.
47. Errington 1988, passim. The miner, Edward Rymer, suggested the pits did occasionally lie idle, but he mentioned just "days now and then." See: Rymer 1898, p. 5.

See also the discussion in Burt 1924, p. 112. See, however, Timothy Mountjoy, who noted that at one point "the summer trade was so bad, we only worked two, sometimes three, days per week, and we could not see when these bad times would come to an end." Mountjoy 1887, p. 18.
48. Oliver 1914, p. 18.
49. Arch 1966, p. 50.
50. Anderson 1896, p. 9.
51. Lovekin, 1:452, no. 4.
52. Powell 1865, p. 10.
53. Whittaker 1884, p. 26.
54. Dodgson, May 19, 1956.
55. "Colin" 1864, pp. 36, 60.
56. Swan 1970, pp. 42–102, p. 51.
57. Johnston 1885, p. 92.
58. For more on unemployment, see Burnett 1994, pp. 54–63, 87–121.
59. Griffin 2018.

REFERENCES

Anon. [A Self-Reformer], 1850. "A working man's experience," *The Working Man's Friend and Family Instructor*, March 2, 1/9, pp. 284–5.

Anon. [Cameron, William], 1888. *Hawkie, the Autobiography of a Gangrel*, ed. John Strathesk. Glasgow: David Robertson & Co.

Anon. [Gooch, Richard], 1844. *Memoirs, Remarkable Vicissitudes, Military Career and Wanderings*. Norwich: Thorndick & Co.

Anon. [Holkinson, Jacob], 1857. "The Life of Jacob Holkinson, Tailor and Poet, written by himself," *The Commonwealth*, 24, January 31.

Anon. [Wright, William], 1893. "Adventures and Recollections of Bill o'th' Hoylus End. Told by Himself." *Keighley Herald*. June 2–December 8.

Anon. "Colin," pseud. 1864. *The Wanderer Brought Home. The Life and Adventures of Colin. An Autobiography.* Edited by the Rev. B. Richings. London: W. Tweedie.

Anon. "Life of a cotton spinner, written by himself." 1856. *The Commonwealth*.

Anon. "Life of a journeyman baker, written by himself." 1856. *The Commonwealth*, 13, December 20. no.4.

Anon. "Life of handloom weaver." 1857. *The Commonwealth*, April 25.

Anon. *An Exposition of the Nefarious System of Making and Passing Spurious Coin . . . Being the Confessions of a Coiner.* Preston, n.d.

Anderson, Isaac. 1896. *The Life History of Isaac Anderson. A member of the peculiar people.* N.p.

Arch, Joseph, 1966. *Joseph Arch: the Story of his Life, Told by Himself.* Edited by the Countess of Warwick. London: Macgibbon & Kee.

Askham, John. 1893. *Sketches in Prose and Verse.* Wellinborough: S. S. Campion

Bates. John, 1895. *John Bates, the Veteran Reformer: A Sketch of his Life.* Queensbury: Feather.

Bennett, John. "Manuscript autobiography of John Bennett of Bristol." Bristol Record Office.

Bent, Charles. 1866. *Autobiography of Charles Bent, a Reclaimed Drunkard.* Sheffield: D. T. Ingham.

Berg, Maxine. 1993. "What difference did women's work make to the industrial revolution?" *History Workshop Journal.* 35: 22–44.

Bezer, John James. "The autobiography of one of the Chartist rebels of 1848." In Vincent, ed., *Testaments of Radicalism.*

Bodell, James. 1982. *A Soldier's View of Empire: the Reminiscences of James Bodell, 1831-92.* London: Bodley Head

Buckley, John. 1897. *A Village Politician. The Life-Story of John Buckley.* Edited by J. C. Buckmaster. London: T. F. Unwin.

Burn, James Dawson. 1978. *The Autobiography of a Beggar Boy, 1855.* Edited by David Vincent. London: Europa Publications.

Burnett, John, David Vincent, and David Mayall. 1984. *The Autobiography of the Working Class. An Annotated Critical Bibliography, 1790-1900,* i. New York: Harvester.

Burnett, John. 1994. *Idle Hands: The Experience of Unemployment, 1790-1990.* London: Routledge.

Burt, Thomas. 1924. *Thomas Burt: Pitman & Privy Councillor; an Autobiography.* London: T. Fisher Unwin.

Campbell, Charles. 1828. *Memoirs of Charles Campbell, at Present Prisoner in the Jail of Glasgow.* Glasgow: James Duncan & Co.

Carlyle, Thomas. 1845. *Past and Present.* 2nd ed. London: Chapman and Hall .

Carter, Thomas. 1845. *Memoirs of a Working Man.* Edited by Charles Knight. London: Charles Knight & Co.

Catton, Samuel. 1863. *A Short Sketch of a Long Life of Samuel Catton once a Suffolk Ploughboy.* Ipswich: Arpthorpe.

Chadwick, Edwin. 1843. *Report on the Sanitary Condition of the laboring Population of Great Britain.* London: W. Clowes.

Chadwick, William. 1974. *Reminiscences of a Chief Constable.* Longdendale: Scholar Press.

Cinnirella, F. 2008. "Optimists or pessimists? A reconsideration of nutritional status in Britain, 1740–1865," *European Review of Economic History*, 12/3:325–54.

Clark, Gregory. 2005. "The Condition of the working-class in England, 1209–2004," *Journal of Political Economy.* 113/6: 1307–1340.

Collyer, Robert. 1908. *Some Memories.* Boston: American Unitarian Association. *Commonwealth.*

Cooper, George. 1974. *George Cooper, Stockport's Last Town Crier, 1824–1895,* Presented by Anne Swift.

Croll, James. 1896. *Autobiographical sketch of James Croll, with Memoir of his Life and Work.* London: Edward Stanford.

Crowe, Robert. 1986. "Reminiscences of Robert Crowe, the octogenarian tailor." In Dorothy Thompson, ed., *Chartists Biographies and Autobiographies.* New York: Garland.

Davis, Edward G. 1898. *Some Passages from My Life.* Birmingham: White & Pike Ltd.

Dodd, William. 2007. *A Narrative of the Experiences and Sufferings of William Dodd, A Factory Cripple, Written by Himself 1851.* In James R. Simmons and Janice Carlisle, eds., *Factory Lives: Four Nineteenth-Century Working-Class Autobiographies.* Ontario: Broadview Press.

Dodgson, Joshua. 1956. "Diary of Joshua Dodgson." *Halifax Weekly Courier and Guardian.*

Doolittle, Megan. 2009. "Fatherhood and family shame: masculinity, welfare and the workhouse in late nineteenth-century England." In Lucy Delap, Ben Griffin, and Abigail Wills, eds., *The Politics of Domestic Authority in Britain from 1800.* Basingstoke: Palgrave Macmillan, pp. 84–110.

Engels, Friedrich. 1987. *The Condition of the Working Class in England.* Edited by Victor G. Kiernan. Harmondsworth: Penguin.

Errington, Anthony. 1988. *Coals of Rails or the Reason of my Wrighting. The Autobiography of Anthony Errington from 1778 to 1825.* Edited by P. E. H. Hair. Liverpool: Liverpool University Press.

Farish, William. 1996. *The Autobiography of William Farish. The Struggles of a Handloom Weaver. With Some of his Writings.* London.

Feinstein, C. H. 1998. "Pessimism perpetuated: real wages and the standard of living in Britain during and after the industrial revolution." *Journal of Economic History.* 58: 625–58.

Floud, Roderick et al. 2011. *The Changing Body: Health, Nutrition, and Human Development in the Western World since 1700.* Cambridge, UK: Cambridge University Press.

Frost, Thomas. 1880. *Forty Year's Recollections. Literary and Political.* London: Sampson Low.

Gagnier, Regenia. 1991. *Subjectivities: A History of Self-Representation in Britain, 1832-1920.* Oxford, UK: Oxford University Press.

Gammage, R. G. 1983. *Reminiscences of a Chartist, Robert Gammage.* Edited by W. H. Maehl [Barnsley]: Society for the Study of Labor History.

Gazeley, I. and Horrell, S. 2013. "Nutrition in the English agricultural laborer's household over the course of the long nineteenth century," *Economic History Review,* 66: 757–784.

Gibbs, John. 1827. *The Life and Experience of the Author and some Traces of the Lord's Gracious Dealings towards the Author.* Lewes: Lower.

Goodliffe, Arnold. "Memoirs of Arnold Goodliffe." Leicestershire Record Office.

Griffin, Emma. 2013. *Liberty's Dawn: A People's History of the Industrial Revolution.* New Haven, CT: Yale University Press.

Griffin, Emma. 2018. "Diet, hunger and living standards during the British industrial revolution." *Past and Present.* 239, no. 1:71–111.

Gwyer, Joseph. 1877. "Life and Poems of Joseph Gywer." In *Sketches of the Life of Joseph Gywer, Potato Salesman, with his Poems.* Penge.

Hackett, Nan. 1985. *Nineteenth-Century British Working-Class Autobiographies: An Annotated Bibliography.* New York: Ams Press.

Hanby, George. 1874. *Autobiography of a Colliery Weighman.* Barnsley: Brewin & Davis.

Hanson, William. 1884. *The Life of William Hanson, Written by Himself.* Halifax: J. Walsh.

Hemmingway, John. "The Character or Worldly experience of the writer from 1791 to 1865." Norfolk Record Office.

[Holkinson, Jacob]. 1857. "The Life of Jacob Holkinson, Tailor and Poet, written by himself." *The Commonwealth*, 24, January 31.

Horler, Moses. 1900. *The Early Recollections of Moses Horler.* Edited by M. F. Coombs and H. Coombs. Radstock.

Innes, William. 1876. "Autobiography of William Innes." In *Memorials of a Faithful Servant, William Innes.* Edinburgh: privately published.

Jewell, Joseph. 1964. "Autobiographical memoir of Joseph Jewell, 1763-1846." Edited by Arthur Walter Slater. *Camden Miscellany*, vol. 22.

Johnston, David. 1885. *Autobiographical Reminiscences of David Johnston, an Octogenarian Scotchman.* Chicago: n.p.

Langdon, Roger. 1909. *The Life of Roger Langdon, Told by Himself.* London: Elliot Stock.

Lincoln, John. "Memoirs of John Lincoln." In Norfolk Record Office.

Livesey, Joseph. 1868. "The Author's Autobiography." *The Staunch Teetotaler*.

Love, David. 1824. Fourth Edition. *The Life, Adventures, and Experience, of David Love, Written by Himself.* Nottingham.

Lovekin, Emmanuel. "Some Notes of my Life." Brunel University Library.

Lowery, Robert. 1979. "Passages in the life of a temperance lecturer." In Brian Harrison and Patricia Hollis, eds., *Robert Lowery, Radical and Chartist.* London: Europa Publications.

M'Gonagall, William. *The Authentic Autobiography of the Poet M'Gonagall.* Dundee, n.d..

Mallard, George . "Memories." Northamptonshire Record Office.

Marcroft, William. 1886. *The Marcroft Family.* Manchester: John Heywood.

Mountjoy, Timothy. 1887. *The Life, Labours and deliverances of a Forest of Dean collier, born the 11th day of September, 1824, on Little Dean Hill.* N.p.: Chilver.

Murdoch, James. 1863. "Autobiography". In *The Autobiography and Poems of James Murdoch.* Elgin: James Black.

North, Benjamin. 1882. *Autobiography of Benjamin North.* Aylesbury: Fred K. Samuels.

Oliver, Thomas. 1914. *Autobiography of a Cornish Miner.* Camborne: Camborne Printing Company.

Pearman, John. 1988. *The Radical Soldier's Tale: John Pearman, 1819-1908.* Edited by Carolyn Steedman. London: Routledge.

Pennef, J. 1990. "Myths in life stories," in R. Samuel and P. Thompson, eds., *The Myths we Live By*. London: Routledge.

Powell, J. H. 1865. *Life Incidents and Poetic Pictures*. London: Trubner & Co.

R. Spurr. 1976. "The autobiography of Robert Spurr." Edited by R. J. Owen, *Baptist Quarterly*.

Roberts, Israel. 2000. *Israel Roberts, 1827-1881: Autobiography*. Edited by Ruth Strong. Pudsey: Pudsey Civic Society.

Rogers, Helen and Emily Cuming. 2018. "Revealing Fragments: Close and Distant Reading of Working-Class Autobiography." *Family & Community History*. 21/3: 180–201.

Rushton, Adam. 1909. *My Life as Farmer's Boy, Factory Lad, Teacher, and Preacher*. Manchester: S. Clarke.

Rymer, Edward Allen. 1898. *The Martyrdom of the Mine, or 60 Years' Struggle for Life*. Middlesbrough: Jordison & Co.

Shaw, Benjamin. 1991. Edited by Alan G. Crosby. *The Family Records of Benjamin Shaw, Mechanic of Dent, Dolphin holme and Preston, 1772-1841*. Record Society of Lancashire and Cheshire, vol. 13.

Smith, William. 1966. "The memoir of William Smith." Edited by B. S. Trinder. *Transactions of the Shropshire Archaeological Society*. No. 58:178–85

Steedman, Carolyn. 1992. "History and autobiography: different pasts." In Idem, ed., *Past Tenses. Essays on Writing, Autobiography and History*. London: Rivers Oram Press, pp. 41–50.

Strange, Julie-Marie. 2015a. *Fatherhood and the British Working Class, 1865-1914*. Cambridge, UK: Cambridge University Press.

Idem. 2015b. "Fathers at Home: Life Writing and Late-Victorian and Edwardian Plebeian Domestic Masculinities," *Gender & History* 27, no. 3:703–717.

Summerfield, Penny. 2018. *Histories of the Self: Personal Narratives and Historical Practice*. London: Taylor & Francis.

Swan, William. 1970. "The journal of William Swan, born 1813," in *The Journals of Two Poor Dissenters, 1786-1880*, ed. Preface by Guida Swan and introduction by John Holloway. London: Routledge & Kegan Paul.

Taylor, Arthur J., editor. 1975. *The Standard of Living in Britain in the Industrial Revolution*. London: Methuen.

Taylor, John. 1893. *Autobiography of John Taylor*. Bath: J. Francis.

Teer, John. 1869. *Silent Musings*. Manchester: Ainsworth & Cheetham.

Thompson, John. 1863. *Memoir of Mr. John Thompson*. Sunderland: Forster.

Thomson, Christopher. 1847. *Autobiography of an Artisan*. London: J. Chapman.

Tough, John. 1848. *A Short Narrative of the Life of an Aberdonian*. Aberdeen: N. P.

Townend, Rev. Joseph. 1869. Second edition. *Autobiography of the Rev. Joseph Townend*. London: W. Reed.

Toynbee, Arnold. 1884. *Lectures on the Industrial Revolution of the Eighteenth Century in England*. London: Longmans, Green and Co.

Ure, Andrew. 1835. *The Philosophy of Manufactures; or, an Exposition of the Scientific, Moral, and Commercial Economy of the Factory System of Great Britain*. London: Charles Knight.

Vincent, David. 1981. *Bread, Knowledge and Freedom: A Study of Nineteenth-Century Working Class Autobiography*. London: Europa Publications.

Waters, Chris. 2000. "Autobiography, nostalgia, and the changing practices of working-class selfhood," in George K. Behlmer and Fred Marc Leventhal. Editors. *Singular Continuities: Tradition, Nostalgia, and Society in Modern Britain*. Stanford, CA: Stanford University Press, 178–95.

Watson, James. 1977. "Reminiscences of James Watson." In David Vincent, ed., *Testaments of Radicalism. Memoirs of working-class politicians, 1790-1885*. London: Europa Publications.

Weaver, Richard. 1913. *Richard Weaver's Life Story*. Edited by James Paterson. London: Morgan & Scott.

Whetstone, Charles. 1807. *Truths. No. 1 or the Memoirs of Charles Whetstone*. N.p.

Whittaker, Thomas. 1884. *Life's Battles in Temperance Armour*. London; Hodder & Stoughton.

Wilson, John. 1980. *Memories of a labor Leader: The Autobiography of John Wilson, J.P., M.P*. Edited by John Burnett. Firle: Caliban Books.

Wood, Thomas. 1880. "Autobiography by Thomas Wood, 1822-1880." In Bradford Central Library.

Chapter 4

George Whitefield's Changing Commercial Theology

Kristen Beales (Warren Center, Harvard University)

Benjamin Franklin reluctantly dropping his coppers into George Whitefield's collection plate is one of the most commonly cited anecdotes in early American history. At the time of the collection, Whitefield was traveling through the British North American colonies to evangelize and to raise money for his Georgia orphan house known as Bethesda. Although Franklin "did not disapprove of the Design," he expressed doubts about the prudence of building an orphanage in a colony that "was then destitute of Materials & Workmen." After unsuccessfully attempting to dissuade Whitefield from the project, Franklin "refus'd to contribute" to the orphanage. Shortly thereafter, Franklin attended one of Whitefield's sermons. As the minister began to preach, Franklin "began to soften," and he tossed some coins into the collection plate. "Another Stroke of his Oratory" made the printer "asham'd of that, and determin'd me to give the Silver; & he finish'd so admirably, that I empty'd my Pocket wholly into the Collector's Dish, Gold and all." Franklin may have been skeptical about Whitefield's plan for Bethesda, but he used the story in his *Autobiography* to demonstrate how Whitefield's eloquence gave him "Power over the Hearts & Purses of his Hearers."[1]

Franklin's anecdote has helped make Whitefield's financial collections one of the most well-known aspects of his ministry. But the type of collection that Franklin described was only briefly a part of Whitefield's commercial theology. I use the phrase "commercial theology" to describe the intertwining of commercial practices, economic thinking, and theology that structured how Christians understood God acting in their economic affairs. By emphasizing the ways that religious and commercial beliefs and practices shaped one another, the term tethers economic morality to the practical theologies that it was part of and highlights how seemingly mundane acts and decisions were imbued with providential significance. Whitefield's commercial theology changed dramatically over the course of his ministry. Initially, he believed that collecting spontaneous donations at his sermons allowed God to guide every decision related to Bethesda. But by the time he began offering financial advice to Samson Occom, Eleazer Wheelock, and Nathaniel Whitaker in the 1750s, he had changed his views. Instead, Whitefield now argued that God would best provide for institutions like Bethesda or Dartmouth through methods that emphasized long-term financial planning and financial stability. Whitefield's shifting financial strategy for his Bethesda orphanage reflected a transformation in how he understood God acting in the economic world.[2]

Although scholars have long been interested in Whitefield's interactions with the commercial world, they have portrayed his commercial theology as a static part of his ministry for two reasons. First, historians have focused on Whitefield's role in the revivals of the so-called "Great Awakening" of the 1740s. They have analyzed the economic context of local revivals, examined how itinerant preaching represented an adaptation to commercial modernity, and demonstrated how Whitefield capitalized on new commercial techniques to spread revival.[3] While this approach illuminates some of the most controversial years of his ministry, it downplays the significant changes that occurred in Whitefield's thinking after the revival fires cooled.[4] Second, scholars have analyzed Whitefield as one of the progenitors of evangelicalism. In these accounts, Whitefield's aggressive appropriation of market means to spread the Gospel marked an emerging evangelical approach to the economic world. What matters about Whitefield in this narrative was that he used the market to spread religion, not the changing financial practices that he used to do so. Whitefield's changing financial strategies, however, reflected significant theological changes that complicate the standard narrative that emphasizes the continuities between Whitefield and later evangelicals.[5]

In order to understand the religious and financial advice that Whitefield offered to the founders of Dartmouth College, therefore, we must examine how the minister's commercial theology developed in tandem with his experiences managing Bethesda. From the beginning of his ministry until about 1742, Whitefield designed a funding plan for his Bethesda orphanage that would demonstrate his complete dependence on God. He rejected both institutional support and a "visible fund," his term for any regularized source of income such as a salary or an endowment, and instead relied on occasional collections, like the one described by Franklin, to fund Bethesda. Whitefield faced a series of financial and personal setbacks between 1742 and 1746, however, that changed his commercial theology. By 1747, Whitefield sought out a "visible fund" in the form of a plantation worked by enslaved labor in

South Carolina, began to rely on more dependable private subscriptions to fund Bethesda, and transformed his accounting methods to include regular audits. This evolution did not represent a crisis of faith, but a change in how Whitefield understood God acting in the financial world. His experiences managing Bethesda caused him to believe that long-term financial planning was a providential tool that would allow the orphanage to flourish. And it was this advice that he ultimately passed on to the men funding what would become Dartmouth College.

It is tempting to analyze Whitefield's initial financial collections and the bold theological claims that undergirded them as laying the foundation for the evangelical entrepreneurs and prosperity gospel televangelists who shape the religious marketplace in modern America. But this type of analysis can obscure the significant changes that occurred in Whitefield's commercial theology over the course of his ministry. Examining these changes, rather than focusing on the collections described in Franklin's anecdote, reveals how Whitefield's practical experiences in the marketplace transformed his commercial theology.

Between about 1738 and about 1742, Whitefield designed a financial strategy that he believed would highlight his dependence on God and allow God to shape every decision related to Bethesda. He worried that relying on either institutional support from the Georgia Trustees or another type of "visible fund" to finance Bethesda would demonstrate that he placed his faith in human, rather than godly, means to support the project. He therefore relied on occasional public collections and donations to support the institution. Restoring the theological justifications for Whitefield's initial financial strategy recovers the spiritual power that Whitefield assigned to money and demonstrates how his commercial theology made his collections both pastoral and evangelizing tools.

Whitefield decided to build a Georgia orphanage in 1738 based in part on an idea from his friend Charles Wesley. The Georgia Trustees had founded the colony in 1733 as a humanitarian venture that would provide a home for both the English poor and persecuted European Protestants. The Trustees feared that relying on enslaved African labor would have a deleterious effect on the moral character of white settlers while also leaving Georgia vulnerable to threats from Spanish Florida. Due to these concerns, they banned slavery in the young colony. Whitefield, meanwhile, hoped that Bethesda would care for the souls and bodies of orphaned children as well as evangelize the Native Americans living nearby. It therefore seemed like Bethesda would both complement the goals of the Trustees and serve the needs of Whitefield's ministry. For the Trustees, the orphanage would help create a disciplined workforce, assure anxious parents that their children would be cared for, and help transform Georgia into a Protestant bulwark on the fringes of the British empire.

For Whitefield, the orphanage provided an opportunity to create a new type of institution that reflected his own form of awakened piety.[6]

In order to create an institution that embodied his religious beliefs, however, Whitefield needed to wrest financial control of Bethesda from the Trustees. In January of 1739, he argued that he could fund the orphanage through collections at his sermons "without putting the Trustees to any charge on that account." Whitefield continued to press the Trustees for sole control of the orphanage until May 9, 1739, when he refused a salary for himself and anyone he hired to work in the house. He returned the commission that allowed him to legally collect money for the institution, claiming that he had "not been able to collect a farthing in virtue of it." If the Trustees refused to grant him control over the "management and disposal of" the orphanage, then Whitefield thought it would be "the best way to decline erecting the orphan house in Georgia." When the Trustees consented to Whitefield's demands, the minister and his supporters rejoiced that the itinerant would be able to design his own Godly financial strategy. God "is a Faithfull Paymaster," his supporter J. Griffiths wrote in response, and "Heaven will at Last make you amends for all: you shall reap if you faint not." Although Whitefield would continue to squabble with the Georgia Trustees over control of the orphanage, the funding for Bethesda was now in Whitefield's, and God's, hands.[7]

To help develop their funding model, Whitefield and his associate William Seward researched how God had supported similar charitable projects in recent history. In particular, they looked to the widely-admired Halle orphanage that was founded by the German pietist August Hermann Francke in 1685. By the time its founder died in 1727, the institution housed roughly three thousand people and contained a university, a print shop, an orphan school, and an infirmary that sold medicines across Europe and the colonies. One of the most remarkable aspects of Francke's success, according to Whitefield and Francke's other admirers, was his decision to eschew a "settled" or "visible" fund that could provide a financial base for the project, and to instead rely entirely on God's providence. Cotton Mather, who was one such admirer, wrote in 1715 that Francke showed it was better to "depend upon *God* than upon our *Friends*. And God countenances him in it, with such Displays of his Providence, as no Age since that of *Man's eating the Food of Angels* has ever Parallel'd." Francke's ability to finance his project seemingly through faith alone helped the institution gain fame throughout the Protestant world and encouraged Whitefield to try a similar strategy to fund Bethesda.[8]

Whitefield admired the Halle orphanage's financial strategy so much that he included over sixty pages of the *Pietas Hallensis*, its major promotional tract, in his 1742 financial accounts. He included manicules in the margins that encouraged his readers to see the parallels between Halle's financial strategy and Whitefield's. Francke wrote that his institution was not based "on any settled Fund gathered in before-hand for this Purpose" but instead was "entirely grounded upon the Providence of our great God." In another excerpt, Francke described how God rescued the orphanage when it ran into financial trouble. Francke was preparing to pray for God's help when he received a letter from a merchant "intimating that he was ordered to pay 1000 Crowns to me for the Relief of the Hospital." Francke concluded that "the Providence of God would actually teach me, not to put too great a Confidence in a visible Stock or present Support of Men." Whitefield included a manicule in the margin of the line that contained the phrase "visible Stock" to draw his readers' attention to the similarities between Francke's reliance on God for funding and his own rejection of a "visible fund."[9] Whitefield frequently noted that the Halle orphanage was "so exactly parallel to my present undertaking for the poor of Georgia, that I trust the Orphan House about to be erected there, will be carried on and ended with the like faith and success." By highlighting the connections between the two institutions, Whitefield not only linked his orphanage to a much-admired Protestant project, but also showed that his commercial theology reflected how God had acted in recent history.[10]

While Halle was the model that Whitefield evoked for publicity purposes, he and Seward also researched more obscure charity projects, such as a series of Welsh charity schools run by Griffith Jones. Jones told Seward that he had begun the project around 1730 "with no other fund to defray the Expence of it, than what could be spar'd . . . out of a Small offertory by a poor country congregation at the blessed Sacrament." Despite this modest beginning, Jones reported that by 1738, they had 2,400 students enrolled and had caught the eye (and financial backing) of the Society for the Promotion of Christian Knowledge (SPCK). Jones warned that setting up charity schools that provided spiritual, intellectual, and material necessities for their students was a daunting task. But because it was "the Lord's Work, and all the Good that is done is his doing, there is no Cause to distrust but he will incline the Hearts of his faithful Servants to assist in an Attempt which has perhaps the directest Tendency to promote" the will of "the most Dear Redeemer's Love." Seward used his letterbook to compile information on how God supported the schools, copying down an observation from Jones that "Providence brings in Contributions to carry on the work the same Providence opens a way in some place, or other to lay it out with a promising prospect of great Success, 'tis the peculiar happiness of this undertaking that no pretence of any rational exception can be objected agt. it." Whitefield's and Seward's research seemed to indicate that God would financially bless Bethesda just as he had blessed Halle and the Welsh schools.[11]

Based on this research, Whitefield decided that occasional collections would be the best way to fund Bethesda because they showed that God, not

Whitefield, was in control of the project. In a letter to a supporter in 1740, Whitefield noted that despite housing almost one-hundred people, the institution did not lack for supplies. "The great householder of mankind," he wrote, "gives us all things richly to enjoy, and, I am persuaded, will provide for us whilst we trust in him. I had rather live by faith, and depend on GOD for the support of my great, and yet increasing family, than to have the largest visible fund in the universe." A year later, Whitefield told a Boston preacher that God acted through spontaneous donations to ensure that the orphanage was supported. Although the Spanish had captured a schooner that was loaded with bricks and supplies for the orphanage, he explained, "GOD about the same time stirred up the heart of a planter in *South Carolina*, lately brought home at the orphan house to GOD, to send my family some rice and beef. At other times, when they have wanted food, the *Indians* have brought plenty of venison. GOD, every day, more and more convinces us that this work is of him." When both supporters and detractors thought that Whitefield was foolish for building the orphanage in a colony that Benjamin Franklin described as "destitute of Materials & Workmen," Whitefield countered that "our extremity is God's opportunity." Not only did Whitefield believe that his collections made the institution completely dependent on God, but also that its success in remote Georgia would be a visible sign of God's blessing to believers and skeptics alike.[12]

Collecting for the orphans at his sermons also enabled Whitefield to integrate his fundraising into his broader ministry and encourage his followers to ask how their "new birth" should shape their temporal lives. Whitefield's sermons, however, eschewed the model provided by standard charity sermons. Traditionally, newspapers both advertised these sermons and published follow-up reports that informed readers of the biblical text, the amount raised, and the festivities, such as dinners and concerts, which accompanied the sermon. Ministers tailored their sermon to elicit donations from the wealthy benefactors in the audience who had gathered to support a particular cause. Their sermons stressed the good work done by the organization, how it spent the money, and the spiritual and social benefits for the donors. These charity sermons helped supplement the money that the organization raised through other means, such as "visible funds" or the money earned through the charitable project itself.

Whitefield, however, rejected this style of charity sermon and instead incorporated his fundraising into his regular preaching. Whitefield's sermons emphasized the necessity of the "new birth," a conversion experience that reoriented the heart and life of a new Christian. Many of the itinerant's sermons were dramatic narrative expositions of familiar biblical stories that appealed to the imagination and emotion of his audience. He preached like an actor on stage, reciting his sermons from memory, pausing dramatically at well-rehearsed moments, and using his entire body to convey his message. Instead of composing sermons specifically about the orphans, he intertwined his pleas on their behalf into the sermons that he preached throughout the colonies. In this way, he urged his audience to see their donations to the orphans as visible sign of their new birth and their first act as new spiritual beings. Integrating his calls for donations into his message about the necessity of the new birth enabled Whitefield to use his sermons to both evangelize and pastor his dispersed flock. Collecting for the orphans at his sermons meant that he could model for his audience what the life of a new convert should look like before he left town for his next preaching destination.[13]

Although Whitefield rarely recorded the text that he preached on when he collected for the orphans, he did note that one sermon, "The Conversion of Zaccheus," was a particularly effective fundraiser. Based on Luke 19:9–10, the sermon told the story of the Roman tax collector Zaccheus who was likely both wealthy and "a notorious sinner." These credentials made him an ideal example of God's free grace "because there is nothing to be found in man, that can any way induce GOD to be merciful to him." Immediately following his conversion, Zaccheus gave half his goods to the poor. Whitefield exclaimed that "Every word calls for our notice. Not some small, not the tenth part, but the *half*. Of what? My goods; things that were valuable. *My* goods, his own, not another's. I give: not, I will give when I die, when I can keep them no longer; but, I give now, even now. *Zaccheus* would be his own executor. For whilst we have time we should do good." Zaccheus's donations, the "Noble fruits of a true living faith," served as evidence to Zaccheus and others that a new birth had taken place. An earlier edition of the sermon preached on the same text explicitly stated that financial donations to Bethesda provided evidence that God had awakened the donor. Whitefield exhorted his audience to "shew their faith, by their works" and "offer every one his Mite, this Day, for the Relief of poor Orphans in *Georgia*. . . . Lay up then for yourselves, Treasures in Heaven, where neither Moth nor Rust can corrupt, nor Thieves break thro' and steal. You will have a Treasure that will never forsake you." Seward noted that this specific sermon elicited large donations, recording that on April 20, 1740, they collected "near 90*l*. Sterling, and is more than we ever had at once." Colonists anxious for a sign that they had been awakened, or, like Benjamin Franklin, who were overwhelmed by the power of Whitefield's preaching, eagerly tossed their mites to the traveling evangelist.[14]

Relying on God to financially support Bethesda did not mean that Whitefield and his associates adopted a passive approach to fundraising; on the contrary, they aggressively publicized his collections and exploited controversies about his ministry to enable God to work most effectively. Whitefield and Seward would publish newspaper advertisements that generated interest in Whitefield's sermons and advertised when Whitefield would be collecting for the orphans. Written as third-party news reports, the advertisements typically included his preaching schedule, locations where collections would be held, crowd size, amount of money raised, and audience reactions. These brief paragraphs also designated a local person who was collecting "Money, Provisions, Clothing, Braisiery Ware, or any thing else" from those "disposed" to contribute to the orphanage.[15] Whitefield also relied on his ministerial supporters to encourage their congregations to support the Bethesda orphans. He printed, for instance, an advertisement in October of 1740 that listed the next eleven stops he was going to make on his preaching tour and asked that "if the Ministers of the respective Congregations are desirous he should collect for the Orphan House, they are desired to give their People previous Notice the next Lord's Day." This would not only further alert his audience to the plight of the orphans, but also make sure that they came with money to contribute.[16] The Presbyterian Gilbert Tennent, for example, wrote in an early letter to Whitefield that he "cease[d] not to make mention of you by Name in my public and private Prayer," and considered it his "duty" to mention the intended orphan house to his parishioners so "that God would prosper them, and encline his People to support them." Boston's Benjamin Colman also read letters to his congregation updating them on Bethesda's progress and facilitated some of Whitefield's most successful collections at Colman's Brattle Street Church. By priming his audience with news and advertisements about the orphans, Whitefield ensured that they would bring their money to his sermons and, hopefully, toss it in his collection plate.[17]

Whitefield also capitalized on the controversies around his ministry to elicit more money from his audience. In two of his most famous confrontations, the preacher timed his collections to show how God favored his commercial theology over that of his allegedly pharisaical rivals. On Friday, March 14, 1740, Whitefield visited the home of Alexander Garden, the Anglican Commissary in Charles Town, South Carolina who would emerge as one of his fiercest critics. According to Whitefield's journal, Garden charged him with "enthusiasm and pride" and forbade him from preaching in any "public church" in the province. Whitefield took this warning as seriously as "a Pope's bull" and declared that if Garden refused to denounce Charleston's balls and assemblies, Whitefield would publicly denounce the commissary. Garden shouted "in a very great rage, 'Get you out of my house,'" and Whitefield and his party duly left. That Sunday, Whitefield went to service at St. Philip's church and sat in the pews as Garden denounced him as a Pharisee. The next day, after preaching in the morning more "explicit[ly] than ever in exclaiming against balls and assemblies," Whitefield made his first collection in the American colonies. He spoke "on behalf of my poor orphans" and collected upwards of seventy pounds sterling, his largest collection up to that point, which confirmed that "we shall yet see greater things in America, and that God will carry on and finish the work, begun in His Name at Georgia."[18]

A similar incident occurred the next month as Whitefield made his second trip through Philadelphia. In the morning, he attended a sermon preached by the Anglican Commissary Archibald Cummings from James 2:18 on "Justification by Works." That evening, Whitefield preached on the same text to about fifteen thousand people and "confuted the false doctrines and many fundamental errors contained in the Commissary's discourse." After the sermon, Whitefield collected eighty pounds in local currency "for my children in Georgia. Little do my enemies think what service they do me." The preaching battle was intense enough to catch the eye of the Quaker merchant John Smith, who recounted the dueling sermons in a letter to a friend, dryly noting that "those of the Black Robe Sometimes Display their Different Sentiments."[19] James Habersham, one of Bethesda's managers, remembered this moment fondly thirty-four years later, writing in a letter to the Countess of Huntingdon that Whitefield "never was more usefull, than when he delivered his Masters Message in Philadelphia in the year 1740 in the public Streets and fields."[20]

Whitefield's early financial accounts both manifested and helped spread his commercial theology. He included his accounts in 1739, 1741, and 1742 in promotional packets that he sold for a small profit and distributed gratis to potential donors. The financial accounts themselves consisted of long lists organized chronologically that emphasized how his money came from spontaneous donations and collections at his sermons. For example, while Whitefield was in Bristol in the spring of 1739, he "receiv'd of a Maid Servant" £1.1.0 and, on April 1, a one shilling donation from "a poor woman." These small contributions, which were often listed as the only donations he received that day, seem to reflect the many scenes in his published journals where Whitefield portrayed poor individuals moved by God to find Whitefield and contribute their mites to the Georgia orphans. To be sure that his readers did not miss the theological significance behind the numbers, he included commentary that explained how God was guiding the orphanage.[21] In his 1741 accounts, for example, which revealed that he was over £800 in debt, he included a disclaimer explaining why he was not worried about his arrears. The "Lord will enable me to pay them, and also raise up fresh supplies for the Maintenance of my large Family," he explained to his donors.[22]

In addition to updating his audience on how God supported the Bethesda orphanage, Whitefield used his financial accounts to strengthen the emotional and spiritual bonds between his donors and the orphans. He provided biographical details about the orphans, information on their daily routines, and anecdotes about their religious education. The hymns in Whitefield's 1741 accounts provide an excellent example of how he peddled this connection to keep the orphans in the prayers of his donors. The children sang a thanksgiving hymn to their benefactors that included the lyrics "*For those who kindly this Support / A better House prepare; / And when remov'd to thy bless'd Courts, / Oh let us meet them there.*" Although Whitefield's collections for the orphans happened only sporadically in a given town, his constant advertisement of their plight established a more significant connection between a distant audience and the children they supported.[23]

Whitefield's initial commercial theology invested money with tremendous spiritual power. He believed that God would direct individuals to donate money during revivals as a visible sign of the new birth. These conversions and donations would provide the financial base for institutions such as Bethesda that would then teach children the basics of experimental Christianity and prepare them for their own conversions. This generation of Christians would then continue this cycle of preaching and funding revivals, creating the conditions that would protect Christians from sinking back into rote ritualism. God guided money to help connect dispersed Christian communities and promote true religion. Whitefield hoped that Bethesda's success in being financed through faith alone would demonstrate to Christians around the world that God did indeed work wonders.

Whitefield's faith in his commercial theology, however, began to waver when he faced a series of financial setbacks beginning in 1741. Divisions within English methodism eroded Whitefield's financial base and the continued hostility to methodists from outside the movement made it difficult to reach new donors. William Seward, who had acted as Whitefield's financial adviser, benefactor, and press agent, died suddenly at the hands of one such anti-methodist mob, throwing the minister's precarious finances into disarray. Spanish privateers, meanwhile, had captured a vessel carrying supplies for Bethesda, a setback that halted construction on the orphan house and forced Whitefield to repurchase the expensive supplies. "It has been a trying time for me," Whitefield explained to James Habersham, "a large orphan family, consisting so near a hundred, to be maintained, about four thousand miles off, without the least fund . . . above a thousand pounds in debt for them, and not worth twenty pounds in the world of my own." Although Whitefield had often portrayed financial challenges as "God's opportunity," he now began to worry that he had misinterpreted God's will.[24]

Whitefield's colonial critics latched on to these financial struggles and began to attack his commercial theology in newspapers and pamphlets. Despite the publicity surrounding Whitefield's collections during his first American tour between 1739 and 1741, the colonists published very few critiques of them during these years. In 1742, however, this began to change when a series of supposedly eyewitness accounts bemoaning the dilapidated state of Bethesda began to circulate in colonial newspapers.[25] In 1743,

"Publicola" took to the pages of the *South Carolina Gazette* to demand that Whitefield publish "full, faithful, sufficiently vouched, sworn to, authentickly audited, and attested ACCOMPTS" that would demonstrate how he had spent his donors' money. Newspapers throughout the colonies reprinted Publicola's demands and fixated on the itinerant minister's commercial theology. Whitefield had publicly claimed that God directed his finances, but now, the minister appeared to be deeply in debt. Was Whitefield a fraud, who had lied to his audience to steal their money, or was he an enthusiast, who claimed false inspiration from God? Either of these sins, both friend and foe agreed, would be a damning condemnation of his ministry. Although Whitefield defended himself against these accusations, the combination of his own financial struggles and growing concerns about his commercial theology prompted the minister to overhaul his plan for Bethesda.[26]

Between 1743 and 1747, Whitefield rethought his commercial theology. He questioned whether his original financial strategy had been too dependent on spontaneous action as a sign of God's approval, and worried that he had actually acted according to his own desires rather than God's will. In a letter he wrote while revising his journals for a new printing in 1748, Whitefield lamented that "Alas! alas! In how many things have I judged and acted wrong. . . . I find that I frequently wrote and spoke in my own spirit, when I thought I was writing and speaking by the assistance of the spirit of GOD. I have likewise too much made inward impressions my rule of acting." Without explicitly acknowledging the charges of enthusiasm that his critics threw at him, Whitefield seemed to admit that his previous strategies had been based on his own misunderstanding of how God acted in the financial world. The preacher blamed his own rashness, rather than God, for his past financial troubles. For example, he referenced Luke 14:28 when responding to a friend seeking financial advice. He wrote "take this caution, 'sit down, and count the cost, before you begin to build.' Do not lay out more than you know you can pay. Go the cheapest way to work. . . . You well know what I have suffered running too far into debt for others." Whitefield did not waver in his faith in God, but his financial struggles prompted him to reconsider how God would support Bethesda.[27]

Whitefield's revised commercial theology included three changes that downplayed the providential significance of short-term cash infusions and instead prioritized long-term financial planning as the godliest method to fund Bethesda. He sought out the "visible fund" that he had previously rejected, switched to relying on dependable subscriptions rather than spontaneous donations at his sermons, and began to conduct regular audits of his financial accounts. First, and most significantly, Whitefield obtained Providence Plantation in South Carolina in early 1747 to serve as a visible fund for Bethesda. God "put into the hearts of my *South Carolina* friends," Whitefield wrote, "to contribute liberally towards purchasing a plantation and slaves" in that colony. When Whitefield's supporters John and Hugh Bryan offered to sell, but continue to manage, their 640-acre plantation to the minister at a "very cheap rate," he jumped at the opportunity to provide a visible fund for Bethesda. Slavery was not yet legal in Georgia, and Whitefield believed that a plantation worked by enslaved laborers in South Carolina would be more economically viable than a plantation in Georgia worked by orphans. He hoped "to stock my new plantation in *South Carolina* as a *visible fund* for the *Orphan-house*" so that "my poor heart may no more be oppressed as it has been for many years by outward difficulties." While Whitefield had previously believed that God "put into the hearts" of his supporters to offer small cash infusions for his cause, he now believed that God had prompted the Bryans to provide the "visible fund" that the minister had previously rejected.[28]

The agreement between the Bryans and Whitefield benefitted both White parties. The Bryans's previous attempts to Christianize the enslaved people living on Providence Plantation, along with Hugh Bryan's prophecies of a slave revolt, had prompted rumors among White Carolinians that the brothers were fomenting a rebellion. The Bryans' partnership with Whitefield would hopefully convince their White neighbors that their brand of awakened piety supported South Carolina's slave system. For Whitefield, the enslaved laborers at Providence Plantation would produce wealth that would free him from the mundane financial concerns that had hampered his ministry and enable Bethesda to flourish. Whitefield now believed that enslaved labor was the Godliest way to finance an institution that would be a hub of awakened piety for generations to come.[29]

Whitefield soon worried, however, that using Providence as his visible fund would split his focus between his orphaned and enslaved "families." Although Whitefield used the term "family" to refer to both the orphans and the enslaved laborers who lived on his properties, he was clear that his enslaved "family" was there to serve his orphan "family." The minister certainly encouraged his enslaved laborers to embrace Christianity, but his priority was using their labor to finance the awakenings of White orphans and colonists. He therefore used his new experience as a South Carolina enslaver to pressure the Georgia Trustees into legalizing slavery. In 1748, he wrote a letter complaining that despite the "providence of a good and gracious God" who enabled him to spend "upwards of five thousand pounds" on Bethesda, the orphanage was struggling "entirely owing to the necessity I lay under of making use of white hands. Had a negroe been allowed, I should now have had a sufficiency too support a great number of orphans." Whitefield had eight enslaved laborers working at Providence who he expected to produce more in one year at "a quarter of expence, than has been produced at *Bethesda* for several years past." The minister had already suspected that Georgia would only "flourish" if it legalized slavery, and his experience with Providence confirmed this. If the Trustees refused to legalize slavery, he could not "promise to keep any large family, or cultivate the plantation in any considerable manner" in the colony. Instead, he threatened to move Bethesda to "the other side" in South Carolina.[30] Once Georgia legalized slavery in 1751, Whitefield tried to sell Providence so that he could replace it as a visible fund with his new Georgia plantation named Ephratah, writing that "I do not choose to keep two families longer than needs must." He planned to invest the extra money he earned from Providence's sale in Bethesda. As Whitefield began to believe that God acted through market mechanisms, both enslaved labor and real estate investment became providential ways to fund his orphan "family."[31]

Whitefield's use of enslaved labor to provide a visible fund for Bethesda reflected his changing commercial theology more than any change in his attitude toward the institution of slavery. Throughout his ministry, he emphasized two consistent points: enslavers should Christianize enslaved people and Georgia would be better off with slavery. While he previously believed that relying on a visible fund would indicate a wavering faith, he now believed that a visible fund was *the* Godly way to fund Bethesda. Enslaved labor—which he believed that God had put into the hearts of his White supporters to help him procure—appeared to be the providential provisioning that he had prayed for. He became an enslaver because enslaved labor appeared to be the visible fund that God provided, not because he changed his mind about the morality of slavery.[32]

Second, Whitefield switched from relying on spontaneous donations and public collections at his sermons to focus on obtaining more dependable private subscriptions. These subscriptions had both religious and practical benefits for Whitefield. Theologically, he believed that the subscriptions provided a God-ordained, long-term tool to support the orphanage. Christians could still be moved by God to donate to the cause, but their donations now came in a form that made it easier for the managers of Bethesda to track and plan around. In a letter to supporters in June of 1746, he wrote that "I have sufficient subscriptions" for the "future support" of the orphanage and that "Our Lord I trust is gradually helping me out of my outward embarrassments." Whitefield continued to see God's hand at work, but he understood that God was acting through different means.[33]

Practically, Whitefield believed that these subscriptions would keep his finances out of the press during the peak years of the debates over his commercial theology. In a letter thanking Benjamin Franklin for writing the preamble to his subscription form, Whitefield wrote that "I only object against its being made publick. . . . I think such a procedure would betray somewhat of meaness of Spirit and of a confidence in Him who *hitherto* has never left me in extremity, since I think a private subscription among my Friends here and *elsewhere* would raise as much as I want." In another letter, Whitefield asked the recipient to refrain from publishing his sermons until his audited accounts had been published, speaking to the ways that the debates directly affected his financial strategies. Indeed, on his second major tour of the colonies between 1745 and 1748, he made no public collections for any charity, and instead, relied on subscriptions from friends and supporters. His abstention from making collections at his sermons also affected the style of sermon he preached. Instead of selecting texts based on dramatic appeal on his spring tour of New England in 1745, for example, he preached a more traditional sermon series on the Book of Genesis.[34]

Whitefield did not abandon his commitment that all Christians should participate in Christian charity, but changed how he implemented this. When he returned to preaching charity sermons on his colonial tours of 1754–1755 and 1763–1765, he collected primarily for local causes. One glowing article in 1754 reported that Whitefield had raised approximately £111 sterling for the charity school at the Philadelphia Academy, a collection that was but "*one noble Instance*" of the "*charitable Disposition and great Publick Spiritedness of the Citizens* of Philadelphia! Who, it cannot be doubted, will put in Practice the other Methods the Preacher so well recommended of relieving the Poor." Rather than framing the donations as evidence of conversions, the paper saw the donations as evidence of the generosity of Philadelphians. On his sixth trip, Whitefield collected for the poor in each city he visited and for major colonial causes including the Philadelphia Hospital, and, "notwithstanding the present Prejudices of many People against the Indians," Eleazer Wheelock's Indian School. In addition to advertised collections, Whitefield made contributions to local causes out of his own pocket. When Harvard's library burned in 1764, Whitefield showed that he had forgiven the institution for labeling his commercial theology as enthusiastic in the 1740s, and used his charitable networks and influence to procure "a large number of valuable books" that he donated to the library. Whitefield would occasionally make collections for Bethesda in addition to local causes, but he no longer viewed them as a reliable source of income for his orphanage.[35]

Third, Whitefield made regular audits a part of his accounting practices, thus aligning his own fundraising strategy with the best practices of eighteenth-century fundraising. Whitefield's colonial critics had argued that an audit was the only way that the ministers' donors could be assured that their money was well spent. In May of 1746, Whitefield acquiesced to these demands. William Woodrooffe, William Ewen, and William Russel in

Savanah attested that his accounts "to the best of their Knowledge, contain a just and true Account of all the Monies collected by, or given to" Whitefield, and that the preacher had not "converted or applied any Part thereof to his own private Use and Property, neither hath charged the said House with any of his travelling, or any other private Expences whatsoever." Woodrooffe, Ewen, and Russel testified that they had "carefully and strictly examined all and singular Accounts relating to" Bethesda contained in the forty-one page book entitled *Receipts and Disbursements for the Orphan House* and calculated that Whitefield had collected £4982.12.3 between December 15, 1738 and January 1, 1746, and spent £5511.17.9¼ during the same period. They found that Whitefield had not used any of the money for himself "but, on the contrary, hath contributed to the said House many valuable Benefactions." The auditors concluded that "in Justice to the Reverend Mr. *Whitefield* and the Managers of the said House," they could attest that the money was "faithfully and justly applied to and for the Use and Benefit of the said House only."[36]

While his previous accounts had been published only in pamphlets, he printed his 1746 audit in both newspaper and pamphlet editions to ensure the widest possible audience. Benjamin Franklin's *Pennsylvania Gazette* ran the first printing in May of 1746. In addition to the audit, Whitefield included a preface that stated it was "*a Minister's Duty to provide Things honest in the Sight of all Men, I thought it my Duty, when lately at* Georgia, *to have the whole Orphan House Accounts audited.*" He had only sent "*an Abstract of the whole, with the particular Affidavits, and common seal of* Savannah" to the papers because he claimed that printing every receipt would be too expensive. However, anyone who wanted to see the originals could visit James Habersham in Savannah or, if someone was willing to "*defray the Expence of Printing,*" Whitefield could publish the whole account. The pamphlet edition included a revised autobiography, a history of Bethesda, a discussion of his future fundraising plans, an update on the orphans who had matriculated, and a description of the benefits that the house had brought to Georgia. On the back cover of the pamphlet, he included a note directing future donations to be sent to a network of his supporters.[37]

Whitefield's decision to publish the audited accounts also reflected the minister's new commercial theology. Previously, he printed long lists of financial transactions because each exchange represented a visible sign of how divine grace was shaping Bethesda. Now, however, as he transitioned away from relying on public collections to more dependable private subscriptions and a "visible fund," the individual transactions became less theologically important. Although Whitefield claimed that the 42 pages of receipts would be too expensive to publish, the printed pamphlet that contained the 1746 audit was 63 pages long and the 1742 published accounts were 84 pages. Whitefield did not object to publishing long pamphlets when he believed the information was important. By 1746, however, Whitefield no longer believed that each transaction had enough religious significance to justify their publication.[38]

By the time Whitefield began advising Samson Occom, Eleazer Wheelock, and Nathaniel Whitaker in the late 1750s about how to fund and organize what became Dartmouth College, he was a different man than he had been in the heady days of revival in 1740. And the advice he offered reflected the commercial theology he had developed in the intervening years. While Whitefield had built Bethesda in a remote location to demonstrate that "our extremity is God's opportunity," he now encouraged Wheelock to build his school in Connecticut where "this Institution hath been most encouraged—There it took its rise—There it will be most visible—There most secure."[39] Instead of praising the leap of faith Wheelock took by launching the project under "God only and the charities of Gods people without any settled fund for its support," as Wheelock had described the project in 1762, Whitefield refused to raise money for the school until Wheelock could send him an account detailing a financial plan.[40] Whitefield also chastised Wheelock for rapidly spending money and thus depleting the "visible fund" that he had come to believe was so important for a charity project. "But how came You to draw for so many hundreds this last year? And why no account of the Disbursements. This must be annually and punctually remitted," Whitefield advised him. If Wheelock was drawing "such sums" on a regular basis after the major costs of "Land Buildings &c" had already been paid for, then "where will be a remaining fund" for the institution? Finally, Whitefield insisted that they have their accounts frequently audited. "Mr. Whitefield says," Whitaker reported to Wheelock, that "you should have all your accounts Audited & certified under some publick seal."[41]

Whitefield's advice on how to finance Dartmouth reflected the years he spent learning about God while trying to manage a transatlantic charity project. He had initially designed a financial strategy for Bethesda that, he believed, would allow the orphanage to succeed by faith alone. Whitefield would collect money at his sermons, enabling those in the throes of a new birth to donate to the Bethesda orphans as their first act as a reborn Christian. But after several years of trying to fund Bethesda with this model, Whitefield began to question whether he had misinterpreted God's will. He therefore changed his commercial theology to reflect these experiences. He began to use enslaved labor as the "visible fund" that would provide a financial base for Bethesda, switched to private subscriptions, and began to publish audited accounts. For Whitefield and many others in the eighteenth century, financial decisions reflected and shaped broader theological claims.

Whitefield is often presented as the first in a long line of evangelical innovators who used the market to spread their religion. His early belief that God would bless Bethesda financially, and the tremendous spiritual power that he attributed to money, can appear at first glance to represent an early iteration of the modern prosperity gospel. His powerful preaching, combined with his ability to use the media to amplify his message, have likewise drawn frequent comparisons to Billy Graham. Yet the dramatic changes in Whitefield's commercial theology caution against interpretations that analyze the eighteenth-century minister as the forefather of a single theological orientation. The continuities between Whitefield's eighteenth-century commercial theology and today are perhaps found not in any single religious movement but in the persistent ways that experiences in the marketplace have shaped religious beliefs. The questions that Whitefield faced—including how should one interpret financial success or failure—have haunted Christians across both time and denomination. If God provides financial resources for a project, does that amount to divine sanction for it? If that financial support evaporates, does that mean that God no longer supports the cause? Or, does it mean that the fundraiser has strayed from God's will? As Whitefield found, these were not easy questions to answer. His dogged attempts to do so, however, reveal the profound influence that economic experiences have had on religious life.

NOTES

1. Franklin 1993, 109–110. For Franklin and Whitefield's relationship, see Haviland 1945; Dallimore 1980, 2:441–454; Stout 1991b; Lambert 1993.
2. My use of "practical theologies" draws from Holifield 2003, 1–4, 8–10.
3. Stout 1991a; Lambert 1994; Hall 1994; Lambert 1999; Breen and Hall 1998.
4. Although the scholarship still focuses on the early years of his ministry, recent work has begun to shed light on the latter years of his life. See Parr 2015; Hammond and Jones 2016; Choi 2018.
5. Lambert 1994; Brekus 2013; Kidd 2014; Stubenrauch 2016.
6. For Georgia's origins, see Wood 1984, 1–23; Choi 2018, 17–41. For orphans in Georgia, see O'Connell 1970.
7. *Manuscripts of the Earl of Egmont. Diary of Viscount Percival Afterwards First Earl of Egmont* (London: His Majesty's Stationary Office, 1923) 3:3, 56, 58; J. Griffiths to George Whitefield, 4 May 1739, DDSe44, The Letters of William Seward, Methodist Archive and Research Centre, John Rylands Library, the University of Manchester.
8. Mather 1715, 3. For Halle, see Ward 1992, 302–303, 61–62; Wilson 2000, 15–41; Koch 2015.
9. Whitefield 1742, 37, 47–48.
10. "[Fifth Journal] A Continuation of the Reverend Mr. Whitefield's Journal from his Embarking after the Embargo, to his Arrival at Savannah in Georgia (August 1739-January 1740)," in Whitefield 1965, 334; Whitefield 1742, 29.

11. Griffith Jones to William Seward, 30 March 1738, GB 135 DDSe4, *The Letters of William Seward*, Methodist Archive and Research Centre, John Rylands Library, the University of Manchester; "Extract from a Lettr. from the Revd. Mr. Griffith Jones at Llandowrer in Carmarthenshire," 6 Dec. 1738, in Letters of William Seward.

12. Whitefield to Mr. M---, New Brunswick, 28 April, 1740, in Whitefield 1771, 1:167; Whitefield to the Rev. Mr. C---, Good Hope, South Carolina, 1 Jan. 1741, in *Works of Whitefield*, 1:230; Franklin 1993, 109; Whitefield to Rev. Mr. B. I., Savanah, 28 March, 1740, in *Works of Whitefield*, 1:158.

13. For overviews of Whitefield's preaching, see Stout 1991a, 37–43, 79–81, 93–95, 105–107.

14. "The Conversion of Zaccheus," in Whitefield 1771, 6:49–50, 57, 58; Whitefield 1739, 14; Seward 1740, 9. This was the same day, although at a different time, as Whitefield's confrontation with a Philadelphia Anglican over James 2:18 discussed below. Harry Stout analyzes "The Conversion of Zaccheus" as an ideal example of Whitefield's preaching style. See Stout 1991a, 104–105. Later editions of Whitefield's sermons and journals usually edited out references to the orphans. Compare, for example, his journal entry for June 5, 1740, printed in contemporary newspapers with the version published in his collected journals. "*Extract from Mr.* WHITEFIELD'S JOURNAL. Thursday, June 5, 1740," *THE AMERICAN WEEKLY MERCURY*, no. 1077, Aug. 14 to Aug. 21, 1740, [1]-[2], and "[Sixth Journal]," in Whitefield 1965, 430–432.

15. "BOSTON," *New England Weekly Journal*, no. 702, Sept. 30, 1740, [2]; "[Sixth Journal]," in Whitefield 1965, 409–10; "BOSTON," *THE New England Weekly JOURNAL*, no. 703, Oct. 7, 1740, [2]. For a discussion of Whitefield and Seward's printing strategies, see Lambert 1994, 52–69, 103–110; Smith 2012, 102–111.

16. "[Sixth Journal]," in Whitefield 1965, 409–410; "BOSTON," *THE New England Weekly JOURNAL*, no. 703, Oct. 7, 1740, [2].

17. See for example "BOSTON," *New England Weekly Journal*, no. 702, Sept. 30, 1740, [2]; Gilbert Tennent to George Whitefield, New Brunswick, 1 December 1739 in Whitefield 1739, 12; Whitefield to Rev. Mr. C., Good Hope, 1 January 1741, in Whitefield 1771, 1:230.

18. "A Continuation of the Reverend Mr. Whitefield's Journal From His Embarking after the Embargo, to his Arrival at Savannah in Georgia (August. 1739—January, 1740)," in Whitefield 1965, 357; "[Sixth Journal]. A CONTINUATION of the Reverend MR. GEORGE WHITEFIELD'S JOURNAL After His Arrival at GEORGIA to a few Days after his Return thither from PHILADELPIA (January, 1740—June, 1740)," in Whitefield 1965, 400–402.

19. 7th day of the 1st mo. 1739, John Smith Diaries, vol. 31, Smith Family Papers, 1660–1941, Library Company of Philadelphia; John Smith to John Wardell, 23 May 1740, John Smith Diaries, vol. 31.

20. "[Sixth Journal]," in Whitefield 1965, 409–410; "BOSTON," *THE New England Weekly JOURNAL*, no. 703, Oct. 7, 1740, [2]; James Habersham to the Countess of Huntingdon, 8 April 1774, A3/6/14, The Countess of Huntingdon Papers, Westminster College, Cambridge (hereafter cited as Huntingdon Papers).

21. Whitefield 1741, 17.

22. Whitefield 1741, 5–6; Whitefield 1742, 26–84.

23. Stevens 2004, 7–22; Whitefield 1741, 6; *"Extract of a Letter from* Charlestown *in* South Carolina, *Dated* March 20th. 1742–3," *The Boston Evening-Post*, no. 405, May 9, 1743, [4].

24. Whitefield to Mr. G[ilbert] T[ennant], Gloucester, 2 Feb. 1742, in Whitefield 1771, 1:362; Undated and unaddressed letter in Whitefield 1771, 1:440; Whitefield to Mr. J[ames] H[abersham], London, 25 March 1741, in Whitefield 1771, 1:256–57. Whitefield partly blamed John and Charles Wesley for prejudicing his former friends against him. See Whitefield 1771, 1:256. Whitefield to Rev. Mr. B. I., Savanah, 28 March, 1740, Whitefield 1771, 1:158.

25. Eyewitness accounts of Bethesda *"Extract of a Letter from* Charlestown *in* South Carolina, *Dated* March 20th. 1742–3" *The Boston Evening-Post*, no. 405, May 9, 1743, [4]; James Hutchinson, "BOSTON," *The Boston Evening-Post*, no. 407, May 23, 1743, [2]; "A Declaration of Capt. *James Hutchinson's* concerning *Whitefield*'s Orphan-house in *Georgia*, having been inserted in the *Boston* Evening-Post, No. 497 in the *New York* Weekly Post-Boy, No. 755. "The following Remarks thereon, we judge worthy a Place in our Paper, and hope they will not be disagreeable to any of our kind Readers," *The Pennsylvania Gazette*, no. 756, June 9, 1743, [2]; Caldwell 1743, 17.

26. *"To the* MANAGERS *of the* ORPHAN-HOUSE *in* Georgia, *in the Absence of Mr.* Whitefield," *SUPPLEMENT TO THE SOUTH-CAROLINA GAZETTE*, no. 484, July 4, 1743, [1]. For a more complete chronology of the debates surrounding Whitefield's commercial theology and the debates over his accounting practices, see Beales 2019, 324–50.

27. Whitefield to "Rev. Mr. S---," The Betsy, 24 June 1748 in Whitefield 1771, 2:143; Whitefield to Mrs. C---, Islington, 27 July 1756, in Whitefield 1771, 3:188. Whitefield to Mr. L---, Bristol, 4 Aug. 1749, in Whitefield 1771, 2:270.

28. Whitefield to "a generous Benefactor unknown," Charles Town, 15 Mar. 1747, in Whitefield 1771, 2:90; Whitefield to "My very dear, dear Brother," New York, 29 Jan. 1747, in Whitefield 1771, 2:110; Whitefield to Mr. H---B---, London, 7 Jan. 1753, in Whitefield 1771, 2:471–72. For more on Providence, see Koch 2015, esp. 385; Kidd 2014, 199; Gallay 1989, 47–54. For Whitefield and slavery more broadly, see Choi 2018, 115–151.

29. Gallay 1989, 49.

30. Whitefield to the Honourable Trustees of Georgia, 6 Dec. 1748, in Whitefield 1771, 2:208–209.

31. Whitefield to Mr. J. B., 1 Feb. 1753, in Whitefield 1771, 3:3.

32. My argument in this paragraph builds on Koch 2015, esp. 381–85. For Whitefield's early critique of slaveowners, see *"A Letter from the Rev. Mr.* GEORGE WHITEFIELD, *to the Inhabitants of* Maryland, Virginia, North *and* South Carolina," *The Pennsylvania Gazette*, no. 592, 17 Apr. 1740. Whitefield began the letter by noting that he would not "take upon me to determine" whether "it be lawful for Christians to buy Slaves, and thereby encourage the Nations from whence they are bought, to be at perpetual War with each other" because he was "sure" that "it is sinful, when bought, to use them as bad nay worse than as they were Brutes." Apart

from the muted critique of the slave trade, which he seemed to separate from slavery itself, Whitefield offered no critiques of the institution of slavery, only of the slave owners. For his early complaints about Georgia's prohibition of enslaved labor, see Whitefield 1741, 5. For more on Whitefield and enslavement, see Parr 2015, 61–80; Choi 2018, 127–168.

33. Whitefield to Mr. Thomas Jones, Bohemia, 16 June 1746, in Christie 1954b:256.

34. Whitefield to Mr. Sims, Christen Bridge, 12 June 1746, in Christie 1954b: 252–53; Whitefield to Benjamin Franklin, Philadelphia, 23 June 1747, *Founders Online,* National Archives, https://founders.archives.gov/documents/Franklin/01-03-02-0064, in Franklin 1961, 143–44. For earlier uses of subscriptions, see Seward 1740, 2; Whitefield to Mr. Smith, Phil[adelphia], 4 June 1746, in Christie 1954a: 186. Whitefield collected for causes such as the Philadelphia Academy, Philadelphia Hospital, Boston fire victims, the poor of New York, and Eleazer Wheelock's Indian School. See "Sunday last the Reverend Mr. WHITEFIELD," *The Pennsylvania Gazette*, no. 1344, Sept. 26, 1754, [2]; "NEW-YORK, JANUARY 23," *The BOSTON Post-Boy & Advertiser*, no. 338, Feb. 6, 1764, [3]; "NEW-YORK, Jan. 2," *The BOSTON Post-Boy & Advertiser*, no. 335, Jan. 16, 1764, [2]; "*Boston, February* 27 1764," *The BOSTON Evening-Post*, no. 1486, Feb. 27, 1764, [3]; 16 April, 20 April, 22 April, 24 April, 1745, Jonathan Willis Diary, Massachusetts Historical Society, Boston, MA.

35. "Sunday last the Reverend Mr. WHITEFIELD," *The Pennsylvania Gazette*, no. 1344, Sept. 26, 1754, [2]; "NEW-YORK, JANUARY 23," *The BOSTON Post-Boy & Advertiser*, no. 338, Feb. 6, 1764, [3]; "NEW-YORK, *Jan.* 2," *The BOSTON Post-Boy & Advertiser*, no. 335, Jan. 16, 1764, [2]; "*Boston, February* 27 1764," *The BOSTON Evening-Post*, no. 1486, Feb. 27, 1764, [3]; Quincy 1860, 2:493.

36. Whitefield 1746, [65]. All three auditors had ties to both Whitefield and the Georgia Malcontents, a group of colonists upset with the Trustees' decision to ban slavery. Seward and Whitefield lobbied in 1740 for Woodrooffe to be named a magistrate and Woodroffe donated money and goods to the orphanage. See Seward 1740, 53–54; Historical Manuscripts Commission, *Diary of the First Earl of Egmont (Viscount Percival)*, Vol. 3: 1739–47 (London: His Majesty's Stationary Office, 1923), 149; Coulter 1958, 132; Whitefield 1741, 29, 32. William Ewen came to Georgia in 1734 as an indentured servant and rose to prominence as a merchant. Throughout his career he served on Malcontent committees, as commissioner for Ebeneezer, superintendent of Savannah, and vendue master for Georgia. He also held offices in his parish for the Church of England. See *New Georgia Encyclopedia*, s.v. "William Ewen (cs. 1720–1776/1777)," by Sam Fore, last edited August 21, 2013. http://www.georgiaencyclopedia.org/articles/history-archaeology/william-ewen-ca-1720-177617774. William Russell had been involved in the "Publick Accompts" for the colony of Georgia earlier in the 1740s, but by November of 1742 "resolved to quit that Business." See Coulter 1958, 133.

37. "Mr. FRANKLIN," *The Pennsylvania Gazette*, no. 910, May 22, 1746, [1]; "*From the* Pennsylvania GAZETTE, May 22. 1746," *The Boston Evening-Post*, no. 565, June 9, 1746, [1]-[2]; "Mr. FRANKLIN," *THE Boston Gazette, OR Weekly JOURNAL*, no. 1266, June 17, 1746, [1]; Whitefield 1746, [65].

38. Whitefield 1746.
39. Whitefield to Rev. Mr. B. I., Savanah, 28 March, 1740, in Whitefield 1771, 1:158; George Whitefield to Eleazer Wheelock, 9 Feb. 1767, "The Occom Circle," accessed 17 Aug. 2019. https://collections.dartmouth.edu/occom/html/diplomatic/767159-4-diplomatic.html.
40. Eleazar Wheelock to Denys DeBerdt, 18 Dec. 1762, "The Occom Circle Project," accessed 8/16/2019, https://collections.dartmouth.edu/occom/html/diplomatic/762668-1-diplomatic.html.
41. Nathaniel Whitaker to Eleazar Wheelock, 12 Feb. 1767, "The Occom Circle Project," accessed 8/16/2019, https://collections.dartmouth.edu/occom/html/diplomatic/767162-1-diplomatic.html.

REFERENCES

The American Weekly Mercury.
Anonymous. 1739. *THREE LETTERS TO THE Reverend Mr.* George Whitefield. Philadelphia: Andrew Bradford.
Beales, Kristen. 2019. "Thy Will Be Done: Merchants and Religion in Early America, 1720-1815." PhD dissertation, College of William & Mary.
The Boston Evening-Post.
The Boston Post-Boy & Advertiser.
Breen, T. H. and Timothy Hall. 1998. "Structuring Provincial Imagination: The Rhetoric and Experience of Social Change in Eighteenth-Century New England." *The American Historical Review* 103, no. 5 (Dec.): 1411–1439.
Brekus, Catherine A. 2013. *Sarah Osborn's World: The Rise of Evangelical Christianity in Early America.* New Haven, CT: Yale University Press.
Caldwell, John. 1743. *AN ANSWER to the APPENDIX OF The Second Edition of Mr. Mc. Gregore's Sermon on the Trial of the Spirits, &c.* Boston: Rogers and Fowle.
Choi, Peter Y. 2018. *George Whitefield: Evangelist for God and Empire.* Grand Rapids, MI: William B. Eerdmans Publishing Company.
Christie, John W., ed. 1954a. "Newly Discovered Letters of George Whitefield, 1745-6, II." *Journal of the Presbyterian Historical Society* 32, no. 3 (Sept.): 159–186.
Christie, John W., ed. 1954b. "Newly Discovered Letters of George Whitefield 1745-1746, Part III." *Journal of the Presbyterian Historical Society* 32, no. 4 (Dec.): 241–270.
The Countess of Huntingdon Papers. Westminster College, Cambridge.
Coulter, E. Merton, ed. 1958. *The Journal of William Stephens 1741-1743.* Athens, GA: University of Georgia Press.
Dallimore, Arnold A. 1980. *George Whitefield: The Life and Times of the Great Evangelist of the Eighteenth-Century Revival.* Edinburgh: The Banner of Truth Trust.
Founders Online, National Archives, https://founders.archives.gov/documents/Franklin/01-03-02-0064.

Franklin, Benjamin. 1961. *January 1, 1745, through June 30, 1750*. Vol. 3 of *The Papers of Benjamin Franklin*. Edited by Leonard W. Labaree. New Haven, CT: Yale University Press.

Franklin, Benjamin. 1993. *Autobiography and Other Writings*. Edited by Ormond Seavey. Oxford, UK: Oxford University Press.

Gallay, Alan. 1989. *The Formation of a Planter Elite: Jonathan Bryan and the Southern Colonial Frontier*. Athens, GA: University of Georgia Press.

Hall, Timothy D. 1994. *Contested Boundaries: Itinerancy and the Reshaping of the Colonial American Religious World*. Durham, NC: Duke University Press.

Hammond, George and David Ceri Jones, eds. 2016. *George Whitefield: Life, Context, and Legacy*. New York: Oxford University Press.

Haviland, Thomas P. 1945. "Of Franklin, Whitefield, and the Orphans." *The Georgia Historical Quarterly* 29, no. 4 (Dec.): 211–216.

Historical Manuscripts Commission. 1923. *Diary of the First Earl of Egmont (Viscount Percival)*, Vol. 3: 1739–47. London: His Majesty's Stationary Office.

Holifield, E. Brooks. 2003. *Theology in America: Christian Thought from the Age of the Puritans to the Civil War*. New Haven, CT: Yale University Press.

Kidd, Thomas S. 2014. *George Whitefield: America's Spiritual Founding Father*. New Haven, CT: Yale University Press.

Koch, Philippa. 2015. "Slavery, Mission, and the Perils of Providence in Eighteenth-Century Christianity: The Writings of Whitefield and the Halle Pietists." *Church History* 84, no. 2 (June): 375–380.

Lambert, Frank. 1993. "Subscribing for Profits and Piety: The Friendship of Benjamin Franklin and George Whitefield." *The William and Mary Quarterly* 50, no. 3 (July): 546–47.

Lambert, Frank. 1994. *"Pedlar in Divinity": George Whitefield and the Transatlantic Revivals, 1737-1770*. Princeton, NJ: Princeton University Press.

Lambert, Frank. 1999. *Inventing the "Great Awakening."* Princeton, NJ: Princeton University Press.

Mather, Cotton. 1715. *Nuncia Bona e Terra Longinqua. A Brief Account of Some Good & Great Things a Doing For the* Kingdom of GOD *In the Midst of EUROPE. Communicated in a Letter to--*. Boston: Printed by B. Green for Samuel Gerrish.

The New England Weekly Journal.

The Occom Circle Project, https://collections.dartmouth.edu/occom/html/diplomatic/767162-1-diplomatic.html

O'Connell, Neil J. 1970. "George Whitefield and Bethesda Orphan-House." *The Georgia Historical Quarterly* 54, no. 1 (Spring): 41–62.

Parr, Jessica M. 2015. *Inventing George Whitefield: Race, Revivalism, and the Making of a Religious Icon*. Jackson, MS: University Press of Mississippi.

The Pennsylvania Gazette.

Quincy, Josiah. 1860. *The History of Harvard University*. Boston: Crosby Nichols, Lee, & Co.

Seward, William. 1740. *JOURNAL OF A VOYAGE FROM SAVANNAH to PHILADELPHIA, AND FROM PHILADELPHIA to ENGLAND*. London, 1740.

Idem. *The Letters of William Seward.* Methodist Archive and Research Centre, John Rylands Library, the University of Manchester.
Smith Family Papers, 1660-1941. Philadelphia: Historical Society of Pennsylvania.
Smith, Lisa. 2012. *The First Great Awakening in Colonial American Newspapers: A Shifting Story.* Lanham, MD: Lexington Books.
South Carolina *Gazette*.
Stubenrauch, Joseph. 2016. *The Evangelical Age of Ingenuity in Industrial Britain.* New York: Oxford University Press.
Stevens, Laura M. 2004. *The Poor Indians: British Missionaries, Native Americans, and Colonial Sensibilities.* Philadelphia: PA: University of Pennsylvania Press.
Stout, Harry S. 1991a. *The Divine Dramatist: George Whitefield and the Rise of Modern Evangelicalism.* Grand Rapids, MI: William B. Eerdmans Publishing Company.
Stout, Harry S. 1991b. "George Whitefield and Benjamin Franklin: Thoughts on a Peculiar Friendship." *Proceedings of the Massachusetts Historical Society*, 103: 9–23.
Ward, W. R. 1992. *The Protestant Evangelical Awakening.* Cambridge, UK: Cambridge University Press.
Whitefield, George. 1739. *An EXHORTATION to come and see JESUS: A Sermon Preached at MOOREFIELDS, May 20, 1739.* London: Printed for C. Whitefield.
Whitefield, George. 1741. *AN ACCOUNT OF Money Received and Disbursed FOR THE ORPHAN-HOUSE IN GEORGIA. To which is prefixed A PLAN OF THE BUILDING.* London: Printed by W. Strahan for T. Cooper.
Whitefield, George. 1742. *A CONTINUATION OF THE ACCOUNT OF THE ORPHAN-HOUSE in Georgia, From January 1740/1 to June 1742. To which are also subjoin'd, Some EXTRACTS from an Account of a Work of a like Nature, carried on by the late Professor Franck in Glachua near Hall in Saxony.* Edinburgh: Printed by T. Lumisden.
Whitefield, George. 1746. *A FURTHER ACCOUNT Of GOD's dealings with the Reverend Mr. George Whitefield, From the Time of his ORDINATION to his EMBARKING for GEORGIA. TO WHICH IS ANNEX'D A brief ACCOUNT of the RISE, PROGRESS, and PRESENT SITUATION OF THE Orphan-House in Georgia. In a LETTER to a FRIEND.* Philadelphia: W. Bradford.
Whitefield, George. 1771. *THE WORKS OF THE REVEREND GEORGE WHITEFIELD, M. A. Late of PEMBROKE-COLLEGE, OXFORD, and Chaplain to the Rt. Hon. the Countess of HUNTINGDON.* Edited by [John Gillies]. 7 vols. London: Edward and Charles Dilly.
Whitefield, George. 1965. *George Whitefield's Journals: A new edition containing fuller material than any hitherto published.* London: The Banner of Truth Trust.
Willis Diary, Jonathan. Massachusetts Historical Society, Boston.
Wilson, Renate. 2000. *Pious Traders in Medicine: A German Pharmaceutical Network in Eighteenth-Century North America.* University Park, PA: The Pennsylvania State University Press.

Wood, Betty. 1984. *Slavery in Colonial Georgia, 1730-1775*. Athens, GA: The University of Georgia.

Chapter 5

Religious Conversion, the Stamp Act, and Revolution in New England

Mark Valeri (Vanderbilt University)

In the spring of 1775, Eleazer Wheelock apprised John Thornton, treasurer of the Dartmouth College Corporation in London, that New Englanders in general, and the residents of the town of Hanover in particular, were set on independence from Great Britain. It was the Stamp Act, Wheelock explained, that first broke New England's loyalty to the kingdom. He may have had in mind a burst of correspondence from the fall of 1765 through the spring of 1766 among the officers and fundraisers for the college. Fundraiser Nathaniel Whitaker described a violent uproar in Boston in response to the Act. Nathaniel Eels, a Connecticut advisor, related to Whitaker that "the Spirit of Opposition" to the act was so intense that "thousands and thousands" of New Englanders would resist it to the point of death. As Wheelock informed Thornton in 1775, the recent murder of New Englanders by redcoats had turned resistance into outright rebellion. Now, as he wrote, a recent surge of religious conversions had fired zeal for New England's "Liberties" along with "confidence" that God would be on New Englanders' "side" as they "determined" that they would "not be slaves" to imperial tyrants.[1]

It is well known, of course, that Wheelock and his cohort were hesitant to sever bonds with their advocates and supporters among England's elite, Lord Dartmouth included. Wheelock was no firebrand. Britain's imperial system had sustained support for the college and its mission. In political-economy terms, both transatlantic commerce and patronage for English institutions in America, such as Dartmouth's, bolstered England's Protestant empire and its defense against Catholic France. Evangelical merchants from New England depended on a full participation in that system. How, then, could the very instruments of Britain's economic empire be parsed with accusations of enslavement? What provoked English subjects in America not merely to protest a duty on paper but to choose what must have appeared as a dreadful disaffiliation from the kingdom?

To answer, we must reconsider the issue of religion and the Revolution. That issue might appear to have suffered enough historical analyses by now—or, we have suffered enough of it to wish for another subject.[2] There is no need to rehash old debates about which Protestant groups or theologies best served the patriot cause. Yet the issue is worth some reconsideration because Protestant preoccupations with religious conversion—a motif that ran through Wheelock's correspondence—inflected the meaning of idioms that were crucial to revolutionary discourse: choice, moral freedom, and liberty. We can use the outbreak of patriotic fervor along with religious revival in Hanover, as well as similar convergences in nearby Connecticut and Massachusetts, to rethink the very meaning of liberty in revolutionary America. In so doing, we might challenge what is at present a tendency for historians to overlook religion in accounts of the American Revolution.[3] A popularized version of philosophical liberty, conveyed through the Protestant discourse of conversion, deconstructed the logic of economic dependence and broke the claims of imperial loyalties and English identities on New Englanders.[4]

American Protestants, to be sure, described the dynamics of conversion in various ways—from evangelicals' sense of emotional crisis to rationalists' description of a gradual process of spiritual and moral maturation. Yet the texts examined in the following account—many of which came from writers who had associations with Dartmouth and its leaders such as Wheelock—help us to identify what stood as conventional and common assumptions by the time of the Revolution. They may be divided into three inter-related topics. First, many religious leaders assumed that conversion rested on moral freedom and competence. They often put this in formal terms as the uncoerced use of reason or liberty of conscience. Second, they referred to a person's sense of dissatisfaction or unease with his or her inherited social identities and religious status, often using a vocabulary of sin, bondage, or humiliation. Third, they identified the importance of a choice to separate from one's old community and form new social alliances. They often elucidated this notion of choice in Christian terms, such as trusting Christ, accepting his offers of mercy, and coming to love God and God's people. Throughout, they anticipated some form of happiness or redemption as the outcome of this disaffiliation from old loyalties and affiliation with a new community.

LIBERTY OF CHOICE

Samuel Langdon's 1775 sermon on the occasion of the election of Massachusetts representatives to the provincial congress clearly drew on these three dimensions of religious conversion to prompt a change in political loyalties.[5] Graduated from Harvard in 1740, Langdon served as a schoolteacher, chaplain to a New Hampshire militia regiment that joined the 1745 campaign against the French at Louisbourg, and pastor in Portsmouth. He was instrumental in the founding of Dartmouth, the mission of which centered on the conversion of Native peoples. As the Secretary of the Sons of Liberty in Portsmouth after 1764, he wrote on behalf of resistance to the taxation policies of Parliament, Courts of Admiralty, proposals for the appointment of an Anglican bishop in America, and decrees of toleration for the Catholic Church in Quebec (the Quebec Act). He lobbied New Hampshire representatives to oppose the Townshend Acts. Appointed President of Harvard in 1774, he served as chaplain to the Continental Army in Cambridge at the request of the Committee of Safety.[6]

In his 1775 sermon Langdon urged delegates from Massachusetts to confirm that they had changed their loyalties from British king to American Congress. He grounded his appeal on what we have described above as the first quality of a religious conversion: it presumed the moral freedom and ability of individuals to make such choices. Just as religious converts were enlightened by reason and the Bible to select the best means to their eternal happiness, so too the representatives had the "invaluable privilege of chusing" that "form of government which to them may appear most conducive to their common welfare." They were to consider "the public good," that is, the government in which "all the people are happy." They were "able," Langdon insisted, to determine their allegiances according to their collective reason, apart from previous attachments. Threats of British military intervention, legal stricture, or economic sanction to coerce or repress those decisions violated natural and divine law and merely enhanced the case for independence.[7]

Langdon drew on multiple meanings of moral freedom or liberty, concepts that had been contested and popularized over the course of the eighteenth century. Debates about freedom and liberty encompassed philosophical questions such as the nature of volition, theological matters such as the relation between divine grace and obedience to divine law in conversion, and long-standing concerns about moral conscience and religious establishment.[8] In explicitly political discourse, Anglo-American commentators defined liberty and freedom, in different contexts, as the prosperity and security of Britain as an empire, adherence to constitutional principles such as representation in legislative and executive decisions, protection of property rights, enforcement of contracts, fair or equitable judicial decisions and legal proceedings, and defense of long-acknowledged privileges of certain social classes, commercial organizations, and municipal governments.[9]

A vigorous philosophical and theological debate from the 1720s through the 1750s expanded and sharpened the political connotations of liberty, especially in New England. The terms of debate included the Calvinist reading of divine election or predestination, codified in the decrees of the Synod of Dort and the Westminster Confession, and what contemporaries called Arminianism, or the interpretation of religious faith as in some sense a free, willful choice in response to divine grace. Anglicans, liberal congregationalists, and critics of the revivals of the 1740s often accused evangelical Calvinists of being irrational bigots whose fixation on predestination obscured the commonsense mandate to uphold the reasonableness of moral liberty. Calvinists in return charged their detractors with holding Arminian ideas that implied an abandonment of the most salient aspects of Christian belief, including the saving work of Christ. Newspaper stories of ecclesiastical trials and controversies, satirical accounts of religious disputes, and frequent publication of theological pamphlets and sermons circulated the terms Arminianism and predestination. Religious controversy had made the nature of religious choice a *cause célèbre*.[10]

Many of the most heated arguments reflected a widespread commitment to conversion and with it a robust idea of moral liberty in some form. To be sure, admirers of latitudinarian ideas such as Boston's Jonathan Mayhew, evangelical Calvinists such as Jonathan Edwards and Hopkins, Anglicans, and radical revivalists often accused each other of theological errors, including either an over-emphasis or under-emphasis on the role of human moral effort in the spiritual life. The rise of missionary societies and efforts, evangelistic preaching, and publications devoted to an apology for the reasonableness of Christianity, however, all pointed to a common concern. Whatever their stance on the revivals, American Protestants wanted people to choose Christ, and they described that choice in various ways: the conversion of the younger generation to piety, skeptics and atheists to faith, Roman Catholics to true doctrine, un-evangelized Native peoples to the gospel, self-deluded enthusiasts to genuine religion, Muslims to Christianity, and lifeless, materialistic, or otherwise distracted Protestants to spiritual rebirth.[11]

Furthermore, they parsed the meaning of conversion as a free choice in one sense or another, whether it depended ultimately on God's intervention or any other preceding cause, such as ancestry or upbringing. As Mayhew put it, the "choice of our religion," be it "Trinitarian," "Unitarian," "Papist," "Protestant," "Mahometan" or "Heathen," was a matter of personal and individual responsibility. Geographic and familial identities ought not to override deliberate moral conviction. Reason "obliged" every person—it was a "*duty*," he reiterated—to "think and judge" for themselves about the "truth and falsehood," and the prospect for "happiness," offered by different religious communities. Like his contemporaries, Mayhew used a jumble of verbs to convey the willfulness of these choices, such as "embrace," "assent," and "yield."[12]

All of this required the inheritors of Puritanism to transpose the Reformed language of divine sovereignty and depravity of will. In order to promote the conversions so needed in New England, Mayhew contended in 1755, "the perplexing question concerning *human liberty*" had to be answered "by those, who can *fully* reconcile our freedom" with "God's fore-knowledge, and eternal counsels." It was no longer possible to "answer the difficulty, by *denying* human freedom" on one side, or "providence" on the other. A consensus among most Protestants emerged by the late 1750s: the validity of religious, social, and political association, including conversion, depended on an affirmation of moral freedom.[13]

Mayhew spoke not only for the rationalist wing of Boston's clergy but other Protestants in New England. Even self-styled Calvinists began to fashion what they maintained was a reasonable form of Reformed teaching: true to New England's Puritan origins yet in accord with current philosophical notions of moral freedom and accountability. In his 1753 treatise on *Freedom of the Will*, Jonathan Edwards conceded that the issue of the day did not involve a choice between moral freedom and supernatural grace but, rather, the proper way to configure these two tenets. Speaking for much of New England's religious establishment, Ezra Stiles, a Newport pastor and later President of Yale, told a clerical convention in 1760 that old disputes between "calvinism and arminianism" were but a dying echo. All New England ministers, he hoped, affirmed both divine grace and "the moral liberty and free agency of man" as essentials.[14]

Samuel West, the pastor in Dartmouth, Massachusetts, most fully illustrated the political implications of this consensus among Protestant preachers and political commentators. West, like Jonathan Mayhew the son of a missionary to Algonquin peoples in New England, promoted the idea of religious conversion and, with it, the philosophical assumption of free will. He also joined the ranks of patriot preachers, became an army chaplain, gave millennial forecasts of an American victory, incurred harassment by the British, and joined the Massachusetts constitutional convention in 1779.[15]

West grounded his case for independence on contemporary philosophies of moral choice. Preaching on the occasion of the election of the Massachusetts Council in May, 1776, he invoked definitions also used by many of his theological opponents, including Edwards and his New Divinity followers such as Samuel Hopkins in Newport, Baptists such as Isaac Backus, and Anglicans to the south. He argued at length that Americans were morally free—despite the threat of British force—to form "themselves into a body politic, and assume the powers of legislation" as their moral consciences determined. In making that argument, he asserted that all people were competent to make such choices. Using the language of the Scottish moral philosopher Francis Hutcheson, West maintained that every person had "moral powers and faculties, by which we are enabled to discern the difference between right and wrong." In particular, people had "tender and social affections, with generous and benevolent principles." This meant that common people had social sensibilities and therefore the capacity to determine which form of government or which leaders best promoted the commonwealth.[16]

Protestant preachers such as West often blurred the precise formulations of philosophers: Locke, say, on the power of self-determination or Hutcheson on the Moral Sense. Like Real Whig agitators against absolutism in England, they imprecisely blended the ideas of Hutcheson with republican theory, religious dissent, and constitutional argument in order to promote liberty.[17] Writers such as Hutcheson gave West a language to express the legitimacy of moral choice in contexts that demanded profoundly unsettling decisions about social loyalties.

West proceeded to link to political matters the "perfect freedom" of people "to order all their actions . . . as they think fit, within the bounds of the law of nature, without asking leave or depending on the will of any man." He defined "right judgment," reasonableness, true discernment, proper affections, and the "fitness" of things as regard for the common good and protection of the "natural rights" of others. To be sure, West maintained, people often judged wrongly and made selfish or irrational moral choices. They were, in theological terms, sinners. That in part explained the need for law and government in the first place. They still had the capacity to know, sense, and select the good. Listening to preachers or reading moral philosophy enhanced their judgments. With repeated reference to Locke, West then made quick work of contending that submission to Britain amounted to bad judgment, a concession to tyranny. A choice for independence amounted to good judgment. Americans were free to choose, but the choice was virtuous only if it secured the liberties of people.[18]

In conflating religious choice, moral volition, and political self-determination, West and his contemporaries affirmed what had become by the 1760s a common and not always precise mélange of philosophical, religious, and political meanings of freedom and liberty. Spiritual and civil concepts of liberty overlapped explicitly in frequent protests by non-Anglican ministers against Anglican missionary societies and proposals for a bishopric in America. The admixture of religious and political authority claimed by bishops, critics charged, threatened the liberty of conscience that was essential for conversion. Religious establishments of the sort enjoyed by the Church of

England, so the argument went, furthermore menaced the freedom necessary to a republican commonwealth.[19]

The political implications of conversion and moral freedom, moreover, ranged beyond matters of religious establishment to other aspects of imperial policy, especially the Stamp Act.[20] We can take, for just one example outside of Hanover, the activities of the Lyme, Connecticut, pastor Stephen Johnson. Throughout the Fall of 1765, Johnson excoriated Britain's Parliament for the Stamp Act and recent trade regulations. Such "evils" imposed on "two millions of free people," he warned in a series of newspaper editorials, threatened to "destroy the good affections and confidence" between Parliament, King, and America.[21] In December, he preached a fast-day sermon that elucidated the meaning of disrupted "affections." The "present crisis," he admitted, was "perplexing and exercising" because it compelled American colonists to choose between loyalty to Britain and their "great, provincial, continental, or national purposes." He put it boldly: "if there be left to the colonies but this single, this dreadful alternative,—slavery or independency,—they will not want time to deliberate which to choose." Johnson reiterated the need for moral deliberation. As he argued in his newspaper pieces, the "liberty of free inquiry is one of the first and most fundamental [liberties] of a free people." Johnson repeated his provocation—that New Englanders ought to be prepared to determine their political allegiance—as a simple question: "what shall we do?"[22]

This question implied more than the possibility of resistance to parliamentary regulation. It hinted at independence from the British empire. Johnson asked his parishioners, the people of Connecticut, and all Americans to imagine a complete transformation of political loyalties, a renunciation of their status as subjects of the English monarchy. He contended that they had the moral capacity—the liberty—to change their allegiances. He urged them to reconsider their social identities and inherited status, often established by hundreds of years of family history. He maintained that they had a responsibility to examine their political affiliations, determine the boundaries between servile patriotism and liberty, and choose accordingly, for the sake of their happiness.

In his sermon, Johnson admitted that making such choices was an ordeal. It was difficult to fathom being "unmade" as an English subject and "made up again" as somebody else.[23] He labored, then, to clarify such decisions by invoking an experience that the religious revivals of the 1740s had made familiar to the people of eastern Connecticut. Many of those people, including one of Lyme's most powerful magistrates, Matthew Griswold, had undergone religious conversion, and the language of conversion drove Johnson's sermon.[24]

EVANGELICAL HUMILIATION

As religious conversion legitimated the very idea of choice for Americans during the crisis with Britain, so too it suggested the necessity of an awakening to the deceits and corruptions of imperial rule. This reflects the second facet of a Protestant paradigm for conversion, what eighteenth-century spiritual writers called evangelical humiliation. They counseled self-scrutiny—the observation, in the moral language of the day, of one's own mind, inclinations, and affections—and a recognition of one's sinful and endangered state. Humiliation implied dissatisfaction with the status quo and desire for change.

We can return to Samuel Langdon's 1775 sermon to illustrate. As Langdon argued that Americans ought to renounce their current status as subjects of the Crown, he attempted to demonstrate how unbearable was the American position. Taxation policies, trade restrictions, blockades, confiscation of American arms, admiralty courts, and the occupation of Boston all amounted to an assault on the "Liberty" that Langdon had expounded at the beginning of his sermon. Imperial rule had become corrupt and tyrannical.[25]

To bring home his analysis, Langdon summoned the sensation of sin that initiated religious awakening: the realization of one's bondage to evil, depraved affections, and self-delusions. Just as converts came to know that they had falsely trusted in their status as churchgoers and dutiful children of saints for their salvation, so Americans had come to see that they had been "deluded with a meer phantom of liberty" under "the British nation." Their government in England had "degenerated," with "vast public treasuries continually lavished in corruption" and "an absolute monarch" who disdained the rights of his people and subjected them to "shameful abuse." To "defend America from slavery," they had to disown their current status. This included a confession of Americans' own "corruptions": the "bribery" and "artifaces" that elevated some colonists into positions of "honor and profit" in their governments. Moreover, British rule "should be discarded." Langdon recalled that religious conversion involved a renunciation of idols, which misled and enslaved, like the gods of Babylon. Americans similarly could now detect the true colors of Britain: "the enemy" that "made a mock" of genuine religion, their "mouths . . . full of horrid blasphemies," and "malice and barbarity." The sense of sin led to a profound unease. It provoked a revulsion against one's own spiritual state and one's political condition. Langdon implored delegates to Congress to refuse further negotiation with London or concede to British demands to surrender their arms.[26]

Other preachers attacked counter-arguments—coming from London, from British evangelicals such as John Wesley, and from some American circles—that colonists ought to remain loyal because of their identities as English subjects of a King and ruling class who ruled by inherited authority. The pattern of conversion, beginning with the recognition of depravity even among those who identified as church members, informed criticism of such excuses. According to Mayhew, assertions of inherited privilege and traditional status often masked religious hypocrisy, as it did political fraudulence. The two cases were "exactly parallel," as he put it, and it was his job to expose the "fabulous and chimerical" nature of the Crown's appeal to divine right, as it was for all preachers to provoke people into a sense of their sin whatever their religious background.[27]

These judgments appeared time and again in revolutionary tracts through the early 1770s. John Cleaveland, the separatist evangelical from Ipswich, argued in 1771 newspaper editorials that one's political loyalties were no more fixed by geographical and familial origins than one's religious faith. "Our civil Subjection to his Britannic Majesty and State is *voluntary*" and does not "arise," as he put it, from "Residence in a State" or "Birth." John Allen, preacher for a Baptist congregation in Boston, seared King, Admiralty, and Ministry for sending armed schooners to seize American sloops accused of smuggling off of Rhode Island in 1772. Neither King nor Parliament could hide the hypocrisy of their claims to "hereditary right" and customary privilege as they committed such atrocities. Americans had "liberty" to "judge" by moral standards that transcended ancestral status and privilege. Jonathan Edwards, Jr., the Calvinist pastor in New Haven, reasoned in the same fashion about the priority of moral facts over received identities. "We are no longer Englishmen," he announced two years before the Declaration. The very name obscured the truth: Americans were "as slaves as the inhabitants of Turkey or the subjects of the Great Mogul," "threatened" with "poverty" and "desolation" by the "arbitrary will of our masters." Moral scrutiny led to the abandonment of any pretense based on notions of ancestry or social privilege.[28]

As commentators drew on the diagnosis of sin, they overlaid specifically political observations—abrogation of natural rights, violation of constitutional principles, nullification of charter precedents—with *ad hominem* denunciation of British officials. Accusations of corrupt minds and malicious intentions served as the political corollary to the awful realization of depravity of soul that preceded conversion. Bad rule, West complained in his moral-philosophical diction, stemmed from the same "corruption" of disposition as did the unconverted life, and it was to be equally exposed as such. Like evangelists who convicted their hearers to the point of spiritual desperation, patriot commentators exposed King and Parliament as hopelessly vile and depraved.[29]

The moral scrutiny implied in conversion partly explains how the rhetoric of the 1770s became so charged. Eighteenth-century critics attributed the colonial policies of King and Parliament to bad dispositions and vicious affections. This led to allegations that rulers in London were not merely incompetent or financially strapped, but malevolent.[30] Even decisions that on the face of it deserved a good riot at most and a shrug of the shoulders at least—such as a tax on tea, arrest of smugglers, quartering of soldiers, or consideration of a Church of England bishop—provoked indictments of perfidy, enmity, and evil. The language of sin informed the critique that presaged independence.

COMMITMENT TO THE NEW COMMUNITY

Conversion furthermore gave Americans a pattern for separation from their old way of life and attachment to a new community. In evangelical terms, the believer who repudiated self-reliant religiosity also disclaimed a church that opposed the gospel. As they embraced Christ, they joined a congregation that promoted salvation. In missionary parlance, the convert rejected non-Christian religions and associated with the godly. As a corollary, patriots rejected their status as subjects of the Crown and committed themselves to the government assembled under the name of the Continental Congress. The dislocation of loyalties from Britain, as arduous as spiritual rebirth, led to liberation.

Langdon made this, the third facet of conversion, the centerpiece of his *Government Corrupted by Vice, and Recovered by Righteousness*. The depth of parliamentary malfeasance, he argued, ought to compel Americans not merely to rebuff current colonial policy but to alter their political and national commitments. They faced a choice between "submission to the despotic power" of Parliament and fidelity to the Congress. The American body clearly had the better case: it had begun to put "into execution the spirited resolutions of a people too sensible" or morally reasonable "to deliver themselves up to oppression and slavery." It was "rational and necessary," then, for Americans to confide in Congress. The newly formed body, like a congregation favored by a convert, merited such trust: it had the "wisdom, religion, and public spirit" to "determine what may be done" to establish a "government" of "law and justice." Something like a creed, even scripture, guided it: "the collected wisdom" of the delegates. Congress in fact had become as "authentic" as "a long established parliament" and had "gained all the confidence of the people."[31]

Other preachers made the decision for independence sound like joining a new church, the public and corporate mark of conversion. Elisha Williams' reflections on revival-era disputes provided them with a precedent. The son of a minister, Williams underwent an intense conversion after graduation from Harvard and a stint preaching to fishermen in Nova Scotia. He became a pastor in Wethersfield, Connecticut, rector of Yale in 1725, friend of prominent English divines such as Isaac Watts and Philip Doddridge, and acquaintance of evangelical leaders in England such as George Whitefield and the Countess of Huntington. He eagerly supported the evangelization of Native Americans and the revivals of the early 1740s. After his retirement from Yale, he was elected to the Connecticut Assembly and appointed to the Supreme Court of the colony. He became a full-time military officer, colonel and commander of Connecticut forces raised for a campaign against Quebec in 1746, and, after election as a deputy and the Speaker of the House, sat with the 1754 Albany Congress.[32]

Quick on the heels of the revival controversies and burst of missions in the mid-1740s, Williams asserted close parallels between conversion and political affiliation. He did so most clearly in a lengthy polemic against a 1742 Connecticut anti-revival statute that prohibited outsiders from preaching anywhere in a parish without the permission of the local minister. He contended that the colony of Connecticut, as a civil government, had no business—neither interest nor right—in passing such laws. The statute violated the moral freedom for all people to choose their religion.[33]

In making his case Williams drew analogies from the convert's membership in a church to the citizen's membership in a civil order. He maintained that Christian believers voluntarily—according to their conscience—submitted themselves to Christ, and to a proper "worshipping assembly" and its pastors. As they did so, they determined to "set aside and renounce all other authority," that is, churches. This was the disaffiliation and affiliation of conversion. They were accordingly free to invite itinerants to preach in separate churches, their houses, or public spaces. It "holds equally true with respect to religious or civil societies," he argued. If a man immigrated from France to England and became "an Englishman," he subjected himself "to the crown and laws of England" and "disowns and renounces all obedience" to France. Just as they "transfer" their allegiance to a new "community" in religious choice, they do the same in political choices.[34]

By Williams' reasoning, then, the voluntary nature of religious adherence suggested the nature of political association. In each case, individuals made a moral determination to leave one community and submit themselves to another. Williams' *Essential Rights and Liberties of Protestants* legitimated what would become a potent political contention: national affiliations were as voluntary and changeable as were the convictions of someone undergoing religious conversion.

That contention inflected much of the commentary of Lyme's Stephen Johnson. In his sermon and editorials, Johnson used the idioms of awakening and religious decision to suggest the possibility of rejecting British political identity and embracing of a new one. Americans felt "the weighty concern" of the crisis—a phrase often used to describe spiritual awakening. In such a moment, they could apprehend that Christ offered them "mercy and salvation" and promised to deliver them "from the jaws of destruction" through "his great grace" if they would pursue "repentance," a transformation of mind and heart. Johnson spoke here of a change in American political fortunes, all the while using a vocabulary of spiritual regeneration. A decision for a new political existence—to "associate" as they wished, as he put it—resembled the choice to forsake one's old spiritual position for new life in Christ.[35]

Johnson's words struck home. The Lyme town meeting renounced implementation of the Stamp Act and demanded the removal of Connecticut's stamp distributor. The *New London Gazette* and *Connecticut Courant* printed Lyme's resolves, which paraphrased and quoted from Johnson's sermon. Judge Griswold, a member of Johnson's church, vocally supported revolution during the early 1770s, led the local Council of Safety, and was forced into hiding by British soldiers. Patriot sentiments flourished in eastern Connecticut and across the border into Newport, Rhode Island, where Johnson's sermon was printed.[36]

Conversion also suggested a new identity defined by the history of the community and its collective wisdom or instruction. For Protestants, this entailed assent to the Bible as interpreted by the community: a rule for behavior, subject for meditation, and guide to salvation. Preachers maintained that new believers ought to identify with the biblical narrative of creation, sin, wandering in the wilderness, suffering, repentance, and salvation. Political commentators drew the corollary accordingly. Membership in the movement for American nationhood implied credence in a common history. Americans ought to read themselves into a record of liberty lost and recovered from the Protestant Reformation through the trials of the Stuart monarchy, rebirth in the Glorious Revolution, betrayal by George III, and revocation of the Stamp Act. From this perspective, the Bible provided a precedent for claims not so much to America's unique and providential status—the antitype of Israel—but to Americans' obligations to fulfill their political conversion.

West claimed along these lines that Americans were like the Gentiles that Paul described in Romans 2, who did not have the Mosaic law but still had divine law. They had "become a law unto themselves" and were "regulated by the law of God written in their hearts." Americans had undergone a parallel experience. Disinherited from the constitutional privileges of English law, they came together under the law of nature and reason. He then rehearsed the script of that law in biblical cadences. He invoked Israel's great lawgiver, Moses, to provide a text for America: "our fathers fled from the rage of prelatical tyranny" and "came into this land"—clear echoes of the exodus from Egypt--in order to "enjoy" God and "find a harbor or place of refuge." Charles Turner did the same. In a 1774 thanksgiving sermon, he recounted the Puritan history at Plymouth as testimony to saintly behavior—the "piety, charity, and liberty"—that ought to guide an America severed from its English origins.[37]

Joseph Emerson, the patriot pastor in Pepperrell, Massachusetts, sketched the history of Anglo-America in light of the repeal of the Stamp Act. The defeat of the Spanish Armada, the failure of the Popish Plot, and the Glorious Revolution were "three great salvations," interspersed with "many sufferings" that the godly "endured." Emerson brought the story to New England. He included the wonders of the 1689 uprising in Boston and ouster of William Andros as Governor of the Dominion of New England. He ended with the glories of "1765," when "the friends of liberty exerted themselves" and "combined together, with fixed resolutions not to give up their liberty." "They did these things," Emerson observed, "under the influence of that God who made them free." Emerson told his hearers that commitment to independence entailed deference to the history of the American cause.[38]

Such deference included families. As English spiritual writers counseled believers to "train up a child" in the way of the Lord (Proverbs 22:6), Emerson urged colonists to "train up our children in the noble and generous principles of civil and religious liberty" contained in England's and New England's saga. "Acquaint yourselves," he urged people, "with the history of our nation and land, and rehearse the wondrous things you meet with, in the ears of your children." "*Tell*" your children this history, he pleaded, twice repeating the exhortation. John Dickinson, a Pennsylvania lawyer and delegate to Congress, used the same logic. He moved from an appeal for Americans to dissociate themselves from Britain, to an exhortation to bind themselves to each other under a common history, and then teach their children the same. "Let us consider ourselves," he wrote in his much-reprinted essays, "separated from the rest of the world, and firmly bound together by the same rights, interests, and dangers." Quoting Deuteronomy 6:7, he implored patriots accordingly to "teach them diligently unto your children."[39]

Protestant teaching on post-conversion practice—"sanctification" in theological parlance—suggested other parallels in the civic realm. Converts were called to exercise their faith by conforming themselves, at least in part, to the righteousness and holiness that would one day fully characterize them. The Litchfield pastor Judah Champion exhorted members of the Connecticut Assembly to bind themselves to the new nation in the same way that believers pursued this so-called sanctification: to become—again, in the peculiar grammar of conversion—what God already had declared them to be. Preaching in 1776 about independence, he invoked the end of history, resurrection of believers, and love and unity of the Church in heaven to call Americans to fulfill their political duties: "the time is short—eternity near, and your work great to prepare therefor," so "for Heaven's sake and for our own, let us arouse, my countrymen, and act up to the dignity of our character as free-born

Americans." The charge to become what one already was sounded familiar to people who knew the language of conversion, so Champion returned to the favorite text of patriot preachers, Paul's admonition for the faithful to "stand fast in the liberty" with which they already had been "made free."[40]

Champion conflated sacred-evangelical and political-revolutionary tropes with abandon. The title of the sermon itself—*Christian and Civil Liberty*—suggested this, as did quotations from Jesus and Algernon Sidney on the title page of the published version of his sermon. He urged Americans to set aside regional or colonial differences and second thoughts about independence, and commit themselves to each other under the new governments of Congress and Connecticut. He did so with reference to the effects of faith: the suffering of obedience, the liberty of the saints, and mutual affection. Other preachers followed suit. They implored Americans to unite with patriots from other colonies, pay taxes to the new government, provide provisions to Continental forces, and support local militia. Loyalty to America required the same charity as did dedication to the church. Preachers attuned to conversion admonished Americans, that is, in the most common idioms of sanctification: to persevere, stand fast, contend for the prize, and love each other.[41]

Although the movement for Revolution had intellectual sources—one might even put it crudely as "causes"—other than the discourse of conversion, that discourse had remarkable effects on political actions. We can return to Dartmouth and Hanover, for example, during the crucial buildup to independence in 1774 and 1775, when Wheelock observed a near "universal" concern for conversion in the town: "clearer" than he had ever seen. Still hoping for financial support from Governor Wentworth in 1774, Wheelock was circumspect about rebellion, even though he informed the governor, in a mélange of evangelical and political idioms, that the whole town was as "unanimous and warm" for "the defence of liberty" as was "any part of the Continent." Whitaker, however, a member of the college Corporation and minister in Norwich, Connecticut, was not circumspect. He used the tropes of conversion in his sermons to promote liberty, steel patriot resolve, and denounce loyalism in no uncertain terms. The evangelical preaching of George Whitefield, he claimed in 1770 with a tad bit of exaggeration, had in fact caused the repeal of the Stamp Act because it conjoined spiritual and political liberty. The town of Hanover put such ideas into action. In August 1774 the town meeting implemented non-importation measures. During the following March, it approved measures adopted by the Continental Congress, effectively professing its allegiance to the Congress in place of the kingdom. It also established a Committee of Correspondence to communicate with other patriot communities.[42]

Or, we can move our sights southward to Newport, Rhode Island and the reflections of a Protestant laywoman. The schoolteacher Sarah Osborn had long listened to Newport pastors who blended ideas of conversion into political activism, David Rowland and Samuel Hopkins. A friend of Osborn's, Hopkins spoke forcefully for America's independence and introduced his parishioners to a new type of spinning wheel in support of the non-importation movement, an act of resistance to trade with England. In his sermon on the repeal of the Stamp Act, delivered and published in Providence in 1766, Rowland rehearsed a favorite text of revolutionary preachers, Galatians 5:1: "Stand fast therefore in the liberty wherewith Christ hath made us free, and be not entangled again with the yoke of bondage." He mused on the conversion-like experience of political liberation: the "deliberate and serious reflection" that led to dramatic decisions, the ecstatic "joy" of newfound freedom, and the mandate "to improve" the "enjoyment" of salvation for the common good.[43]

Osborn conveyed her religious and political transformations in comparable terms. She underwent religious conversion, by her account, in 1737, at the age of twenty-three. Just as she recalled exercising her "will" to "choose Christ" after years of attendance at the local Anglican church and frivolous amusements in Newport, she renounced loyalty to her home country, England, and became a fervent patriot. On the tenth anniversary of the repeal of the Stamp Act, she pondered the same text used by Rowland, Galatians 5:1, and applied the tropes of "bondage" and "liberty" to "Church and State," as she put it. She imbibed local newspaper tirades against the Intolerable Acts and other parliamentary misdeeds, joined Hopkins's cadre of non-importing Newport spinners, and defiantly refused to leave the town during British bombardment and occupation. She also predicted a national salvation, America's "redemption" from imperial "captivity."[44]

Formulations of conversion as a free choice, often as a rejection of inherited geographical, political, or familial identities and attachment to a new set of loyalties and obligations, conveyed a sense of freedom to detach oneself from one nation and form a new nation, just as one joined or formed a new church. They offered a potent version of liberty to Osborn and Judge Griswold, as they did to leaders of Dartmouth who otherwise might have remained dependent on the economic largesse of patrons in Britain.

Yet the conceptions of conversion and liberty traced here reflected a deep paradox. They signaled a remarkable departure from seventeenth-century Protestant teaching, according to which liberty meant conformity to divine law. They legitimated what to many eighteenth-century Americans was an otherwise unimaginable break from their past. They gave moral sanction to the rupture of long cherished associations with Britain and to independence from the economic largesse funneled to them from patrons such as Lord Dartmouth. They compelled independence from Britain's imperial moral economy.

The discourse of liberty, however, had its limits. Late eighteenth-century Protestants never imagined modern notions of the moral autonomy of individuals apart from religious, social, and national attachments. Nor, for that matter, did they ponder the contradictions of their claims to moral freedom in a society fettered by unfreedom for African slaves, Indigenous people, and the indigent. Our recognition of such contradictions, however, is also a mark of the salience of the discourse itself. It served at times as a rule by which to measure disparities between religious and political ideals and social realities. Although it remained partial, and incompletely applied, such was its potency that it could move people such as Dartmouth's Thornton and Wheelock to resituate their loyalties with revolutionary hope.

NOTES

1. Nathaniel Whitaker to Eleazer Wheelock, Dec. 18, 1765; Nathaniel Eels to Nathaniel Whitaker, Jan. 16, 1766; and Eleazer Wheelock to John Thornton, April 29, 1775: all from the Wheelock Papers, Baker-Berry Library, Dartmouth College, Hanover, New Hampshire.

2. For one particularly helpful survey of the immense literature on religion and the American Revolution, see Wood 1997.

3. Many recent histories of the American Revolution have in fact nearly omitted discussions of religious discourse following the Stamp Act. For one example, see Taylor 2016. Gray and Kamensky 2013 have only a single chapter out of thirty-three that concerns religion, and that chapter downplays the role of religion in the Revolution: Juster 2013. For a compelling critique of the temptation to reduce cultural expressions to mere political forces, see Wilson 1993.

4. Other moral and theological ideas, of course, also informed political revolution. Many arguments for independence, including those of Thomas Paine's *Common Sense*, never addressed the philosophical issue of moral freedom. As James Smylie argued, Presbyterian clergy from Pennsylvania, New Jersey, and New York thought that a robust notion of divine dominion or sovereignty, which they claimed from their Calvinist vantages, provided a hedge against any claims to sovereignty by king and parliament. Smylie 1970.

5. Langdon 1775.

6. Entry on Samuel Langdon in Shipton 1958, 10:508–528.

7. Langdon 1775, 5, 12.

8. Oakes 2016, esp. 184–209. Despite its title, Clark 1994 has little to say about essential definitions, especially philosophical debates.

9. In his 1755 dictionary, for example, Samuel Johnson nearly equated liberty and freedom, quoted John Locke to provide the philosophical definition of liberty as "the power in any agent to do" or act as they had "preference," and then focused on political privileges and immunities: Johnson 1979, entries on "liberty" and "freedom." William Blackstone, the author of the authoritative legal dictionary from the period,

similarly included descriptions of moral competency along with specific political liberties: Blackstone 1756, 7, 105.

10. Oakes 2016, 10–11, 26, 29, 37–81.

11. For examples from non-evangelicals who made conversion a central issue, see Chauncy 1765, 338–39; and Oakes 2016, esp. 21–22, 127–56. Many histories of the period posit a fourfold division in American Protestantism during the eighteenth century: New Lights or evangelical Calvinists, radical evangelicals or separatists such as Baptists, Old Lights or moderate Calvinists who rejected the revivals but maintained much of Calvinist teaching, and religious liberals or rationalists. Although this is a helpful typology of theological differences vis-à-vis the revivals, it does little to explain religious developments after 1750. See, e.g., Holifield 2003, 127–156.

12. Mayhew 1750b, 20, 43–45, 51; see 18, 48–49 for comments on geography and family.

13. Mayhew 1755, quote from 291–92. Many passages out of Mayhew on the nature of moral choice, just like passages from the evangelical Edwards, rested on Lockean epistemology and the moral philosophy of Francis Hutcheson and his so-called Moral Sense school. For the currency of Lockean epistemology and the transformation of it into the Moral Sense school, see Fiering 1981.

14. Stiles 1799 [1761], 65–66.

15. "Samuel West" in Shipton 1958, 13:501–510.

16. West 1776, 278–79, 267.

17. Robbins 1959.

18. West 1776, 270.

19. For arguments against an Anglican bishop and missionary societies, see Oakes 2016, 130–40, 146–48, 160–61.

20. So too with the Sugar Act. In his fulminations against the 1764 Act, the Rhode Island lawyer, sometimes governor, chief justice, and signer of the Declaration Stephen Hopkins insisted that the contest with Parliament demanded a right philosophy of the will, an affirmation that "liberty solely consists in an independency upon the will of another." Hopkins 1765, 4, quoting Sidney 1698.

21. [Johnson] 1765, in Bailyn 1970, in "Appendix B," 144–69. The quotations are from 147–48, 152–53. Bailyn provides biographical information on Johnson, 125–39.

22. Johnson 1766, 20, 37–38; *New London Gazette*, quoted in Bailyn 1970, 162.

23. Johnson 1766, 38.

24. The religious revivals of the 1740s were especially intense in eastern Connecticut, including Lyme: Bushman 1967, 191; Winiarski 2017, 333–52; and Ifkovic 1977, esp. 98–99.

25. Langdon 1775, 6; 22–24 on negotiations; *passim* for British policies.

26. Langdon 1775, 11, 16, 20, 22, 27–28.

27. Mayhew 1750a, 35–36.

28. Eremo 1771, quoted in Botein 1980, 32; [Allen] 1773, xxii-xxiii, xxvii; Edwards 1774.

29. West 1776, 300.

30. Wood 1982.

31. Langdon 1775, 10, 24–26.

32. For biographical information on Williams: Shipton 1958, 5: 1701–1712; and Weaver 1988.
33. [Williams] 1774, 53–118.
34. [Williams] 1774, 101, 65–66.
35. Johnson 1766, 40, 45.
36. Ifkovic 1977, 104–119; and Baldwin 1928, 178.
37. West 1776, 304, 311; Turner 1774, 29.
38. Emerson 1766, 19, 30.
39. Emerson 1766, 28–30; Dickinson 1774, 128–29.
40. Champion 1776, 30–31.
41. These terms are scattered throughout Revolutionary-era sermons and pamphlets. For two examples, see Champion 1776, 31; and Edwards 1774.
42. Chase 1891, I: 329 (Wheelock quotation on conversions); 326 (Wheelock to Wentworth); 320–21 (town meetings); 330–31 (the militia); 336–48 (Wheelock's loyalty to Congress). For Whitaker, see especially Whitaker 1774 and Whitaker 1777.
43. Rowland 1766, 27, 31; Baldwin 1928, 154n1; Valeri 1989, 741–69; and, for a brief biography of Rowland, Dexter 1912, 1:744–746. For a statistical summary of favorite patriot texts, see Byrd 2013, 170.
44. Sarah Osborn to Samuel Hopkins, n.d., Letters 69 and 70 in Osborn and Anthony 1807, 149; Sarah Osborn to "The Rev. Mr. F___," n.d., in Ibid., 156, 158. For her conversion, see Osborn 1799, 21–24. For the other details here, see Brekus 2014, 22, 63–65 (bad associations in Newport), 93–118 (conversion), and 290–301 (political views and engagement in the American Revolution).

REFERENCES

Allen, John. 1773. *An Oration Upon the Beauties of Liberty*, 3rd ed. New London.

Bailyn, Bernard. 1970. "Religion and Revolution: Three Biographical Studies." Pp. 85–169 in *Perspectives in American History* 4. Cambridge, MA: Charles Warren Center for Studies in American History.

Baldwin, Alice M. 1928. *The New England Clergy and the American Revolution.* Durham, NC: Duke University Press.

Blackstone, William. 1756. *An Analysis of the Laws of England*. Oxford.

Botein, Stephen. 1980. "Natural Rights Reconsidered." Pp. 13–34 in *Party and Political Opposition in Revolutionary America*, edited by Patricia U. Bonomi. Tarrytown, NY: Sleepy Hollow Press.

Brekus, Catherine. 2014. *Sarah Osborn's World: the Rise of Evangelical Calvinism in Early America*. New Haven, CT: Yale University Press.

Bushman, Richard. 1967. *From Puritan to Yankee: Character and Social Order in Connecticut, 1690-1765.* Cambridge, MA: Harvard University Press.

Byrd, James P. 2013. *Sacred Scripture, Sacred War: The Bible and the American Revolution*. New York: Oxford University Press.

Champion, Judah. 1776. *Christian and Civil Liberty.* Hartford.

Chase, Frederick. 1891. *A History of Dartmouth College and the Town of Hanover.* 2 vols. Edited by John K. Lord. Cambridge, U.K.

Chauncy, Charles. 1765. *Twelve Sermons.* Boston.

Clark, J. C. D. 1994. *The Language of Liberty: Political Discourse and Social Dynamics in the Anglo-American World.* New York: Cambridge University Press.

Dexter, Franklin Bowditch. 1912. *Biographical Sketches of the Graduates of Yale College.* 6 vols. New Haven, CT: Yale University Press.

Dickinson, John. 1774. *Letters from a Farmer.* Philadelphia.

Edwards Jr., Jonathan. 1774. Sermon on Ecc. 7:14. Box 166, Folder 2735, Item 75758, Sermon #390. Jonathan Edwards, Jr. Sermons, Hartford Seminary, Hartford, Connecticut.

Eels, Nathaniel. " Nathaniel Eels to Nathaniel Whitaker, January 16, 1766." Letter from Baker-Berry Library, Dartmouth College, The Wheelock Papers, 1772–1827.

Emerson, Joseph. 1766. *A Thanksgiving-Sermon Preach'd at Pepperrell, July 24, 1766.* Boston.

Eremo, Johannes [John Cleaveland]. 1771. Essex *Gazette*, April 9.

Fiering, Norman S. 1981. *Jonathan Edwards's Moral Thought and Its British Context.* Chapel Hill, NC: The University of North Carolina Press.

Gray, Edward G. and Jane Kamensky, editors. 2013. *The Oxford Handbook of the American Revolution.* New York: Oxford University Press.

Holifield, E. Brooks. 2003. *Theology in America: Christian Thought from the Age of the Puritans to the Civil War.* New Haven, CT: Yale University Press.

Hopkins, Stephen. 1765. *The Rights of the Colonies Examined.* Providence.

Ifkovic, John W. 1977. "Matthew Griswold: Lyme's Revolutionary Magistrate." Pp. 96–136 in *A Lyme Miscellany, 1776-1976*, edited by George J. Willauer. Middletown, CT: Wesleyan University Press.

Johnson, Samuel. 1979. *A Dictionary of the English Language.* New York: Arno Press.

Johnson, Stephen. 1765. "*New London Gazette,* Sept. 6, Sept. 20, Oct. 4, Oct. 11 and Nov. 1, 1765." Reprinted in Bailyn 1970, "Appendix B," 144–69.

Idem. 1766. *Some Important Observations.* Newport.

Juster, Susan. 2013. "The Evangelical Ascendency in Revolutionary America." In *The Oxford Handbook of the American Revolution,* edited by Edward G. Gray and Jane Kamensky. New York: Oxford University Press.

Langdon, Samuel. 1775. *Government Corrupted by Vice, and Recovered by Righteousness.* Watertown, MA.

Mayhew, Jonathan. 1750a. *A Discourse Concerning Unlimited Submission.* Boston.

Idem. 1750b. *Seven Sermons.* Boston.

Idem. 1755. "Sermon IX." Pp. 256–307 in *Sermons Upon the Following Subjects.* Boston.

Oakes, John S. 2016. *Conservative Revolutionaries: Transformation and Tradition in the Religious Thought of Charles Chauncy and Jonathan Mayhew.* Eugene, OR: Pickwick Publications.

Osborn, Sarah. 1799. *Memoirs of the Life of Mrs. Sarah Osborn.* Worcester, MA.

Osborn, Sarah and Susanna Anthony. 1807. *Familiar Letters, Written by Mrs. Sarah Osborn, and Miss Susanna Anthony.* Newport.

Paine, Thomas. 1775. *Common Sense.* Philadelphia.

Robbins, Caroline. 1959. *The Eighteenth-Century Commonwealth man: Studies in the Transmission, Development and Circumstance of English Liberal Thought from the Restoration of Charles II until the War with the Thirteen Colonies.* Cambridge, MA: Harvard University Press.

Rowland, David S. 1766. *Divine Providence Illustrated and Improved.* Providence.

Shipton, Clifford K. 1958. *Sibley's Harvard Graduates.* 18 vols. Boston: Massachusetts Historical Society.

Sidney, Algernon. 1698. *Discourses Concerning Government.*

Smylie, James H. 1970. "Presbyterian Clergy and the Problems of 'Dominion' in the Revolutionary Generation." Pp. 161–75 in *Journal of Presbyterian History* 48.

Stiles, Ezra. 1799 [1761]. *A Discourse on the Christian Union.* Boston.

Taylor, Alan. 2016. *American Revolutions: A Continental History, 1750-1804.* New York: W.W. Norton Co.

Turner, Charles. 1774. *A Sermon Preached at Plymouth.* Boston.

Valeri, Mark. 1989. "The New Divinity and the American Revolution." Pp. 741–69 in *William and Mary Quarterly* 46.

Weaver, Glenn. 1988. "Elisha Williams: The Versatile Puritan." Pp. 119–233 in *The Connecticut Historical Society Bulletin* 53.

West, Samuel. 1776. *A Sermon Preached before the Honorable Council.* In *The Pulpit of the American Revolution: Political Sermons of the Period of 1776*, edited by John Wingate Thornton. Boston, 1860.

Wheelock Papers. From Baker-Berry Library, Dartmouth College.

Whitaker, Nathaniel. 1774. *A Confutation of Two Tracts.* Boston.

Idem. 1777. *An Antidote against Toryism.* Newbury-Port.

Williams, Elisha. 1774. "The Essential Rights and Liberties of Protestants." Pp. 53–118 in *Political Sermons of the American Founding Era, 1730-1805*, edited by Ellis Sandoz. Indianapolis: Liberty Press, 1991.

Wilson, John F. 1993. "Religion and Revolution in American History." Pp. 597–613 in *Journal of Interdisciplinary History* 23.

Winiarski, Douglas L. 2017. *Darkness Falls on the Land of Light: Experiencing Religious Awakenings in Eighteenth-Century New England.* Chapel Hill, NC: University of North Carolina Press.

Wood, Gordon S. 1982. "Conspiracy and the Paranoid Style: Causality and Deceit in the Eighteenth Century." Pp. 401–44 in *William and Mary Quarterly* 39.

Idem. 1997. "Religion and the American Revolution." Pp. 173–205 in *New Directions in American Religious History*, edited by Harry S. Stout and D. G. Hart. New York: Oxford University Press.

Chapter 6

The Making of a "Rebel Lady"

Gender, Virtue, and Bloodshed in Mercy Otis Warren's Radicalization, 1769–1772

J. Patrick Mullins, PhD (Marquette University)

On February 15, 1777, American writer Mercy Otis Warren wrote English historian Catharine Macaulay with a much-needed lift to wartime morale: General George Washington's successful crossing of the Delaware River and victory at Trenton on Christmas Day. In conclusion, she remarked how deeply she valued writing her friend Macaulay, "yet lest she should suffer any inconvenience from a real or suspected correspondence with a *rebel lady*, I shall suspend any attempt for further intercourse until hostilities cease and peace again shews her welcome face on both sides of the Atlantic." The letter did not reach Macaulay, likely intercepted by Crown authorities, and she made no attempt to reach out to Warren after hostilities began between Britain and the thirteen American colonies in 1775. Parliament had banned correspondence with Americans. Following the suspension of habeas corpus, Macaulay lived in dread of arrest for treason and espionage as an English defender of the American cause. Mercy Warren was not at great risk of imprisonment as a rebel, but she continually worried for her husband James, a member of the Massachusetts Provincial Congress, if he should fall in the hands of the king's troops.[1]

Like Macaulay, Mercy Warren was a public advocate of colonial rights in an era when political activity was considered the proper province of gentlemen like James Warren and Macaulay's brother, member of Parliament James

Sawbridge. Moreover, both women were startlingly radical in their political claims. While Macaulay justified English resistance to King Charles I in her *History of England*, Warren justified American resistance to King George III's colonial officers years before the war began. In the spring of 1772, her play *The Adulateur* described in heroic terms an uprising of patriots against a fictional tyrant who represented Thomas Hutchinson, royally appointed governor of Massachusetts. It was Warren's first published writing and the first in a series of "pamphlet plays" colonists wrote over the Revolutionary era to advance their political causes.[2]

The radicalism of *The Adulateur* can be explained in part by reference to Warren's radical Whig political principles and view of history. She did however defend the use of armed, lethal force against Crown government in advance of the other Boston Whigs who shared those principles, let alone the typically more moderate Patriots of the mid-Atlantic and southern colonies. To understand Warren's readiness, not just to address politics publicly as a woman but to justify revolution as early as spring 1772, one must consider *The Adulateur* in the contexts of her ideological framework as well as other factors, namely, the physical assault and mental deterioration endured by her brother James Otis, Jr., the killing of ten-year-old Bostonian Christopher Seider, Governor Hutchinson's centralization of power in Massachusetts, and the personal example and transatlantic prestige of Catharine Macaulay as a politically active woman. The often-gendered nature of Warren's radicalization by the events of 1769–1772 helps explain the incendiary message of *The Adulateur*. It also illuminates her development, in the wake of its publication, of an argument for female patriotism which broadened the basis for elite women's participation in politics and affirmed her own public persona as "a rebel lady."

Fundamental to Mercy Otis Warren's understanding of politics throughout her adult life was the premise that human nature is uniform and immutable across time and place, and that there is "a noble principle implanted in the nature of man, that pants for distinction." In her 1805 *History of the Rise, Progress, and Termination of the American Revolution*, she wrote that this principle of action "operates in every bosom, and when kept under the control of reason, and the influence of humanity, it produces the most benevolent effects." When this innate "love of distinction" is not controlled by "conscience," however, as when "the moral sense [is] weakened by the sudden acquisition of wealth or power," it drives humans to dominate and exploit their fellows. She continued:

> Thus when we look over the theatre of human action, scrutinize the windings of the heart, and survey the transactions of man from the earliest to the present period, it must be acknowledged that ambition and avarice are the leading

springs which generally actuate the restless mind. From these primary sources of corruption have arisen all the rapine and confusion, the depredation and ruin, that have spread distress over the face of the earth from the days of Nimrod to Cesar, and from Cesar to an arbitrary prince of the house of Brunswick.[3]

From the publication of her masterwork near the end of her life back to her first political writing in 1772 and earlier, Warren held the view of human history as driven by a struggle between corrupt tyrants who give free rein to the will to power and virtuous citizens who defend liberty at all costs.

Warren shared this understanding of the political world with her fellow radical Whigs in Massachusetts during the years leading up to the Revolutionary War. In his 1765 pamphlet against the Stamp Act, her friend John Adams wrote that the "love of power" has "always prompted the princes and nobles of the earth, by every species of fraud and violence, to shake off all the limitations of their power," while a determination to preserve their liberty has "always stimulated the common people to aspire at independency, and to endeavor at confining the power of the great within the limits of *equity* and *reason*." Similarly, his wife Abigail Adams wrote him ten years later, "It seems Humane Nature is the same in all ages and Countrys. Ambition and avarice reign every where and where they predominate their will be bickerings after places of Honour and profit." Through this ideological framework, it seemed that Massachusetts politics bore out the lessons of history, from Biblical and classical antiquity to the British Empire in the seventeenth and eighteenth centuries. Mercy and James Warren, their friends the Adamses, James Otis, and the other leading Massachusetts Patriots shared the conviction that ultimately only civic virtue—rooted in rational self-mastery—could preserve liberty by restraining the thirst for power within the human soul and the body politic.[4]

Mercy Otis Warren admired her older brother, James Otis, Jr., as an exemplar of civic virtue. Within the ideological framework of eighteenth-century Whiggism, citizens could preserve liberty by exercising civic virtue through such public services as arms bearing, office-holding, and political oratory on behalf of the common good. True to his principles, Otis resigned his position as acting Advocate General for Massachusetts in protest when Thomas Hutchinson accepted Governor Francis Bernard's appointment as chief justice while retaining his offices as lieutenant governor, provincial councilor, and probate judge. In essays submitted to the *Boston Gazette*, Otis decried Hutchinson's concentration of judicial, legislative, and executive power in his own hands, accusing him of seeking wealth and power at public expense. He represented Boston merchants in a suit against the customs service to stop the use of general search warrants to suppress smuggling. As a member of the Massachusetts assembly, Otis led relentless opposition to Bernard's policies, and his pamphlets challenged Parliament's Sugar Act of 1764 and Stamp Act of 1765 for violating the colonists' natural, charter, and English rights.[5]

American liberty never seemed more gravely in danger than by the Townshend Acts of 1767–1768, which established new excise duties on imports like tea, a bureaucracy of customs collectors armed with general search warrants for efficient collection of the tax, and a vice-admiralty court for the vigorous prosecution of smugglers. These new Crown officers would be paid out of the taxes they collected or the cargoes and ships they seized. As historian Patrick Griffin has explained, the acts were intended less to raise revenue than to assert "the superiority of the Crown" and Parliament over the colonies by subjecting them to a new, permanent "system" of imperial governance. Boston merchants vowed not to import taxed goods until the laws were repealed, while urban crowds styled the Sons of Liberty enforced non-importation through intimidation of customs commissioners and importers. When the crowd rioted on June 10, 1768, assaulting customs commissioners to prevent confiscation of a merchant ship, Governor Bernard called for regiments of the British regular army to restore civil peace in Boston. For James Otis and the leading Boston radicals, Bernard's prorogation of the Massachusetts legislature at the end of June and the arrival of the king's troops in October generated gloomy thoughts that physical resistance might be the only way to prevent the complete loss of liberty.[6]

At this darkening historic moment, Massachusetts Patriots found an eloquent and devoted ally in Catharine Sawbridge Macaulay, the famous English author of a political history of seventeenth-century Britain, which she wrote in eight volumes over twenty years. Published early in 1769, the fourth volume offered her account of the defeat of King Charles I and his execution one hundred and twenty years earlier. Macaulay praised the commonwealthmen who replaced the monarchy with a republic as "the partisans of liberty," committed to the principle that government is "instituted for the protection of the people, for the end of securing not overthrowing the rights of nature." When a prince exceeds "the limits of that power with which he is vested for the protection of his people," Macaulay explained, his rights to govern are "forfeited" and the subject's allegiance is "dissolved." At that point, the subject "may justly, by the right of self-preservation, take very probable mean[s] to secure himself from the lawless power and enterprizes of the tyrant." Macaulay contended that Parliament "had a right to oppose the tyrant to the utmost" in the English Civil War. And the New Model Army had a right to execute Charles I in 1649, as "never any prince had laid deeper schemes against the freedom of the constitution" than he. Her unsparing portrayal of Charles I as a corrupt tyrant, and her defense of his execution as "that eminent act of justice" cost Macaulay the favor of moderate Whigs in Britain, not least because they found her lack of sympathy for the king unfeminine.[7]

Many American colonists, however, honored Macaulay for her fearless endorsement of such radical Whig principles as the sovereignty of the people, the natural rights of man, and the right of resistance to tyranny. On April 27, 1769, she shipped the first four volumes of her *History of England* as a gift to James Otis, Jr., with a letter praising him as "the great Guardian of American Liberty." Describing her fellow British radicals with the same term she had described the seventeenth-century republicans, Macaulay informed him that "every partizan of liberty in this Island simpathizes with their American Brethren." She assured Otis that his "defense of the rights of your fellow Citizens claim[s] the respect and admiration of every Lover of their Country and Mankind." Coming from an Englishwoman esteemed in Britain for her political principles and scholarly achievement, Macaulay's letter cheered despondent colonists with her affirmations that their cause was just and they were not alone in their struggle. On June 19, the *Boston Chronicle* reported breathlessly that "Mr. Otis has lately received a very polite letter from the celebrated Mrs. Macaulay, the great patroness of liberty in England, with a copy of her history elegantly bound." Over the following weeks, this report was repeated in newspapers throughout New England, in New York City, and as far south as Savannah, Georgia.[8]

Macaulay had written with the expectation Otis would circulate her letter among Boston Whigs, and Otis responded with a lengthy account he hoped would strengthen support for America among British radicals. In his missive of July 27, 1769, Otis praised her as the greatest scholar of British history of either sex and as "a most illustrious proof" that God and Nature have "been equally kind to both Sexes," "at least in point of genius," and that only "the Tyranny of Custom" prevented more women from "rivalling gentlemen in the arts and sciences." Confirming that the American colonies were "really distressed as you justly conceive," he criticized Governor Bernard and "the rest of ye Tory tools." Outlining the impact of the Townshend Acts, Otis described the customs commissioners as "to ye last degree oppressive." He was dismayed that the royal revenue service preyed on the shipping of Boston merchants as if they were "traitors" and "rebels," and that accused merchants were subjected to the "Caprices of a sole uncontroulable Judge" paid out of the "Confiscations he shall decree." "Good GOD! This is British liberty & felicity with a vengeance," he bemoaned. "People may bear these things for this generation, but it will be marvelous if those that are rapidly rising should." Otis assessed the Townshend duties as damaging to American commerce and therefore Britain's wealth, and he warned that the current ministerial policy of colonial "subjugation" would bring about the fall of the British Empire. While Otis hoped this appeal to British self-interest would prompt public support for repeal of the Townshend Acts, he noted obliquely that imperial policy might ultimately provoke a colonial revolt.[9]

Otis read the fourth volume of Macaulay's *History of England* with enthusiasm, noting in his letter, "you have so true an Idea" of the oppressiveness of Britain's Stuart kings. On September 4, 1769, the *Boston Gazette* published an exuberant recommendation of her book under the pseudonym "John Hampden!" In *Boston Gazette* essays against the Stamp Act four years earlier, Otis had used the pseudonym of John Hampden—the statesman and soldier who opposed royal taxation in Parliament and died fighting King Charles I's troops in the Parliamentarian cause. The recommendation has Otis's distinctive tone. "Mrs. Macaulay's History is a work of inexpressible Merit," Otis chimed brightly. "It is written in the true spirit of Liberty." Echoing his letter to Macaulay, he observed that the fourth volume justly condemned the Stuart dynasty as "a race of Tyrants." "This Book is recommended to every Son and Daughter of Liberty in North-America," he concluded. The peculiar inclusion of an exclamation point in his use of the Hampden pseudonym suggests that Otis's mind at the time was exuberant, if not fervid.[10]

Over the preceding few years, Otis had displayed to his family and friends worrisome signs of mental deterioration, including erratic behavior, bursts of temper, and excessive drinking. His internal condition then took an explosively public form. On the same page of the *Boston Gazette* edition as the anonymous recommendation of Macaulay's *History of England* appeared a piece which Otis submitted to the editors under his own name. Otis had heard that customs commissioner John Robinson charged him with being "inimical to the Crown." He wrote in response that if Robinson "misrepresents me, I have a natural right if I can get no other satisfaction to break his head." In a more lucid frame of mind, Otis would have realized that threatening physical retaliation—rather than appealing first to the courts for redress—did not follow from the Lockean natural-rights doctrine that he, Macaulay, and his fellow Whigs espoused. Having thrown down the glove in a very public forum, he came looking for Robinson on September 5, seeking satisfaction for his offended honor.[11]

Spoiling for a fight, Otis entered the British Coffee House, Boston's gathering place for provincial officials, customs collectors, and officers of the royal army and navy. When Robinson entered and observed Otis, the two men exchanged angry words. Robinson seized Otis by his nose, and then they fenced with canes before their duel turned into a general brawl. Some men restrained Otis while Robinson struck him in the head with a blow that cut down to the skull and left him drenched in blood. Otis's assailants appear to have been an army officer and a naval officer. A gentleman observing Otis's beating tried to intervene, but he was injured and driven off. One of the provincial officers rescued a dazed and battered Otis from the coffee house.[12]

In the first of her letters to survive intact, Mercy Otis Warren expressed horror at her brother's savage beating. "You know not what I have suffered for you within the last twenty four hours," she wrote James. Mercy imagined him "slain by the hands of merciless men," his wife widowed and children orphaned, and "your country in tears for the man who had sacrificed interest[,] health, and peace, for the public weal." Approaching this affair of honor between Otis and Robinson within the context of the larger political crisis, Warren wondered whether "we have men among us under the guise of officers of the Crown, who have become open assassins?" She charged Robinson with attacking "a gentleman alone and unarmed with a design to take away his life." The British Crown had sent the army and navy to Boston purportedly as "*conservators* of the peace," but in the coffee house, royal officers had behaved like "a band of ruffians." Warren knew well that the "errand" of the king's troops in Boston was "to uphold villainy, and protect villains," that is, to protect the customs commissioners from the Sons of Liberty. But she never imagined that they would "stand by" and allow a "miscreant" like Robinson "to spill the blood of citizens, who criminate the designs, and their measures."[13]

While Warren expressed outrage at Otis's beating as the attempted assassination of a virtuous patriot, she was well acquainted with his fits of temper and likely appreciated the part which his mental condition played in the incident. Warren feared that her brother would respond to the assault by challenging Robinson to a lethal duel of honor. She insisted that duels were contrary to "the laws of reason and the laws of God" as well as civil law. She urged him, "with a sisterly affection," not to allow "either public oppression or private wrongs, the injustice of a few in power, or the folly of the many who are out" to "ruffle and discompose a man," who, when his mind was "calm and steady," could still serve "the greatest good of his fellow creatures—and in consequence thereof to secure to himself, eternal felicity." Warren worried that Otis's ordeal would provoke him to retaliatory violence or send him deeper into madness. She asked him to excuse her candor as "one who has your welfare more at heart, after very few exceptions, than that of any other person in the world." Warren understood this incident in light of both radical Whig ideology and family loyalty. She addressed Otis with the civic-minded voice of the outraged patriot as well as the gendered voice of a loving sister and woman of sensibility.[14]

In the months following the assault, John Adams observed that his friend Otis enjoyed greater clarity of mind than earlier. On January 16, 1770, however, Adams lamented in his diary that Otis was "in confusion yet; he loses himself; he rambles and wanders like a ship without a helm." He added on February 26th that Otis "has been, this afternoon, raving mad; raving against father, wife, brother, sister, friend, &c." Otis displayed a steady decline in judgment and self-control over the early months of 1770. Sarah Prince Gill—a Boston lady whose brother-in-law, John Gill, was co-publisher of the *Boston Gazette* and an American edition of Macaulay's *History*—had recommended in December 1769 that Macaulay seek information on the colonies from Otis, "the Cato of America." In March 1770, she wrote Macaulay, "It gives me Pain to mention the Malloncholly Fact that my Worthy Friend Mr Otis Labours under such Infirmities as deprives us in a great measure of His Assistance in this Exigence of our Public Affairs!" Gill encouraged her to contact John Adams instead. Massachusetts had long looked to Otis to keep his hand firmly on the helm of public affairs, but he could no longer exercise that rational self-mastery which civic virtue required.[15]

Roiling with conflicting passions, Boston itself seemed to have lost self-mastery and begun staggering toward the precipice. There, as in other port cities, tensions continued to build between royal enforcers of the Townshend Acts and the Sons of Liberty. On February 19, 1770, Bostonians learned of the so-called Battle of Golden Hill, a large-scale brawl in New York City which occurred a month earlier between Sons of Liberty and the British regulars who tried to pull down their liberty pole. On February 22, 1770, a crowd of men and boys were picketing the retail shop of Theophilus Lillie, one of the few merchants who continued importing and selling taxed goods. They planted in front of the shop, facing a busy street, a sign naming the remaining violators of the non-importation agreement. Ebenezer Richardson, one of the "friends of government," observed the picketing of his neighbor's store, challenged the protesters, and struggled unsuccessfully to pull the sign up from the ground. Richardson was notorious among Massachusetts Whigs as a paid informer for the customs commissioners and subsequently a customs employee. He gave up removing the sign and headed home, running into Sons of Liberty who denounced him as a perjurer for his anti-smuggling testimony years earlier. Their angry exchange in the street attracted idle boys, as school let out early on market days. The boys crowded outside of Richardson's home, shouting "Informer!" After he ordered them to disperse, they began throwing rubbish at the house. When Richardson lobbed a brick at the boys, the crowd began to grow and hurled stones at his house, breaking windows and hitting his wife. The increasingly angry crowd had not attempted to enter his home, but Richardson presumably felt in danger of life and limb. He pointed a musket out of a second-story window and fired into the mass of men and boys.[16]

This discharge of a weapon into the crowd was the first use of lethal force in the Imperial Crisis between Britain and the American colonies. The spray of birdshot struck two spectators, nineteen-year-old Samuel Gore and ten-year-old Christopher Seider. Just released from school, Seider had run to the crowd to see what was going on and was hit almost immediately. While

Gore had minor injuries, Seider was struck in the chest and belly. One of the eleven pellets punctured Seider's lung, and attending physician Dr. Joseph Warren was unable to prevent his death that night. After the now furious crowd subdued the cutlass-brandishing Richardson and prepared to hang him on the spot, a Whig gentleman prevented his lynching and delivered him to civil magistrates. On the testimony of doctors who performed the autopsy, including Dr. Warren, the coroner pronounced Seider's killing an act of murder, and Sons of Liberty raised a sign at Liberty Tree calling for the "death" of the "murderer." Although a child of poor German immigrants, Seider received a funeral procession of about two thousand participants, "the largest perhaps ever known in America" in Thomas Hutchinson's estimation. An anonymous contributor to the *Boston Gazette* pronounced Seider "this little hero and first martyr to the noble cause." The *Gazette* compared his death to that of William Allen, the innocent boy whose killing by Scottish troops in London precipitated the 1768 Massacre of St. George's Fields. On March 5, just eleven days after Seider's death, the cause of American Whiggism received additional martyrs when British regulars fired into a crowd on King Street, killing four Boston men and one seventeen-year-old boy.[17]

Boston's radical Whigs pressed for prosecution of the arrested British soldiers and their commanding officer for murder. Thomas Hutchinson, who became acting governor upon Bernard's departure in August 1769, insisted on postponing trial for the March 5th killings until after Richardson's trial, which began on April 20 before a jury drawn from outside of Boston. Three of the four judges concluded that Richardson had committed manslaughter, but Justice Peter Oliver found that he acted justifiably in self-defense. The Whigs who inflamed the mob and the magistrates who failed to suppress the mob were actually to blame for the boy's death, Oliver maintained. The jury deliberated all night and the next morning pronounced Richardson guilty of murder, defying the judges' instructions for a finding of manslaughter. The judges reluctantly recorded the verdict but declined to pass sentence. If the Whigs were aggravated enough by justice delayed for Richardson, they did not take the news well of justice denied when juries in October and November 1770 acquitted the British soldiers and their commanding officer of murder charges.[18]

Despite removal of two of four regiments from Boston and repeal of all Townshend duties except the tea tax, the Whig cause was in retreat. Repeal took the steam out of the non-importation movement. While radicals urged boycott of the taxed tea, public support for resistance had waned by the fall of 1770. On March 14, 1771, Thomas Hutchinson's royal commission as Massachusetts governor took effect. His brother-in-law Peter Oliver replaced him as Chief Justice of the Superior Court, and his younger brother Foster Hutchinson also sat on the court. His other brother-in-law, Andrew Oliver, was promoted from provincial secretary to lieutenant governor. Hutchinson chose his nephew, notorious importer Nathaniel Rogers, as Andrew Oliver's replacement. When Rogers died before he could assume office, the place of provincial secretary went instead to Thomas Flucker, one of the few officers in the new administration who was not related to Hutchinson. These appointments confirmed for Mercy Otis Warren her brother's prediction nine years earlier that Hutchinson "would never cease engrossing places of power & profit for himself, his family, and dependents, 'till he had set the province in a flame."[19]

If Hutchinson managed to centralize power in his own hands and then rendered himself unaccountable to the people by accepting a royal salary out of the tea revenue, Warren and the radicals worried, he could commit abuses and permit crimes with no check from the people's representatives. As if to confirm their worst fears regarding the consequences of his rise to dominance, Hutchinson saved Ebenezer Richardson from the gallows. The Superior Court judges were unable to hold a new trial for him and unwilling to execute him on a charge of murder. Hutchinson had kept Richardson in jail while requesting a pardon for him from the Crown. On March 10, 1772, after two years' confinement, Richardson received his royal pardon. He paid bail and fled town immediately with the mob at his heels. Long a threat which Otis had hoped to avert by lawful means, the permanent abrogation of Americans' natural, charter, and English rights by acts of Parliament appeared to be close at hand, with few remaining routes for redress. For Warren, the cause of liberty in Massachusetts seemed all but lost, and defensive force might be the only way to save it.[20]

Warren's radicalization between 1769 and 1772 cannot be understood solely by reference to her political principles, principles also held by Whig leaders like John Adams and John Hancock who did not believe that circumstances in the spring of 1772 warranted force. Warren interpreted the events of this tumultuous period not only in terms of ideology and statecraft but also family and gender. The decline of public liberty in Massachusetts was closely related in her mind with the mental decline of her brother, whose virtuous commitment to public liberty since 1760 seemed its best security. She was not alone in her esteem for him. Boston voters continued to choose James Otis as a town selectman, and Middlesex County voters kept returning him to the provincial assembly. On March 14, 1770, nine days after the Boston Massacre, merchant John Rowe reported in his diary that Otis "got into a mad freak to-night, and broke a great many windows in the Town House." On April 22, 1770, the day after Ebenezer Richardson's trial concluded, "Mr. Otis behaved very madly, firing guns out of his window, that caused a large number of people to assemble about him." A threat to civil peace rather than its guardian, Otis was removed by his family to the countryside under the care of a physician. Before seeking his replacement, the Boston Town Meeting thanked him "for his undaunted Exertions in the Common Cause of the Colonies from the beginning of the present glorious Struggle for the Rights of the British Constitution." Warren shared the people's admiration for Otis as a champion of their rights.[21]

She also lamented his condition as a devoted sister who, as she had written him the previous year, "has your welfare more at heart, after very few exceptions, than that of any other person in the world." Warren remarked to a friend, "to see the mind of a man so superior, thus darkened, and that man a most affectionate brother, is grief beyond expression." By the spring of 1771, Otis had partially recovered and returned to office, but by the end of the year he suffered a mental collapse which required his permanent isolation to the country, out of public view. Not everyone was heartbroken by the fall of James Otis, Jr. On December 3, 1771, Hutchinson crowed to Bernard that "Otis was carried off to-day in a post-chaise, bound hand and foot. He has been as good as his word,—to set the Province in a flame, and perished in the attempt." If he thought that the Otis family would no longer be a thorn in his side, Hutchinson was mistaken. Mercy Warren's biographer Rosemarie Zagarri has argued that Otis's fall was her principal spur to take up her brother's cause by becoming an activist in her own right. With her brother incapacitated and her father elderly, Warren carried on the family quarrel with the Hutchinson-Oliver faction which had sidelined the Otises by consolidating control over the executive and judiciary offices of the province. For Warren, the political was the personal.[22]

The Hutchinson administration was monopolizing power, seizing property, and curtailing liberty. Most critically for Warren, though, it had shed patriot blood. In 1769 and 1770, men representing the British Crown had beaten her brother savagely, killed a ten-year-old boy, and shot five Bostonians, and none of these men received what Warren considered a fitting punishment. If, as American Whigs agreed, allegiance to the Crown went hand in hand with protection by the Crown, such incidents of bloodshed challenged Warren's patriotic confidence in the British monarchy as defender of rights and dispenser of justice. Crown officers, acting in the king's name, had seemingly declared war on the people they were sworn to protect. If the king would not protect the colonists against his own men, the colonists would have to protect themselves. By spring 1772, Warren concluded that bloodshed by Crown government justified defensive force against Crown government.

Warren published the first installment of *The Adulateur* three weeks after Ebenezer Richardson was released from jail. The Boston Massacre—infamous throughout the colonies and across the Atlantic—figures only dimly in *The Adulateur* as an anticipated calamity. Central to the play's narrative, by contrast, is the murder of a boy called Seider by a man named Ebenezer.

Notably they are the only two characters in the play whose names are not changed from their real-world counterparts. Richardson's killing of a child, and Hutchinson's attainment of a pardon for the killer from the British Crown, seared Warren to the core. More than anything, this little remembered incident in Massachusetts history estranged her from provincial Crown government and drove her to political action as a literary activist. One may speculate reasonably that the incident was so compelling for Warren because, as the mother of five sons, she felt a peculiar horror at the wrongful killing of a little boy and the moral failure of men in power to avenge it. In *The Adulateur*, she would use her pen in place of the sword to gain justice for Christopher Seider, the massacre victims, her brother, her family, and her country.

Purporting to be excerpts submitted to advertise a stage performance overseas, Warren's *Adulateur* took the form of two short "dramatic sketches" published in the March 26 and April 23 issues of *The Massachusetts Spy*. The *Adulateur* was published with no author given, and its attack on Hutchinson and his allies was set in an unspecified era in the land of "Upper Servia." Commentators on Warren's *Adulateur* have described this setting as "mythical," "fictional," and "imaginary," but "Servia" is an alternate spelling of Serbia. "Upper Servia" is a sub-region of Serbia, lying between two tributaries of the Morava River, and the seat of a late medieval Christian uprising against Ottoman Turkish rule. Warren described her arch-villain as "the Bashaw of Servia" and his military henchman as the "Captain Bashaw," and she called the courtroom in which a corrupt judge presides a "Divan" (an Ottoman judicial chamber). This comparison of Massachusetts under Crown rule with Turkish-occupied Serbia—and, by extension, of the British Empire with the Ottoman Empire—was itself profoundly subversive.[23]

As the principal newspaper for the Sons of Liberty, *The Massachusetts Spy* had faced threats of prosecution from Governor Hutchinson before, and Warren took care to immunize herself and the newspaper against a charge of seditious libel. In addition to publishing anonymously and setting the play in a distant land, she disguised her targets with fictional names. Her heroes are Cassius and Marcus, named for classical Roman heroes (the assassin of Julius Caesar and the son of Cato). Warren restyled Francis Bernard and Thomas Hutchinson as Brundo and Rapatio. Meanwhile, the remaining villains have comically satirical English names: Andrew Oliver is Limpet (a spongy mollusk), Chief Justice Oliver is Chief Justice Hazelrod (a branch used for beatings), Thomas Flucker is Dupe, Justice Foster Hutchinson is Meagre, and Captain Gripeall is Admiral John Montagu, a British naval officer much hated in New England for his seizure of merchant ships. The last antagonist, "Ebenezer, a friend to Government," is the undisguised Richardson. If providing foreign or buffoonish names served to provide Warren deniability in her criticism of Massachusetts' ruling faction, the real-world referents of these characters were unmistakable to Warren's readers within the political context of the time[24]

Long criticized by Otis for political avarice, Hutchinson is depicted in *The Adulateur* as a rapacious despot, and the other provincial officers as his "myrmidons." In a soliloquy, Bashaw Rapatio ponders how "from my youth ambition's path I trod,/. . . and lust of power is still my darling lust,/Despotic rule by first, my sovereign wish." A collaborator with the Turks, he is approaching the completion of a long-term conspiracy to enslave "Servia's freeborn sons,/Destroy their boasted rights," subjugate his "native land,/And revel on its spoils!" Rapatio is aided in his "deep-laid schemes" by a "venal herd" of office-holding lackies, corrupted through the bashaw's patronage, who flatter and serve him. For example, on encountering Chief Justice Hazelrod, Warren's caricature of Peter Oliver, Rapatio greets him as "My friend, my brother, or still dearer name,/Thou firm abettor of my grand design,/Thy sanction now will cover what the world call *crimes*." Hazelrod is said to preside as judge over "the Star-Chamber," the judicial chamber commemorated by Macaulay as an engine of tyranny in King Charles I's reign.[25]

True to her Whig view of history as a struggle between virtue and corruption, liberty and power, Warren's *Adulateur* pits Rapatio against a freedom-loving citizenry. An homage to James Otis, Jr., the "virtuous senator" Cassius weeps for his "poor country" in a soliloquy, crying out that he "would have fought for thee,/And emptied ev'ry vein" if it would prevent the triumph of despotism. The previous bashaw Brundo (Governor Bernard) prepared "manacles" for Servia, and Cassius despairs that "Cruel Rapatio, with more fatal arts,/Has fix'd, has rivetted them beyond redress." In the absence of legal redress, Cassius concludes that the only way to stop the bashaw from consolidating total power is through his violent overthrow. "Servia's virtuous sons," he says, will "execrate" Rapatio as a "shameless tyrant" for seeking to "enslave/A gen'rous, free and independent people." But Cassius is not yet ready to organize insurrection against Rapatio and his henchmen, instead appealing to God to "crush, crush these vipers,/Who singled out by a community/To guard their rights—shall for a grasp of oar [ore]/Or paltry office, sell them to the foe." While Warren provided legitimation for the violent overthrow of Hutchinson as a "tyrant" and a "viper," the hero of her play ended the first installment hoping for divine intervention rather than plotting revolution.[26]

In the second installment of *The Adulateur*, Warren presented the character of Ebenezer in a jail cell, awaiting execution for killing a child named Seider. Rapatio had promised him "honors, places, pensions" in return for killing the bashaw's opponents. Ebenezer soliloquizes that Rapatio guaranteed a pardon if he would "glut *your* vengeance, for the cause was *yours*/On weeping innocence." Warren represented her villain Ebenezer as a tool in Rapatio's hands, indirectly blaming the Hutchinson faction for the death of Christopher Seider. In a satire of Oliver's defense of Richardson at trial, Chief Justice Hazelrod visits Ebenezer in his cell and informs him that his judges approved of the child's murder. "When Seider bled/We snuff'd the rich perfume.—The groans of youth/Gods! they were music in our ears," and Hazelrod vows that the jury verdict will soon be negated with a pardon. Rapatio will release Ebenezer soon to play his grisly part, "Again with pleasing scenes of blood and carnage,/To glut *our* vengeance." Hazelrod's fellow judges are part of Rapatio's conspiracy to "crush the friends of Freedom, extirpate/The dear remains of Virtue, and like Nero,/At one dread blow to massacre his millions." Implying that the Boston Massacre was part of a British plot to subdue Boston, Warren attributed to her fictionalized Hutchinson a plan to slaughter the populace.[27]

As for Warren in March 1772, it is the pardon of a child-murderer which prompts the play's protagonist to take action against a despotic regime. Cassius is horrified to learn of the impending release of Seider's killer from jail. "To see the Patriot/Reeking in Gore excites the keenest pleasure" for Rapatio and his minions, he roars. Again addressing his "poor country," he asks, "when will it be,/When high-soul'd honour beats within our bosoms,/ And calls to action; when thy sons, like heroes,/Shall dare assert thy rights, and with their swords,/Like men, like freemen, pave a way to conquest,/Or on thy ruins gloriously expire." Cassius had already acknowledged that the violent overthrow of the regime was justified, but now he accepts personal responsibility for taking revolutionary action. He urges the "young patriot" Marcus, "When I am gone, as soon perhaps I may be," to remember that the time may "soon arrive, when murders, blood and carnage/Shall crimson all these streets. . . forbid it Heaven!" But in this bloody struggle, Cassius hopes, "may these monsters find their glory fade,/Crush'd in the ruins they themselves have made." Alluding to the destruction of Samson along with his captors, Warren ended her second sketch on an uncertain note, with a chilling prediction of civil war which would claim both the righteous and the wicked.[28]

Warren wrote *The Adulateur* to assert the rightfulness and urgency of the Whigs' opposition to the Hutchinson administration at the time when their morale, and public support, was lowest. Following Hutchinson's consolidation of power and pardon of Richardson, she felt compelled by civic virtue to carry on her family's cause when her brother and father were no longer able to do so. Rather than offering another appeal to the intellect with dry arguments drawn from constitutional law or natural-rights philosophy, Warren adopted the literary form of drama. She applied the florid language of heroic tragedy to appeal directly to emotion, aiming to stoke her readers' resentments, remind them of their grievances, and move them to action. The play's repeated exhortation to "crush" Hutchinson, the Olivers, and their allies as "vipers" and "monsters" conveys the unfeigned vehemence of Warren's very personalized hatred for the ruling faction as traitors to Massachusetts and abettors in her brother's assault, Seider's death, and the Boston Massacre. Meanwhile, *The Adulateur* honored James Otis Jr., in the form of Cassius as an exemplar of civic virtue whom New Englanders should imitate in this time of crisis.

Indeed Warren's "Cassius" is the first appearance of the political revolutionary as a new heroic type in American drama. Through the rhetoric of Cassius, Warren claimed that violence against Hutchinson and his allies, and more generally the revolutionary overthrow of their corrupt regime, were morally legitimate, perhaps even obligatory. Justice required that honorable men take up the sword and fight to the death, even if liberty could not be restored. Warren's Cassius remained oblique about whether he was preparing an assassination of Rapatio, like his ancient Roman namesake, or organizing a large-scale revolt. He refrained from specifying just when the time would be for patriots to draw the sword and take action. *The Adulateur* fell just short of being an incitement to violence.

The Adulateur was not only one of the earliest examples of political writing by an American woman, it was one of the first public defenses of armed resistance to a provincial Crown government during the Imperial Crisis. Acting from her civic roles as a radical Whig and Massachusetts patriot and her gender roles as a sister, mother, and loyal member of the Otis family, Warren produced her first published writing in response to her brother's beating and mental collapse, the killing of seven Bostonians (including a boy and an adolescent), Hutchinson's centralization of power and the decline of the Whig opposition to it, and the pressing need for bold intellectual leadership in Otis's absence. *The Adulateur* was Warren's response to the crisis of the moment, and it must be interpreted in the context of the events of 1769 to 1772. But Warren continued writing as the Imperial Crisis took new forms, and *The Adulateur* was only the first in a cycle of three plays. Published in two editions of the *Boston Gazette* in 1773, her play *The Defeat* described the downfall of Rapatio at the hands of Cassius and other patriots based on James Warren, John Adams, John Hancock, and other Whig leaders. Early in 1775, she completed a final installment called *The Group* in response to the Coercive Acts and the military re-occupation of Boston, but war broke out before she could publish it. She then turned her attention to research for a complete history of the war, aspiring to be a historian like the illustrious Catharine Macaulay.[29]

Unfolding political events, interpreted within the framework of her political convictions, account for Warren's conviction that her plays would be a public service. The question remains, however, as to why Warren thought that she should respond to the Imperial Crisis by personally entering public political debate. Taking up her fallen brother's cause was certainly a motive. Considering the taboo against political commentary by women, however, it is curious that Warren did not leave that task to her husband and the other gentleman-politicians whom she honored as patriotic heroes in *The Defeat* and *The Group*. March 1772 was not exactly a Joan of Arc moment, in which Mercy Warren would have felt compelled to take action herself due to male inaction or incompetence. Warren reached the conclusion that it was fitting for herself—despite being a married woman of genteel rank—to enter politics as a literary activist alongside and in support of the existing Whig political leadership.

It seems likely that she reached this unorthodox conclusion thanks to the personal example of Catharine Macaulay, whom Warren knew as a politically engaged woman of scholarly accomplishment and transatlantic prestige, admired by Whigs throughout the British Empire. In September 1767, the *Boston Gazette* advertised for sale an "elegant Edition of Mr. Macaulay's History of England." With release of the controversial fourth edition of her *History* early in 1769, and growing conflict over the Townshend Acts, there could be no mistaking this author as "Mr. Macaulay." As the transatlantic crisis deepened after 1769, "Macaulay was increasingly celebrated as the incarnation of liberty," according to philosopher Karen Green, "and as the foremost champion of the natural rights of humanity." Although a woman publishing on politics in her own name, Macaulay won esteem from the colonial Whig leadership for the merit and ambition of her scholarship, the Whiggishness of her historic interpretation, and the zeal of her pro-American sympathies. In his first letter to her (August 9, 1770), John Adams praised Macaulay as "one of the brightest ornaments, not only of her Sex, but of her age and Country." Macaulay demonstrated to both men and women the measure of accomplishment and approval possible for an educated, intellectually ambitious woman within the male political world.[30]

In the summer of 1773, Adams forwarded to Macaulay a letter from Mercy Warren, whom he honored in similar terms as "one of the ornaments of her Sex in the Country, and not the less amiable, for being attentive to public affairs, and a Friend to Liberty." He also introduced her as the wife of patriot leader James Warren and sister of "your Friend Mr Otis of Boston who has Sacrificed himself his Fortune & family in the Cause of his Country." In her letter of June 9, 1773, Warren offered thanks to Macaulay for her previous attention to Otis and indicated that her "bosom has been long warmed with affection and respect for your distinguished literary career." She vented her outrage at Britain for "making illegal encroachments on her loyal subjects, and by every despotic measure urging these populous, brave, and extensive colonies, to a vigorous union in defence of their invaded rights." Warren went so far as to predict, if Britain did not change its policies, the outbreak of war between Britain and the colonies. Evoking the spirit of *The Adulateur*, she prayed that "Heaven may yet avert the dread calamity of Civil War; and prevent the sad alternative of either bowing beneath the *bands* of slavery or of repurchasing our plundered rights by the blood of the virtuous citizens." Like Otis and Adams, Warren hoped to have some impact on public opinion in London through correspondence with Macaulay. By making clear that Americans were prepared to fight for their liberty, perhaps civil war could be averted.[31]

Warren's early correspondence with Macaulay is suggestive of her new thinking about the political role of women. In the first letter, she asked if the "Genius of Liberty which once pervaded the bosom of each British hero" has "forsaken that devoted Island," or if she has "only concealed her lovely form" until such time as she will reappear to "lift her avenging hand to the terror of every arbitrary despot and to the confusion of their impious minions on each side of the Atlantic." Macaulay answered that, as the Coercive Acts of 1774 indicated, liberty was in full retreat in Britain. The civic virtue which eighteenth-century Britons considered necessary for the preservation of liberty was, as historian Ruth Bloch explained, "male public spirit," the "willingness of citizens to engage actively in civic life and to sacrifice individual interests for the common good." By law and convention, women could not exercise civic virtue by casting ballots, holding office, or holding forth on the assembly floor, like James Otis and James Sawbridge. But Macaulay had shown how women could serve as public advocates for liberty through political writing.[32] If civic-minded women could not bear arms on the town green or the battlefield, Macaulay had shown how they could write in defense of armed resistance, as she had done in her vivid description of Charles I's downfall. It is suggestive of Warren's new thinking about civic virtue for women that, in her letter to Macaulay, she personified liberty as a goddess who is "lovely" and feminine but not gentle or retiring. Liberty is a warlike goddess: an avenger of violated rights and a terror to despots. Warren could not "lift her avenging hand" against Robinson, Richardson, Bernard, Hutchinson, or the other enemies of her family, town, and country, but she could inspire the appeal to arms by appealing to the hearts of men through emotionally charged literature.

Warren's response to Macaulay's 1774 letter adapted civic virtue and patriotism to her sex through passionate advocacy of armed resistance, in the same spirit as *The Adulateur*. As British expeditionary forces descended upon Boston to enforce the Coercive Acts, she interpreted the current crisis as another episode in the world-historical struggle between virtue and corruption, liberty and power. Warren's letter of December 1774 assured Macaulay that "America Stands Armed with Resolution & Virtue" against the Crown's policy of subjugation. America "still Recoils at the thought of Drawing the sword" against the mother country, however, and Warren expressed hope that the next Parliament would favor reconciliation. But if members of the Commons remained "the Dupes of Venality and Corruption," "they will soon see the Genius which once Animated their Hambdens, Haringtons, & Pyms, has taken up for Residence on their Distant shores." Like Macaulay in her *History of England*, Warren held up the Parliamentarians and commonwealthmen of the 1640s as an inspiring example of English resistance to royal tyranny. Warren boasted of the "united Millions ready to Pour out the Warm Blood as a Libation at the Shrine of Freedom Ere they would submit to become the slaves of arbitrary power." The time was fast approaching, it seemed, that Cassius would need to answer the call to action.[33]

In developing a concept of female patriotism, though, Warren took care to balance the language of civic virtue, armed resistance, and blood sacrifice with that of feminine sensibility. Macaulay, after all, had endured from British moderate Whigs the criticism of displaying "a troubling feminine bellicosity" in her unsympathetic depiction of Charles I's execution. It was not with relish, Warren made clear to Macaulay and the London radicals, that she trumpeted the necessity and justice of preparations for war against Britain. She foresaw America as "an Innocent Land drenched in Blood" in which civilians like herself would have to flee "plundered cities," "taking refuge in the forests." Warren anticipated that she might well have to make a sacrifice not only of domestic tranquility but of her family blood. With America and Britain standing at the brink of war, "none can wonder that a timid Woman should tremble for the consequences, more Especially one who is connected by the tenderest tie to a Gentleman whose principles & Conduct in this province may Expose him to fall an Early Victim." Her feminized brand of civic virtue was gendered in its poignant homage to marriage, domesticity, and peace, but at the same time radically Whiggish in its threat of military force and offer of a libation of blood—even that of her cherished husband—to "the Shrine of Freedom."[34]

By December 29, 1774, only a few months from the outbreak of war, Warren was ready to act on the proposition she communicated in her 1772 play. Armed revolt against Crown rule was morally justified, and she would support it with firmness, as a literary political activist in peacetime, and as a Spartan wife and mother in wartime. Warren embraced the legitimacy of revolutionary violence against provincial Crown government well ahead of most Boston radicals. She reached this conclusion in reaction to the physical assault on and mental collapse of James Otis, the Boston Massacre, the killing of Christopher Seider and pardon of his killer, the centralization of power by the Hutchinson-Oliver faction, and the resulting low state of Whig morale. The example of Catharine Macaulay, as much as the example of James Otis, inspired Warren to take the next step and respond to these developments by entering public debate. In the years between publication of *The Adulateur* and the outbreak of war, Warren began developing a concept of civic virtue which would empower elite women to participate in politics while keeping traditional gender roles ostensibly intact. Even before the Revolutionary War began, she was a *"rebel lady"*—while taking care not to lose the "lady" in the "rebel."

NOTES

1. Mercy Otis Warren to Catharine Macaulay, February 11, 1777, in Richards and Harris, eds., 2009, 92–93, 95. For Macaulay's failure to receive Warren's wartime letters, see Green, ed. 2020, 158n. For Macaulay's fear of arrest due to intercepted correspondence, see Davies 2005, 11–12, 139–40. For examples of Warren's fear of the British threat to her husband's life, see Warren to Hannah Quincy Lincoln, September 3, 1774, and Warren to Catharine Macaulay, December 29, 1774, in Green, ed., 2020, 34, 39.

2. For *The Adulateur* as the first political play of the Revolutionary era, see Shaffer 2006, 3–4, 7–9.

3. Warren 1989, I: 3; the spelling "Cesar" is in the original. For the fullest account of Warren's theory of history, see Cohen 1980.

4. John Adams, "A Dissertation on the Feudal Law," No. 1, August 12, 1765, in Taylor et al, eds., 1977, 1:111–12; Abigail Adams to John Adams, November 5, 1775, in Butterfield et al, eds., 1:321; errors of spelling and punctuation are in the original.

5. For the best short overview of the political career of James Otis, see Richard Samuelson, "The Life, Times, and Political Writings of James Otis," in Otis 2015, vii-xv.

6. Griffin 2017, 115–17, 119–21, 124–31, 142–48; Hinderaker 2017, 54–56, 69–71, 73; Carp 2007, 43–50; Zobel 1970, 62–63, 69–76, 80–81, 94, 99. For the thesis that Otis, Samuel Adams, and other Boston radicals plotted armed insurrection in the fall of 1768, see Miller 1934.

7. Macaulay 1769, 415–20; Davies 2005, 147–49; Green 2020, 83–86.

8. Green 2020, 79–80; Catharine Macaulay to James Otis, Jr., 27 April 1769, in Green, ed., 2020, 98 (errors of spelling are in the original); the *Boston Chronicle*, June 19, 1769, 195. For other examples of the reprint of this report, see the *Essex Gazette* (Salem, Massachusetts), June 20, 1769, the *Boston News-Letter*, June 12, 1769, the *Providence Gazette, and Country Journal* (Providence, Rhode Island), June 24, 1769, the *Boston Gazette and Country Journal*, June 26, 1769, the *New York Gazette or Weekly Post-Boy*, June 26, 1769, the *New York Journal or General Advertiser*, July 6, 1769, and the *Georgia Gazette* (Savannah, Georgia), July 26, 1769.

9. James Otis to Catharine Macaulay, July 27, 1769, in Green, ed., 2020, 98–101.

10. Otis to Macaulay, July 27, 1769 in Green, ed., 2020, 101; *Boston Gazette, and Country Journal* (September 4, 1769), 2; Tyler, 1986, 91–92.

11. *Boston Gazette, and Country Journal* (September 4, 1769), 2.

12. Zagarri 2015 [1995], 52–53; Zobel 1970, 147–50; Archer 2010, 155–57.

13. Mercy Otis Warren to James Otis, Jr., [c. September 10, 1769], in Richards and Harris, eds., 2009, 203.

14. Warren to Otis, [c. 10 September 1769], in Richards and Harris, eds., 2009, 4; Zagarri 2015 [1995], 55.

15. Adams 1950, 2:226; Sarah Prince Gill to Catharine Macaulay, December 8, 1769, in Green, ed., 2020, 95; Gill to Macaulay, March 24 [1770], in Green, ed., 2020, 96–97.

16. Archer 2010, 149, 178–79.

17. Archer 2010, 179–81; Zobel 1970, 172–79; Carp 2007, 52. For Christopher Seider's age, see *Boston1775.com*, May 24, 2006, at http://boston1775.blogspot.com/2006/05/christopher-seider-shooting-victim.html.

18. Zobel 1970, 222–26.

19. Zobel 1970, 228, 240; Weales 1979:105–106; *Boston Gazette*, April 11, 1763. For the debate on royal salaries for Massachusetts officials, see Bushman 1992 [1985], 172–75; *Boston Gazette*, April 11, 1763, 2.

20. *Boston Gazette*, March 16, 1772, 3.

21. Pierce, ed., 1895, 74–75. For insights into Otis's 1770 mental breakdown, see *Boston1775.com*, May 8, 2020, at http://boston1775.blogspot.com/2020/05/after-james-otis-behaved-very-madly.html?utm_source=feedburner&utm_medium=email&utm_campaign=Feed%3A+Boston1775+%28Boston+1775%29.

22. Richards and Harris, eds., 2009, xiv, 3–4; Mercy Otis Warren to Sarah Walter Hesilrige, [c. December 1773], in idem, 21; Hosmer 1972 [1896], 221–24; Zagarri 2015 [1995] 50, 54–55.

23. Zagarri 2015 [1995], 57; Nussbaum 2013, 267; Shalev 2009, 66; Shalev 2015:7, at http://journals.openedition.org/transatlantica/7713; Weales 1979, 109–110. For the location and history of "Upper Servia," see King 1885, 671.

24. York 1995:102–103; *Massachusetts Spy*, March 26, 1772, 15; *Massachusetts Spy*, April 23, 1772, 32; Warren, "Plays and Poetry." Note that this Houghton manuscript is written in the hand of Warren's son, James Warren, Jr., in his capacity as amanuensis; it is a verbatim copy of the original manuscript, located in the Mercy Otis Warren Papers, Massachusetts Historical Society, Boston, Massachusetts.

25. *Massachusetts Spy*, March 26, 1772, 15; Warren, "Plays and Poetry," 1.

26. *Massachusetts Spy*, March 26, 1772, 15; Warren, "Plays and Poetry," 1, 5.

27. *Massachusetts Spy*, April 23, 1772, 32.

28. *Massachusetts Spy*, April 23, 1772, 32.

29. For a brief review of Warren's pre-war political plays, see Shaffer 2006, 7–10.

30. Zagarri 2015 [1995], 56; Green, ed., 2020, 150; *Boston Gazette and Country Journal*, September 14, 1767, 3; Green 2020, 86; John Adams to Catharine Macaulay, August 9, 1770, in Green, ed., 2020, 115.

31. Adams to Macaulay, August 9, 1770, in Green, ed., 2020, 115 (errors of punctuation in the original); Mercy Otis Warren to Catharine Macaulay, June 9, 1773, in Green, ed., 2020, 150–51; Zagarri 2015 [1995], 56.

32. Warren to Macaulay, June 9, 1773, in Green, ed., 2020, 150; Macaulay to Warren, September 11, 1774, in Green, ed., 2020, 152; Bloch 1987: 38, 42–47, 56; see also Lewis 1987.

33. Warren to Macaulay, December 29, 1774, in Green, ed., 2020, 153–55 (errors of spelling in the original).

34. Davies 2005, 148–49.

REFERENCES

Adams, Charles Francis, ed. 1950. *Works of John Adams.* 2nd volume. Boston: Charles C. Little and James Brown.

Archer, Richard. 2010. *As If an Enemy's Country: The British Occupation of Boston and the Origins of Revolution.* Oxford and New York: Oxford University Press.

Bloch, Ruth. 1987. "The Gendered Meanings of Virtue in Revolutionary America." *Signs: The Journal of Women in Culture and Society* 13 (11): 37–58.

Boston Chronicle

Boston Gazette and Country Journal

Boston News-Letter.

Boston 1775. http://boston1775.blogspot.com

Bushman, Richard L. 1992. *King and People in Provincial Massachusetts.* Chapel Hill and London: University of North Carolina Press.

Butterfield, L. H., Wendell G. Garrett, and Marjorie E. Sprague, eds. 1963. *Adams Family Correspondence.* 13 volumes to date. Cambridge, MA: Harvard University Press.

Carp, Benjamin L. 2007. *Rebels Rising: Cities and the American Revolution.* Oxford and New York: Oxford University Press.

Cohen, Lester H. 1980. "Explaining the Revolution: Ideology and Ethics in Mercy Otis Warren's Historical Theory." *William and Mary Quarterly* 37 (2): 200–218.

Davies, Kate. 2005. *Catharine Macaulay and Mercy Otis Warren: The Revolutionary Atlantic and the Politics of Gender.* Oxford and New York: Oxford University Press.

Essex Gazette.

Georgia Gazette.

Green, Karen, ed. 2020. *The Correspondence of Catharine Macaulay.* Oxford and New York: Oxford University Press.

Green, Karen. 2020. *Catharine Macaulay's Republican Enlightenment.* Abingdon and New York: Routledge.

Griffin, Patrick. 2017. *The Townshend Moment: The Making of Empire and Revolution in the Eighteenth Century.* New Haven, CT: Yale University Press.

Hinderaker, Eric. 2017. *Boston's Massacre.* Cambridge, MA: Harvard University Press.

Hosmer, James K. 1972. *The Life of Thomas Hutchinson, Royal Governor of the Province of Massachusetts Bay.* New York: Da Capo Press.

King, Edward. 1885. *Descriptive Portraiture of Europe in Storm and Calm.* Springfield, MA: C. A. Nichols.

Lewis, Jan. 1987. "The Republican Wife: Virtue and Seduction in the Early Republic," *William and Mary Quarterly* 44 (4): 689–721.

Macaulay, Catharine. 1769. *The History of England, from the Accession of James I to That of the Brunswick Line.* 4th volume. London: Nourse, Dodsley, and Johnson.

Massachusetts Spy.

Miller, John C. 1934. "The Massachusetts Convention, 1768." *New England Quarterly* 7 (3): 445–474.

New York Journal or General Advertiser

New York Gazette or Weekly Post-Boy

Nussbaum, Martha C. 2013. "Friends, Romans, and Lovers: Political Love and the Rule of Law in *Julius Caesar*." *Shakespeare and the Law: A Conversation among Disciplines and Professions.* Edited by Bradin Cormack, Martha C. Nussbaum, and Richard Strier. Chicago and London: University of Chicago Press.

Otis, James. 2015. *Collected Political Writings of James Otis.* Edited by Richard Samuelson. Indianapolis: Liberty Fund.

Pierce, Edward L., ed. 1895. "Extracts from John Rowe's Diary, 1764-1779," *Proceedings of the Massachusetts Historical Society* (March 1895): 11–108.

Providence Gazette, and Country Journal

Richards, Jeffrey H. and Sharon M. Harris, eds. 2009. *Mercy Otis Warren: Selected Letters.* Athens and London: University of Georgia Press.

Shaffer, Jason. 2006. "Making 'An Excellent Die': Death, Mourning, and Patriotism in the Propaganda Plays of the American Revolution." *Early American Literature* 41 (1): 1–27.

Shalev, Eran. 2009. *Rome Reborn on Western Shores: Historical Imagination and the Creation of the American Republic.* Charlottesville: University of Virginia Press.

Idem. 2015. "Mercy Otis Warren, the American Revolution and the Classical Imagination," *Transatlantica* 2: 1–19. http://journals.openedition.org/transatlantica/7713.

Taylor, Robert J., Mary-Jo Kline, and Gregg L. Lint, eds. 1977. *Papers of John Adams.* 19 volumes to date. Cambridge, MA: Harvard University Press.

Tyler, John W. 1986. *Smugglers and Patriots: Boston Merchants and the Advent of the American Revolution.* Boston: Northeastern University Press.

Warren, Mercy Otis. 1989. *History of the Rise, Progress, and Termination of the American Revolution, Interspersed with Biographical, Political, and Moral Observations, in Two Volumes*, ed. Lester H. Cohen. Indianapolis: Liberty Fund.

Idem. [n.d.]. "Plays and Poetry." Manuscript (MS Am 1354.1). Houghton Library, Harvard University Libraries.

Weales, Gerald. 1979. "The Adulateur and How It Grew." *Library Chronicle* 43 (2): 103–133.

York, Neil L. 1995. "Tag-Team Polemics: The 'Centinel' and His Allies in the 'Massachusetts Spy'." *Proceedings of the Massachusetts Historical Society* 107: 85–114.

Zagarri, Rosemarie. 2015. *A Woman's Dilemma: Mercy Otis Warren and the American Revolution.* Chichester, UK: Wiley.

Zobel, Hiller B. 1970. *The Boston Massacre.* New York and London: W. W. Norton.

Chapter 7

Recovering the Native Origins of Dartmouth College through *The Occom Circle*

Ivy Schweitzer (Dartmouth College)

First, it is important to recognize that Dartmouth College is located on the traditional territory of the Abenaki people, who were its stewards for many centuries, until they were forced to flee north into Canada by European wars and rampant settlement. There is no Abenaki reservation in the United States and no treaty ceding these lands or approving that settlement. The recently renovated Hood Museum of Art at Dartmouth College includes on its new front door a "land acknowledgment," the first statement of its kind to appear on an official Dartmouth building. It reads: "The Hood Museum of Art at Dartmouth is situated upon the ancestral and unceded lands of the Abenaki people. This acknowledgment reminds us of the significance of place, the continued existence of Indigenous peoples, and the museum and Dartmouth's commitment to building respectful relationships with those who call these lands home today" (Silverstein 2019).

Land acknowledgments are delicate gestures of recognition, reconciliation, and reality. According to Métis scholar âpihtawikosisân, they are meant to be "sites of potential disruption" in the sense that they attest to the discomfort of Indigenous people who, at best, have been treated as guests on their ancestral lands, and produce discomfort in non-Indigenous people who have to confront Indigenous priority and come to terms with their own place on others' territory. Furthermore, such acknowledgments can become pro-forma and empty if they do not recognize the present, ongoing reality of colonialism and seek to address it with action. Then, "they can be transformative acts that to some extent undo Indigenous erasure" (âpihtawikosisân 2016).[1] The Hood Museum has acted on the words of its acknowledgment by hiring an associate curator of Native American Art to foreground its Native holdings. It has also started a program of internships to train Native and non-Native graduate and undergraduate students as curators of Native art. This program seeds the pipeline of professionals who can, potentially, change the attitudes and content of museums to better reflect the past, present and future of Native existence and artistic achievement (Office of Communications 2018).

Still, as a gesture of respect for the Abenaki people, I would like to encourage us to view the Hood's acknowledgment from a Native perspective. Arthur Hanchett, who works at Dartmouth College, is also a council member of the Koasek Band of the Sovereign Abenaki Nation, which was officially recognized by the state of Vermont only as recently as 2012. Hanchett responded to the Hood Museum's gesture by saying that the Abenaki "approved" of the acknowledgment and elaborated: "The sentiment attests a commitment everlasting that Dartmouth thrives upon the land of the Abenaki people." This carefully worded recognition of hospitality quietly but firmly asserts that the land remains Abenaki and that Dartmouth is a tolerated, if welcomed, guest (Silverstein 2019).

But the Abenaki do not figure in Dartmouth's origin story, which, as Steven Pincus argues elsewhere in this volume, is part of what he calls "the project of the imperial state." Other Indigenous people do, but often in supporting roles. It has been one of my professional and political missions to bring an awareness of the centrality of Native literature and culture to my field of Early American studies, in order to amend history and, thus, to influence our future. In that decolonizing spirit, I offer this sketch of the *Native* origins of the founding of Dartmouth College, which often go unrecognized or are represented through the distorting lens of myth.[2] To do so, I will use the life and work of Samson Occom (1723–1792), a Mohegan leader, activist, and public intellectual, and I will introduce *The Occom Circle*, http://www.dartmouth.edu/occom/, a digital resource I created with a team at Dartmouth College and launched in 2016 that facilitates further research into these occluded events. This exploration demonstrates how these origins served both the designs of the imperial state in the founding of an elite institution and the survival needs and threatened sovereignty of the region's Native Tribes. Furthermore, it shows that the suppression, cooptation and belittlement of Native sovereignty, even existence, was and still is a tactic of the imperial state.

It is instructive to begin with popular images, which often contain equal amounts of facts and fictions. The latter is often born of a desire for how the present wants to imagine the past. One popular rendition of the founding of Dartmouth College takes the form of a toby jug (to be distinguished from a "mug" by those in the know), commissioned in 1998 by Steve Mullins, a member of the Dartmouth class of 1954 and curator of the American Toby Jug Museum in Evanston, Illinois (https://www.tobyjugmuseum.com/) as a gift for his class.

It features the Reverend Eleazar Wheelock, a Congregational minister and the founder of Dartmouth College, as the vessel of the jug, with Samson Occom, a Mohegan Indian and his famous first Native student, as the handle. This placement literalizes the notion of Natives in a "supporting role." The jug features four other iconic items relevant to the myth of the college's founding, which I will discuss below. This fascinating object sold like hotcakes, according to Mullins, who presented one to retiring President James Friedman, who was himself a collector and collected toby jugs (Mullins 2014).

Let's look at these two major actors in our origin story. Born in 1711 in Windham, Connecticut, Wheelock attended Yale, experienced the "Great Awakening" of religious revivals, and became the popular pastor of the Second Congregational Church of Lebanon, CT.[3] But Wheelock's New Lights

Figure 7.1. Toby Jug, 1998. *Ivy Schweitzer.*

enthusiasm lost him his salary and he began taking in and tutoring students in what became his "Latin School."[4] One of these students was Samson Occom, the eighteen-year-old son of a Mohegan council member. Occom came to live and study with Wheelock in late 1743 and proved to be a brilliant student, mastering Latin and Greek and some Hebrew. But weak eyesight prevented him from matriculating at Yale. In 1749, he moved to Long Island where for twelve years he served as an effective teacher and missionary to the Montaukett people, married, and started what would be a large family.[5]

From this successful educational experiment with Occom, Wheelock formulated a plan to establish a school to educate Native boys to become schoolteachers and missionaries to their people and a "female school," as he called it, to educate Native girls as their wives and helpmates. Wheelock was progressive for his time in that he accepted girls into his school, though they studied a separate, less academic and more domestic curriculum taught by his sister, and he combined his Indian School with the Latin School, which enrolled English youth, making this one of the earliest intercultural and coeducational schools in the colonies.

Still, Wheelock held some of his age's prejudices about Indian inferiority. In 1756, for example, he wrote to Andrew Oliver, an influential Boston merchant, politician and member of several funding societies, seeking support for the Indian school. As evidence of the school's success, Wheelock alluded to aid given to him for Occom's education by the New England Company, a powerful missionary society. About Occom's subsequent mission to the Montauketts, he wrote: "I was not a little Encouraged in the affair by the Success of the Endeavors I [had] by the Assistance of the Honorable Commissioners in ye Education of Samson Occom who had been useful to them beyond what could have been Reasonably expected of an English Man & less than half of ye Expence" (Wheelock 1756).[6] Wheelock recognized, as he argues to Oliver, that English missionaries faced "mighty . . . prejudices" by not knowing Indian languages or customs. They needed interpreters, at additional trouble and expense. Furthermore, educating Indian children as missionaries, he argued, would give Tribes "the most convincing Proofs & Demonstrations of the sincerity of Our Intentions" (Wheelock 1756). Best of all, as he concluded, it could be done at cut rate. In his "Autobiographical Narrative, Second Draft" penned in 1768, Occom complained bitterly about how poorly he was paid for his missionary labors, compared to the pay of English missionaries. He blamed the difference on the racism of his employers (Occom 1768, ms. 768517; J. Brooks 58).

The first Indian students arrived for schooling in Lebanon, Connecticut in 1754, and for the next two decades, Wheelock pursued what he called his "great design." He regarded this as a sacred calling of some personal and national urgency. In another letter written in 1756, "To the Sachems and Chiefs of the Mohawk, Oneida, Tuscarora, and other nations and tribes of Indians," he admitted that, since he was a boy, "I have had you upon my heart," pitying what he saw as the Indians' "worldly poverty" and, most of all, "the perishing case your precious souls are in, without the knowledge of the only true God and Savior of sinners" (Wheelock 1756a in McClure and Parish, 259). In full settler-colonial mode, Wheelock saw his Indian school as an answer to *his* prayers. Furthermore, in an account of the Indian School published in 1763, Wheelock disclosed that he established the School because he felt compelled "to clear myself, and Family, of partaking in the public Guilt of our Land and Nation in such a Neglect of them," the Indians. He dedicated most of his life and his personal fortune to that end (Wheelock 1763, 14).

Wheelock was also responding to the escalating conflicts in Indian country. From the beginning of the French and Indian War in 1754 to Dartmouth's founding in 1769 and beyond, British colonial settlement exploded out of the narrow strip of the original colonies along the eastern seaboard. After 1763, Indian nations resorted to armed defense of their lands, which resulted in violence and major land cessions from the Haudenosaunee (Iroquois) Confederacy in the Treaty of Fort Stanwix. This land grant divided northern and southern tribes, weakening Native resistance to English colonizing and depredations. Always concerned with the bottom line, Wheelock argued in his *Narrative* of 1763 that "the instructed and civilized Party [of Indians] would have been a far better Defense than all our expensive Fortresses, and prevented the laying waste of so many Towns and Villages" (Wheelock 1763, 11). Notice that he is concerned with the loss of English life not Native territory.

Looking to expand his school and make it more permanent with a charter, Wheelock and his supporters hit on the idea of sending Occom, who by this time was living with his large family in Mohegan, Connecticut, to go "begging," as they called it, for donations in Europe. They came to realize that an Indian minister, reclaimed from savagery and speaking like an English gentleman on behalf of the school, would be a sensational enticement to giving and a fine advertisement for the school's accomplishments. So calculated the Rev. Charles Jeffrey Smith, one of Wheelock's most trusted advisors, in a letter to his friend dated March 30, 1764: "When the Indian War is a little abated would it not be best to Send Mr. Occom with another Person home a begging? An Indian minister in England might get a Bushel of Money for the School" (Smith 1764).

In December 1765, Occom crossed the Atlantic, accompanied by Nathaniel Whitaker, a pastor of a church in Norwich, Connecticut, and close associate of Wheelock's. They set up in London at the home of George Whitefield, the leading evangelical minister and no mean fundraiser himself. Occom preached to often enormous and admiring crowds in London and across England and Scotland; he was even mimicked on the London stage. After two and a half years, they raised the staggering sum of nearly £12,000, the equivalent of $2 million today, including two hundred pounds from King George and fifty very important pounds from the Earl of Dartmouth. The trip was, to all intents and purposes, a huge success.

But when Occom returned to Connecticut in 1769, he found that Wheelock had moved his base of operations to New Hampshire, where he had finally secured a royal charter from the young royal governor, John Wentworth, to establish what he now called a "College." Because of a series of developments, recounted in fascinating detail by historian Jere Daniell, Wheelock's plans had "evolved," as we now say. In fact, he came to believe that his educational efforts had largely failed to "purge all the Indian" out of his Native students, as he expressed his objective in a letter to a correspondent (Wheelock 1764, Dartmouth ms. 764560.1). When they left his tutelage and returned to their Tribes as missionaries, they tended to "revert," in his mind, to Native ways (Daniell 1969, 28). Because of this, Wheelock decided to focus his energies on educating English missionaries in his new "College." They could be paired with Indian teachers and interpreters, who had no need of college-level education. But in order to use the large sums collected by Occom and Whitaker, now overseen by a wary "Trust" in England and an even warier Society in Scotland for Propagating Christian Knowledge, Wheelock had to convince these overseers that the Indian School was somehow co-extensive with the new college.[7]

In the official "Dartmouth College Charter," we can see Wheelock maneuvering towards his new goal. He explains the move to New Hampshire by arguing:

> such a situation would be as convenient as any for carrying on the great design among the Indians; and also, considering, that without the least impediment to the said design, the same school may be enlarged and improved to promote learning among the English, and be a means to supply a great number of churches and congregations which are likely soon to be formed in that new country, with a learned and orthodox ministry (Wheelock 1769).

In the section of the Charter Daniell calls "the formal statement of purpose," Wheelock reinforces this impression of co-existence when he declares the purpose of the College to be: "for the education and instruction of youth of the Indian tribes in this land in reading, writing, and all parts of learning which shall appear necessary and expedient for civilizing and christianizing children of pagans, as well as in all liberal arts and sciences, and also of English youth and any others" (Wheelock 1769). But, as Daniell shows, this is the wording of the *final* draft. In the first draft, Wheelock initially reversed the order of the objects of his attention. The passage reads, "for the education & instruction of Youths of the English and also of the Indian Tribes . . ." (Daniell 1969, 29).

By foregrounding Indian education in his list of objectives in the final draft, Wheelock was sending a message to the men who controlled the funds raised by Occom in Europe. In reality, only two Indians accompanied the Wheelocks on their move up north to New Hampshire. Then, in January of 1769, the Oneida Tribe withdrew all of their children from the School because of Wheelock's harsh disciplinary methods and what they saw as his forcing their sons to do manual labor, like farming, rather than study academic subjects like reading and writing, which is what they wanted and Wheelock had promised.

This brings us to what I call "the break-up letter," a long and bitter missive Occom wrote to Wheelock on July 24, 1771, accusing Wheelock of betraying the original mission of the Indian School to educate Indians. A month later, Wheelock responded with denials and indignation. In fact, as Daniell details, Wheelock had lost faith in his design, complaining in letters to other correspondents about Indian backsliding once they returned to their homes (Daniell 1969, 29; Hoefnagel 2006, 26). After this exchange of letters, the long association between Wheelock and Occom cooled significantly. Wheelock established what became a flourishing educational institution, and Occom was remembered, if at all, as a footnote to this story, or, as embodied in the popular imagination of the toby jug, the "handle."

The imagery of this toby jug gives us further insight into the mythology of Dartmouth's origins, which, no matter how comic or entertaining, degrades its Native participants. This imagery draws on a popular drinking song composed by Richard Hovey, Dartmouth class of 1885, which is memorialized in the controversial Hovey Murals.

These murals were commissioned by Dartmouth President Ernest Hopkins and painted in 1938 by Walter Beach Humphrey, Dartmouth class of 1914, as a response to the Orozco Murals, which, when they were completed by the Mexican muralist in 1934, set off a firestorm of complaints for how they satirized American academic rituals and New England culture.

As an alternative, however, Humphrey's vision offers caricatures of Wheelock as well as the Natives he encounters. The first stanza of Hovey's song, which is printed at the bottom of the mural's first panel, sets the stage for the tale and what will become its iconic imagery:

Figure 7.2. Panel 1, Hovey Murals, 1938. *Trustees of Dartmouth College.*

> Oh, Eleazar Wheelock was a very pious man;
> He went into the wilderness to teach the Indian,
> With a Gradus ad Parnassum, a Bible and a drum,
> And five hundred gallons of New England rum (McGrath 2011, 21)

The four elements mentioned here figure prominently in the jug: the drum Wheelock carries, presumably to call the Indians to a gathering; the bible he reads as sign of his missionary intentions; the *Gradus ad Parnassum*, a book of Latin instruction he sits on, which was probably actually used at Wheelock's Latin School; and a keg of rum, which forms part of the handle behind Occom's head. In Humphrey's mural, this keg is enormous; its size humorously suggesting its relative importance in this origin myth and celebrated character of the college. The male Indians in the mural are depicted as savage or confused or drunk. The female Indians are topless and look like pin-ups; apparently their features were based on the faces of some of the faculty wives of the time.[8]

It is perhaps not surprising that these popular depictions of Dartmouth's origins include easily dismissed and denigrating representations of its founding Natives, given that Occom, a historical actor in this origin story, declined to visit Hanover and strongly denounced Dartmouth College's whiteness, as we will see.

Now, let's flip this history and look at it from Occom's perspective. Though the story goes that Occom's mother approached Wheelock to ask if he would educate her son, the context is crucial. That summer, upon his father's death, Occom became a tribal councilor and attended hearings on the Mohegan Land case held in Norwich, Connecticut. This complicated case began in 1640 when Uncas, Sachem of the Mohegans, entrusted a large tract of the Tribe's subsistence territory to the colony of Connecticut, to be overseen by major John Mason, a friend of the Tribe. For years, Mason's heirs resisted the Colony's claims to ownership of this land, and in the 18th century, as the colonists' hunger for land grew, the Mason heirs filed suits and petitions in the English courts against the Colony.

It is a strong possibility that Occom was in the room that summer of 1743 when William Bollen, attorney for the Mohegans, directly connected literacy and land dispossession. Bollen argued that the Colony exploited the Mohegans' illiteracy in English by composing several questionable treaties and transactions, which, he argued, the Colony "doubtless took care to express favorably for their own interest." Thus, the Colony disadvantaged the Mohegan Tribe by the very documents meant to insure the Indians' rights (L. Brooks 2008, 84). After attending these hearings, Occom came to realize that he could best serve the interests of his people and all Native peoples in the region by becoming fluent in English language and law and sharing those skills widely.[9]

This commitment is precisely what Wheelock failed to understand about Occom through their long association. While Wheelock labored to educate and convert Indians in order to deracinate and assimilate them to white Christian "civilization," Occom sought to gain and share the tools of resistance for a collective Native survival in an increasingly hostile white world. Occom never wavered in his commitment. But Wheelock could only ever understand Occom's strenuous activities through an ethnocentric and racist lens characteristic of his age.

For example, one of Wheelock's motivations for sending Occom abroad in 1765 was to curtail his efforts on behalf of the Mohegans in the Land Case. Earlier that year, the Connecticut Board of Commissioners reprimanded Occom for what they called his "ill conduct" and forced him to issue a "confession" in which he formally apologized for his participation in the case. Though he seemed outwardly to capitulate to their demands, in this confession Occom affirmed very strongly that he felt duty-bound to act on behalf of his people: "Although as a Member of the Mohegan Tribe, and, for many years, one of their Council, I thought I had not only a natural & civil Right, but that it was my Duty, to acquaint myself with their temporal Affairs" (Occom 1765; L. Brooks 2008, 97). Furthermore, Occom delayed his departure from England at the end of the fundraising trip for several weeks, in order to attend hearings on the case in London—despite knowing that his large family was in dire financial straits because Wheelock had not kept his promise to support them in Occom's absence.

Although the Crown ultimately decided the case in 1770 *against* the Mohegan Tribe, the resistance efforts it spawned gave Occom and the group of Native activists who fought it, many of them former students at Wheelock's school, vital experience in adapting the imperial technologies of knowledge, rhetoric, law, religion, and politics to their own purposes of communal resistance and survival. Likewise, though a tool of colonial experimentation, Wheelock's Indian School and the missionary efforts it sponsored became an important space for Natives across the region to make connections and share strategies. Quite unintentionally, Wheelock's school became part of a regional network of Native organizing, exchange, and resistance.[10]

The Occom Circle (http://www.dartmouth.edu/occom/) represents my attempt to revise the origin story and relative cultural values assigned to its major players by the toby jug. One of Dartmouth's first born-digital projects, *The Occom Circle* is a freely accessible digital edition of primary handwritten sources held in Dartmouth Libraries by and about Samson Occom. Dartmouth holds about half of Occom's known output of letters, journals, tribal documents, sermons, and hymns and all of the extensive Wheelock papers, which include letters and documents by many of the Native students at the Indian School, including the women. A large, cross-disciplinary group created the project, which was comprised of a project management team, a library team,

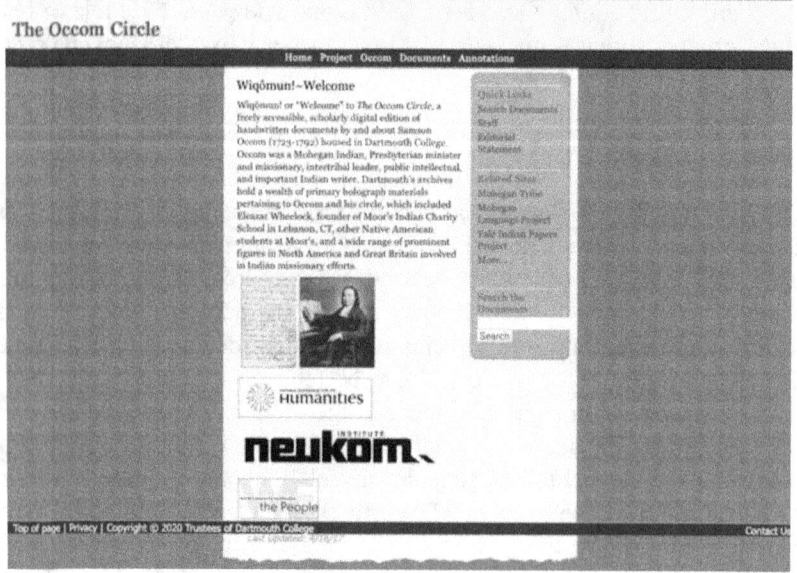

Figure 7.3. Home page, *The Occom Circle*, 2020. Trustees of Dartmouth College.

and a document management team. We also trained graduate and undergraduate students who served vital roles as transcribers and researchers.[11]

In envisioning this project, I took up the challenge of Lisa Brooks, a scholar of this early period and member of the Abenaki Tribe, who asks: "What happens when we put Native space at the center of America rather than merely striving for inclusion of minority viewpoints or viewing Native Americans as part of or on the periphery of America?" (L. Brooks 2008, xxxv.) Accordingly, our team structured the site in response to what Timothy Powell describes as "a post-Eurocentric paradigm," one that decenters dominant national and European perspectives in order to foreground Indigenous knowledge and illustrates "difference and conflict as well as commonality and community" (Powell 1998, 2).

In this spirit, *The Occom Circle* puts Occom at the center of a multicultural and international network of associations, of which Wheelock was just one very important one. It does not merely replace Wheelock with Occom but *displaces* a single prominent white man with a "circle" of diverse voices and events named for Occom. Crucially, *The Occom Circle* presents Occom in context and in conversation, as a member of his community, not as the single, heroic or finished entity often produced by western canonizing collections of "Complete or Collected Works." Because digital editions can present non-linear networks, *The Occom Circle* is an excellent tool for evoking the complex Native origins of Dartmouth's founding.[12]

Having selected the 580 documents included in the project, I must acknowledge that *The Occom Circle* is an act of interpretation—every archive is. My goal was to draw attention to Occom as a public intellectual and to the occluded history of Native struggles for sovereignty. When Wheelock is the center of this history, Occom disappears at the founding of Dartmouth College. With Occom at the center of the story, however, we realize that this is the point when his career really began to flower. His break with Wheelock allowed him the freedom to determine the focus of his energies and to work directly and collectively on behalf of his people.

For example, in 1772, Moses Paul, a Wampanoag man convicted of murdering a white man at a tavern in Connecticut, asked Occom to give the sermon at his execution. It was a sensational event attended by a large audience of Indians and English. The sermon, on the perils of drinking, became a bestseller, was reprinted in over twenty editions and several languages and made Occom a national celebrity. But far from using his fame for personal gain, Occom put it to the service of working with other Natives to create a multi-tribal Christian Indian group called Brothertown, which in the 1780s

Figure 7.4. Documents Landing page, *The Occom Circle*, 2020. *Trustees of Dartmouth College.*

left New England to escape what they saw as pernicious English influences. They settled on land offered to them by the Oneida nation in upstate New York where Occom became their spiritual guide. The story of Brothertown is one of continual dispossession, as the group was forced to move yet again, when the Oneidas sold off the land they gifted to Brothertown. Occom died in New Stockbridge, New York, in 1792 before he could move west with the group, who are currently located in Wisconsin.

The homepage of *The Occom Circle* contains links to more information about the project, its genesis and history, scope, staff, and an editorial statement. The "Documents" landing page demonstrates how we structured the site to give users as many options as possible in terms of accessing and viewing documents. Each document is tagged in XML, an abbreviation for an "extensible markup language" that is readable by humans and machines, according to the field's standard Text Encoding Initiative (TEI) P5 guidelines, making the texts fully searchable. As illustrated by the menu on the right side, users can search for documents in a variety of ways: by type of document (with twenty-one types listed), author, recipient, date, place, events mentioned, organizations mentioned, as well as by the Dartmouth library catalog manuscript (ms.) number, themes, and common words.

Users can view documents in a variety of ways as well. In the menu bar at the top of each document, users can choose different "View" options: either "diplomatic" or literal transcriptions, which reproduce the written text as faithfully as possible, including abbreviations, errors, strike-throughs, insertions, and additions; or a modernized version, which removes the deletions, adds in additions, modernizes spelling and capitalization, and expands abbreviations. It is also possible to see the "Validation" version of the initial markup and download the XML view as well as a scan of the document. Furthermore, users can view documents as text only or as an image of the scanned pages only, with a handy zoom in and out and rotate buttons. Best of all is the ability to see the text and scanned image together, because eighteenth century handwriting is often very difficult to decipher.

Significantly, each document has been annotated. Words and phrases in blue link to boxes of short annotations that identify persons, places, organizations and major events related to Occom's life mentioned in the letters. Each of these boxes also has a link directing users to "Go to the full record," which displays all the information in the annotation, including sources, and will even retrieve related documents. There is a wealth of historical information in these annotations.

It is the contents of the letters, how they network with one another and what this reveals about the politics of this momentous moment in Dartmouth's origin story that advances our exploration. If we search for July 24, 1771, Occom's letter to Wheelock comes up (Occom 1771), which paints a vivid picture of the frosty and bitter feelings that existed between these men after Wheelock's move to New Hampshire and Occom's return from England. We also witness Occom's firm and even forceful resistance to Wheelock's views of his standing in relation to God, the New England Indians and European society. This quite spectacular declaration of independence bears closer inspection.

On the first page, Occom reproves Wheelock for expressing "Sorrow" about Occom's situation in a letter dated January 22, which he has just received—six months after it was sent. While Occom had been suffering from some physical infirmities which kept him confined to his house, he now asserts that his "Standing with the Indians" has substantially increased, and that many of the surrounding Tribes "would put themselves under my Instructions." This boast must have rankled Wheelock, because at this time, his standing with the Indians was at an all-time low, in part because he had begun to send his son Ralph out as his ambassador. Whether because of medical problems (possible epilepsy) or simply temperament, Ralph alienated the Indians he visited by his haughty manner and insensitive speech.[13]

Occom then refuses Wheelock's invitation to go "into the wilderness" to missionize Indians. He indicates his awareness of, as well as contempt for, Wheelock's stinginess when he also refuses on the part of his brother-in-law David Fowler, a graduate of Wheelock's school and a formerly loyal follower of Wheelock's. Occom insists, "he will not go for what you offer" and may, in fact, proffer his services to the rival New England Company, if they will pay him what he rightly deserves. It is significant that Occom makes clear that he and his Native associates will no longer tolerate inadequate compensation for their work based on what he considers morally corrupt notions of racial difference and Indian inferiority.

On the second page of the letter, Occom launches into the central subject of complaint, Wheelock's removal of the Indian School to New Hampshire. Below, I quote a long passage from this letter so that we might get a sense of Occom's voice, style, and character. This passage gathers together many threads to paint an extraordinarily detailed critique of Wheelock's "schemes," hypocrisies and betrayals. The quotation is from the "modernized" version of the letter for easier reading:

> —I am very Jealous that instead of Your seminary Becoming Alma Mater, She will be too alba mater to Suckle the Tawnies, for She is already adorned up too much like the popish Virgin Mary She'll be Naturally ashamed to Suckle the Tawnies for She is already equal in Power Honor and Authority to any College in Europe, I think your College has too much worldly grandeur for the Poor Indians they'll never have much benefit of it, — In So Saying I Speak the general Sentiment of Indians and English too in these parts; a. also many of your missionaries and schoolmasters and Indian Scholars Leaving You and Your Service Confirms me in this opinion, — b Your having So many white Scholars and So few or no Indian Scholars, gives me great discouragement— I verily thought once that your institution was Intended Purely for the poor Indians with this thought I cheerfully ventured my Body and Soul, left my Country my poor Young Family all my Friends and Relations, to Sail over the boisterous Seas to England, to help forward your School, Hoping, that it may be a lasting benefit to my poor tawny Brethren, with this View I went a Volunteer—I was quite willing to become a Gazing stock, Yea Even a Laughing Stock, in Strange Countries to Promote your cause—we Loudly proclaimed before Multitudes of People from Place to Place, that there was a most glorious prospect of Spreading the Gospel of the Lord Jesus to the furtherest Savage Nations in the wilderness, through your institution, we told them that there were So many missionaries and So many schoolmasters already Sent out, and a greater Number would Soon follow (Occom 1771)

The letter continues in this extraordinary vein for three-and-a-half closely written pages, unbroken by paragraph breaks or even full stops. Immediately striking is its thoroughly affronted and relentless tone. Occom was perfectly capable of using English grammar but chose in this instance to link his points by dashes, as if piling up one indignity and outrage onto the other. Wheelock taught his Native students to write letters as evidence of their acquisition of Western subjectivity, and to advertise his school's success to patrons and potential donors.[14] There is, of course, a double edge to this tactic. Brilliant students like Occom could and did "write back," using the master's tools to indict the master in terms he would fully and painfully comprehend.

In this instance, we see Occom using his knowledge of Latin to create a stinging pun denouncing racism. At the beginning of this long passage, Occom accuses Wheelock of making the new College, which he calls an "Alma Mater," or nourishing mother, too "alba," that is, Latin for white, to "suckle" or benefit the "tawny" Indians. This whiteness, which excludes the explicitly colored Indians, is a function of outward shows of wealth and privilege. Occom argues that the College, "adorned" with too much "worldly grandure," has lost its spiritual mission, and like the powerful Colleges in Europe, which Occom had visited, would be "ashamed" to admit Indians. To make his punning accusation even more pointed, Occom compares the new College's grandeur to "the popish Virgin Mary," the paradigmatic Catholic "mother." This is an insult a Protestant like Wheelock would not have taken lightly.[15]

Nor did Wheelock take it lightly. In the next two sentences, Occom adduces two more strong pieces of evidence against Wheelock: so many missionaries and schoolmasters leaving his service and the dearth of "Indian Scholars" at Dartmouth College. In the passage quoted above, notice the "a." and "b." before each of these points. In the manuscript document, it is clear that these references were inserted by another hand and refer to comments written along the tiny left-hand margin—by Wheelock himself. He wrote: "a: N.B. none have left me since I got a Charter. b. I have no white Charity Scholars but such as are fitting for a mission." As Wheelock read this bitter letter, he was already constructing responses, albeit weak ones, to Occom's central charges. What he does not and cannot answer is Occom's stinging sense of personal betrayal, on account of being used as "Indian bait," as Occom complains later in the letter, to collect Wheelock's "bushel of money"; made a "Gazing stock" if not a "Laughing Stock" before all of London; and, perhaps worst of all, made a party to the deception of donors in England and Scotland, who gave generously to an Indian for an Indian School, not for Dartmouth College.

There are many notable moments in this letter that illuminate the tenor of Dartmouth College's founding. One that stands out is Occom's name checking of "that great man of God . . . Mr. Whitefield," the leading Evangelical minister in England at the time. Occom recounts to Wheelock that while in England Whitefield cautioned him: "You have been a fine Tool to get money for them" but will be "set adrift" when he returns home. At this point in Occom's relationship with Wheelock and in the disposition of the Indian School, this warning must have felt eerily prophetic. Likewise, to be suspected of manipulation by one of the most celebrated Evangelical figures in Britain must have stung Wheelock deeply.

One final example clinches the character of the two principal players in Dartmouth's origin story this letter elaborates. A few lines after the long paragraph cited above, Occom upbraids Wheelock for writing critically of him to John Thornton, the treasurer of the English Trust and always a loyal supporter and defender of Occom. At the end of the letter, Occom softened a bit and asked, if he is mistaken about any of the facts he has cited, to be enlightened but added this postscript: "I have not wrote this Sort to any one in England, I choose to let you know my mind first." By stark contrast, even *before* receiving this letter, Wheelock began proactively spinning a complex web of correspondences in response to rumors circulating about Occom's discontent and feelings of betrayal. Wheelock wrote to several Trustees making false accusations and trying to turn them against Occom and deflect attention away from the investigations getting underway about Wheelock's (mis)handling of the Trust's funds. Occom probably heard about Wheelock's machinations to tarnish his reputation from Thornton. Still, even in the face of this scheming, or perhaps because of it, Occom assures Wheelock that he went directly to Wheelock first and has not circulated opinions detrimental to his mentor's reputation—as Wheelock has done to his mentee, is the implication. The contrast in their moral sense and modes of operating in this international and multicultural sphere of influence could not be starker.[16]

I will leave you to read Wheelock's long, defensive letter written in response on August 15 (ms. 771465). That he took Occom's criticism to heart becomes clear when, on September 21, Wheelock wrote to Governor John Wentworth of New Hampshire. He said that to avoid criticism about his use of the English and Scottish Trust funds, many of the hundred students he could now accommodate at Dartmouth College should be Indians, and he solicited the governor's help in recruiting Native students from Canada (Wheelock 1771, ms. 771521).

This promise, however, which was at the heart of Dartmouth's founding, went unfulfilled until John Kemeny, a Hungarian Jew and revolutionizing computer scientist, became the thirteenth president in the Wheelock Succession and established a significant Native American presence at Dartmouth. But Dartmouth has yet to fully reckon with its Native origins.

NOTES

While the English Trust protested Wheelock's maneuverings, they eventually gave him all the funds he requested. The SSPCK was not satisfied with Wheelock's machinations and gave him only a small part of the funds in their trust; years later the remainder of the funds were eventually reassigned to other missions.

1. More information on land acknowledgments as decolonizing practices can be found in Garcia 2018 and the resources at www.landacknowledgements.org.
2. For a more capacious history of the Native presence at Dartmouth from its founding to the present, see Calloway 2010.
3. For an account of Wheelock's biography and early years, see Hoefnagel and Close 2006.
4. Hoefnagel explains in detail the difference between Wheelock's Latin School, which Occom attended, and the "Indian Charity School," also known as "Moor's Indian Charity School," named after a neighbor who donated land with a building on it, which Occom's success inspired. After the Indian School began, however, the two schools "actually existed side by side, causing distinction between them to be difficult to apprehend when the generic term 'school' was used in letters and documents" (10).
5. An excellent source on Occom's biography and an account of his writing is Brooks 2006.
6. All quotations from documents by or about Occom will be given print and on-line sources, where relevant: from Brooks 2006, the Papers of Eleazar Wheelock, and the on-line resource, *The Occom Circle,* where they can be searched by date, author or ms. number.
7. For a detailed description of the English "Trust," its creation and dealings with Wheelock around Dartmouth's founding, and the SSPCK, see the annotations, "The Trust in England" and "Society in Scotland for Propagating Christian Knowledge" on *The Occom Circle,* list of organizations, https://collections.dartmouth.edu/occom/html/ctx/orgography/orgography.html.
8. For more analysis of how Humphrey depicted the Indians in his murals and why, see Kennedy 2011, a collection of essays on the Hovey murals by Dartmouth faculty. Particularly insightful are the essays by Colin Calloway and Mary Coffey.
9. Brooks 2008, 64–110, analyzes this case in detail from the Mohegans' perspective and also grounds it in a regional history of struggles over land rights, linking it to issues of literacy and to Occom's time studying with Wheelock.
10. For more on the doubled legacy of Wheelock's school "as a site within [an Indigenous] network," see Brooks 2008, 86–90.
11. See the "Staff" page at *The Occom Circle* for a complete list.
12. I have written more extensively about *The Occom Circle* in terms of issues of Native sovereignty, the politics of the archive, and digital affordances. See Schweitzer 2016.
13. Wheelock was grooming Ralph as his successor and seemed unaware of the damage he caused, but it was substantial. See Hoefnagel 2006, 96–99 and Calloway 2010, 24–29. Wyss 2012, 65–70, analyzes several letters in her examination of how, at this moment, power was shifting from Wheelock to Occom.

14. Wyss 2012 makes a compelling argument for the centrality of writing in Wheelock's bid for dominance of Native space in New England and Brooks 2006 shows how Native writers like Occom appropriated and adapted this imperial technology.

15. This pun takes on added weight when we realize that Wheelock insisted on teaching his Native students Latin and Greek, despite criticism from many of his colleagues, who thought it was unnecessary. This pun clearly had powerful meaning for Occom, who discussed it and its fraught context in a fundraising letter to John Bailey written in 1784, years after Wheelock's death. For more on this pun and Occom's letter, see Schweitzer 2015, 43–45. For an incisive discussion of Wheelock's classical pedagogy and Occom's use of classical languages and puns, written by a Dartmouth graduate and research assistant on *The Occom Circle,* see Vance 2016.

16. For a more detailed account of Wheelock's epistolary scheming around Occom's letter, see Schweitzer 2015, 44–45.

REFERENCES

âpihtawikosisân. 2016. "Beyond Territorial Acknowledgments." *Law. Language. Culture.* https://apihtawikosisan.com/2016/09/beyond-territorial-acknowledgments/.

Brooks, Joanna. 2006. "'This Indian World': An Introduction to the Writings of Samson Occom." In *The Collected Writings of Samson Occom, Mohegan: Leadership and Literature in Eighteenth-Century Native America,* edited by Joanna Brooks. New York: Oxford University Press.

Brooks, Lisa. 2008. *The Common Pot: The Recovery of Native Space in the Northeast.* Minneapolis: University of Minnesota Press.

Calloway, Colin. 2010. *The Indian History of an American Institution.* Hanover, NH: University Press of New England.

Daniell, Jere. 1969. "Eleazar Wheelock and the Dartmouth College Charter." *Historical New Hampshire* 24 Winter: 3–44.

Garcia, Felicia. 2018. "Guide to Indigenous Land and Territorial Acknowledgments for Cultural Institutions." http://landacknowledgements.org/.

Hoefnagel, Dick with Virginia Close. 2006. *Eleazar Wheelock and the Adventurous Founding of Dartmouth College.* Hanover, NH: Friends of the Dartmouth Library.

Kennedy, Brian. 2011. *The Hovey Murals at Dartmouth College: Culture and Contexts.* Hanover, NH: University Press of New England.

McGrath, Robert. 2011. "American Bacchanal: Myth, Memory, and the 'Hovey Murals.'" Pp. 21-43 in *The Hovey Murals at Dartmouth College: Culture and Contexts.* Edited by Brian Kennedy. Hanover, NH: University Press of New England.

Mullins, Steve. 2014. Personal communication. May 9.

Occom, Samson. 1765. "Confession." In *Minutes of the Connecticut Correspondents, March 12, 1765.* Dartmouth ms. 765212.10. Papers of Eleazar Wheelock. Hanover: Dartmouth College.

———. 1768. "Autobiographical Narrative, Second Draft." Dartmouth ms. 768517. In *The Occom Circle.* Hanover: Dartmouth College. J. Brooks, ed. *Collected Works,* 58.

———. 1771. Letter to Eleazar Wheelock. July, 24, 1771. Dartmouth ms. 771424. In *The Occom Circle.* Hanover: Dartmouth College.

Office of Communications. 2018. "Hood Museum Appoints Associate Curator of Native American Art." Dartmouth College, April 16. https://hoodmuseum.dartmouth.edu/news/2018/04/hood-museum-appoints-associate-curator-native-american-art.

Powell, Timothy. 1999. "Introduction." Pp. 1-13 in B*eyond the Binary: Reconstructing Cultural Identity in a Multicultural Context.* Edited by Timothy Powell. 1-13. New Brunswick, NJ: Rutgers University Press.

Schweitzer, Ivy. 2015. "Native Sovereignty and the Archive: Samson Occom and Digital Humanities." *Resources for American Literary Studies* 38: 21–52.

Idem. 2020. *The Occom Circle.* http://www.dartmouth.edu/occom/. Hanover, NH: Dartmouth College.

Silverstein, Hannah. 2019. "A Renovated and Expanded Hood Museum Opens its Doors." *Dartmouth News.* https://news.dartmouth.edu/news/2019/01/renovated-and-expanded-hood-museum-opens-its-doors.

Smith, Charles Jeffrey. 1764. Letter to Eleazar Wheelock. Dartmouth ms. 764230. Papers of Eleazar Wheelock. Hanover, NH: Dartmouth College.

Vance, E. J. 2016. "Classical Education and the Brothertown Nation of Indians." *American Indian Quarterly* 40.2: 138–74.

Wheelock, Eleazar. 1756. "Letter [to Andrew Oliver]." Ms 756900.1. *The Occom Circle.* Hanover, NH: Dartmouth College. https://collections.dartmouth.edu/occom/html/diplomatic/756900-1-diplomatic.html.

Idem. 1756a. "To the Sachems and Chiefs of the Mohawk, Oneida, Tuscarora, and other nations and tribes of Indians." In *Memoirs of the Rev. Eleazar Wheelock, D.D. Founder and President of Dartmouth College and Moor's Charity School; with a Summary History of the College and School To Which are Added Copious Extracts from Dr. Wheelock's Correspondence.* Edited by David McClure, and Elijah Parish. 259-63. Newburyport: Edward Little, 1811.

Idem. 1763. *A Plain and Faithful Narrative of the Original Design, Rise, Progress and Present State of the Indian Charity-School at Lebanon, in Connecticut.* Boston: R. and S. Draper. Hathi Trust. https://babel.hathitrust.org/cgi/pt?id=osu.32435017812793&view=1up&seq=9.

Idem. 1764. Letter to Mr. Pemberton. Oct. 10, 1764. Dartmouth ms. 764560.1. Papers of Eleazar Wheelock. Hanover, NH: Dartmouth College.

Idem. 1769. *Dartmouth College Charter.* Hanover: Rauner Library, Dartmouth College. https://www.dartmouth.edu/~library/rauner/dartmouth/dc-charter.html.

Idem. 1771. Letter to John Wentworth. September 21, 1771. Dartmouth ms. 771521. Papers of Eleazar Wheelock. Hanover, NH: Dartmouth College.

Wyss, Hilary, 2012. *English Letters and Indian Literacies: Reading, Writing, and New England Missionary Schools, 1750-1830.* College Park: University of Pennsylvania Press.

Index

Page numbers in *italics* indicate illustrations.

Abenaki, 153–54, 162
absolute kingship/divine right of kings/ divine royal authority, 28–30, 32, 39, 114, 117
Adams, Abigail, 131
Adams, John, 131, 135, 136, 138, 143–45
The Adulateur (Warren), 8, 130, 139–43, 145–47
African Americans and Wheelock, 10
Alexandrians, 18
Algonquin peoples, 113
Allen, John, 117
Allen, William, 137
"alma mater" pun, 166–67, 171n15
American colonies: financial activity of British empire in, 48–49; James II and Glorious Revolution, effects of, 29, 30; Royal Dominion, creation and dismantling of, 29, 30, 121; Scottish Enlightenment, influence of, 33, 35; university foundations of 18th century in, 33–35, 36
American Indians. *See* Native Americans
American Philosophical Society, 3, 18, 36
American Revolution: Continental Army, 111, 122; Continental Congress, 34, 35, 118, 122; crossing of Delaware and Battle of Trenton, 129; Declaration of; Independence, 34, 35, 36, 117, 127n20; financial activity of British empire and, 48–49; Macaulay's support for, 129, 144; science, technology, and rational design, political implications of, 36. *See also* revolution and religion in New England; *specific battles, precipitating Acts and events, etc.*; Warren, Mercy Otis
Americas, European discovery of, 2, 22–23
Analects (Confucius), 19, 20
Andros, William, 121
Anglicans, 23, 28–30, 32, 34, 92, 93, 112, 113, 114–15, 123
âpihtawikosisân (Métis scholar), 153–54
Arch, Joseph, 73
Aristotle and Aristoteleanism, 18, 19, 21, 22, 26–27, 31–32
Arkwright, Richard, spinning machine patent, 3, 18, 36
Arminians and Arminianism, 112, 113

173

astronomy, 24–27, 31
Aurangzeb (Mughal ruler), 24, 28
Autobiography (Franklin), 85
Autobiography of the Working Class: An Annotated Critical Bibliography (Burnett), 67
"Axial age," 20

Backus, Isaac, 113
Bacon, Francis, 12, 15, 26
Bacon, Roger, 21, 26–27
Bailey, John, 171n15
Baptists, 28, 113, 117, 127n11
Bartlett, Ichabod, 3, 43
Beales, Kristen, 5–6, 85, 173
Bennett, John, 73
Bernard, Francis, 131–32, 133, 137, 139, 140, 141, 145
Bethesda (orphanage in Georgia), Whitfield's fundraising for, 5, 85–89, 91–100
Birmingham Lunar Society, 18
Bissell, George, 17
Black, Joseph, 33
"black legend" of Spanish colonialism, 11
Blair, James, 34
Bloch, Ruth, 145
Board of Trade, 44, 46, 50
Bollen, William, 161
Bonner, Robert, 40
Boston Chronicle, 133
Boston Gazette, 131, 134, 136, 137, 143, 144
Boston Massacre (1770), 8, 109, 137, 139, 140, 142, 143, 146
Boyle, Robert, 18, 29, 31
Brahe, Tycho, 25, 31
Breen, T. H., 1, 60n37
Britain: Board of Trade in, 44, 46, 50; Civil War (English Revolution/ Puritan Revolution), 7, 27, 132; the "Condition of England," concept of, 65; France, relations with, 110, 111; Glorious Revolution (1688), 28–30;

Jacobite rebellions (1715, 1719, and 1745), 30; political ideology and party divisions in, 60n37, 62n78; Restoration era, 7, 28; Royal Society in, 18, 29; science, technology, and the modern world in, 2–3. *See also* Industrial Revolution in Britain
British Coffee House, Boston, 134–35
Brooks, Lisa, 162, 171n14
Brothertown, 163
Brown University, 35
Bryan, John and Hugh, 96
Buddhism, 19–20
Bull, William, 55
Burn, Robert Dawson, 69
Burnett, John, 67
Bute, John Stuart, 3d Earl of, 44, 48

calculus, development of, 27
Calvinists, 23, 34, 112, 113, 117, 127n4, 127n11
Camden, Charles Pratt, Lord, 44
Carlyle, Thomas, 65
Carté, Kate, 1
caste system in India, 2
Catholics and Catholicism, 6, 7, 11, 23–24, 27–29, 31–32, 34, 110, 111, 112
Catton, Samuel, 70
Chain of Being, 28
Champion, Judah, 121–22
Charles I (king of England), 30, 130, 132, 134, 141, 145
Charles II (king of England), 28, 29
Charleston (SC), College of, 55
charter. *See* Royal Charter for Dartmouth
Chase, Salmon, 17
Châtelet, Emilie du, 7
China: collapse of Ming dynasty and rise of Manchus, 24, 27, 28; Europeans arriving in, 22; footbinding in, 2, 15n6; religion in, 19–20, 28; synchronicities connecting Middle East and Europe

Index

to, in 18th century, 2; traditional authority and its challengers in, 18, 19–20
Christian and Civil Liberty (Champion), 122
Christianity. *See* religion
Cider Tax, 44
Circle of Justice, 28
Civil War, British (English Revolution/Puritan Revolution), 7, 27, 132
Clark, Henry C., 1, 173
Cleaveland, John, 117
Coercive Acts, 143, 145
Colin, John, 74
colleges. *See also specific establishments*; universities and colleges
Collyer, Robert, 72–73
Colman, Benjamin, 92
Columbia University (originally King's College), 35, 55
Columbus, Christopher, 2, 22
commercial theology. *See* Whitefield, George, commercial theology of
Common Sense (Paine), 127n4
the "Condition of England," concept of, 65
confederal model of empire, 4, 48, 55, 56
Confucianism, 19–20, 28
Congregationalists, 28, 53
Connecticut: anti-revival statute in, 119; intensity of religious revivals of 1740s in, 128n24; Lebanon, Wheelock's school in, 40, 54. *See* Moor's Charity School
Connecticut Courant, 120
Constitution, U.S., 18, 36
Continental Army, 111, 122
Continental Congress, 34, 35, 118, 122
conversion dynamics, political implications of idioms of, 110, 111, 115, 117, 119, 120, 122–24
Cooper, George, 72
Copernicus, Nicholaus, 24–25, 36

Corn Laws, 74
Cortez, Hernan, 11
counter-Reformation, 24
Cromwell, Oliver, 28
Cullen, William, 33
Cummings, Archibald, 93

Daniell, Jere, 9, 158–59
Daoism, 20
Dartmouth, William Legge, 2nd earl of, 17, 41, 52, 109, 123
Dartmouth and the world in 1769, 1–11; famous alumni of, 17; founding purposes of college, 3–4, 17, 39–56; Industrial Revolution and, 4–5, 65–76; Native Americans and, 8–10, 153–68; political economy and, 10–11; religious purposes of college, 3, 10; revolution and religion, 6, 109–24; science and technology, importance of, 2–3, 17–36; sestercentennial of founding of college, 1, 11; standards of living in, 1–2, 7–8, 65–67; Whitefield and, 5–6, 85–101; women and gender relations, 7–8. *See also* founding purposes of Dartmouth; Industrial Revolution in Britain, Native Americans at Dartmouth; political economy; religion; revolution and religion in New England; science, technology, and the modern world; Warren, Mercy Otis; women and gender; Whitefield, George, commercial theology of
Dartmouth College v. Woodward (1819), 1, 56
De Revolutionibus (Copernicus), 25
Declaration of Independence, 34, 35, 36, 117, 127n20
The Defeat (Mercy Otis Warren), 143–44
DeLancey, James, 55
Desaguliers, John, 3, 32
Descartes, René, 23, 26–27, 31, 32

Dickens, Charles, 65
Dickinson, John, 121
Diogenes, 18
Dioscorides, 22
Disraeli, Benjamin, 65
Dissenters, 3, 28, 32, 34
divine right of kings/divine royal authority/absolute kingship, 28–30, 32, 39, 114, 117
Dodd, William, 70
Doddridge, Philip, 119
Dodgson, Joshua, 74
Dort, Synod of, 112
duels and dueling, 135
Dutch Reformed Church, 23
Dyer, Eliphalet, 42

educational institutions. *See specific institutions by name*; universities and colleges
Edwards, Jonathan, 112, 113, 127n13
Edwards, Jonathan, Jr., 117
Eels, Nathaniel, 109
Elderkin, Jedediah, 42
Emerson, Joseph, 121
Engels, Friedrich, 65–66
England. *See* Britain
English Trust, 41, 42–43, 52, 158, 167–68, 170–71n7
Enlightenment: in England, 17; in Scotland, 3, 6, 10, 17. *See also* science, technology, and the modern world
Ephrata Plantation, Georgia, 97
Epicurus, 18
equality, origins of 18th century concern with, 7
Essential Rights and Liberties of Protestants (Williams), 119
Euclid, 18
European Marriage Pattern, 7
evangelical humiliation/self-scrutiny, 110, 116–18
Evangelicals, 6, 34, 86, 110, 112, 117, 127n11

Ewen, William, 98–99, 107n36

factory employment and wages, 4, 69–71
Filmer, Robert, 30
Flucker, Thomas, 138, 140
footbinding in China, 2, 15n6
Fort Stanwix, Treaty of, 157
founding purposes of Dartmouth, 3–4, 17, 39–56; governing body of college and, 53; Great Awakening and, 35; in Hovey Murals, 159–60, *160*; implementation of Patriot ideology in New Hampshire and, 48–52; John Wentworth's Patriot ideological commitments and, 43–48; Moor's Charity School, relationship of Dartmouth to, 3, 10, 40–43, 54; naming of college for 2nd earl of Dartmouth, 3–4, 17, 39–56; Native Americans, evolution of Wheelock's educational plans away from, 54, 158–59; Occom's perspective on, 160–63; private institution narrative, 3–4, 39–43, 53–54, 56; religious test, lack of, 4, 53; road construction in New Hampshire and access to college, 50, 51–52; Royal Charter, 4, 6, 9, 17, 39–40, 42–43, 51, 52–54, 158; significance of state/public standing, 54–56; as state/public institution, 3–4, 39–43, 50–56; toby jug commissioned by Steven Mullins and, 154–55, *155*, 159. *See also* Native Americans
Fowle, Daniel, 47–48
Fowler, David, 165
France, 27, 28, 32, 110, 111
Francke, August Hermann, 88–89
Franklin, Benjamin: *Autobiography*, 85; on Georgia's lack of materials and workers, 85, 90; Grenvillian political economy critiqued by, 47; *Pennsylvania Gazette*, 99; as president of American Philosophical

Society, 3, 18, 36; University of
    Pennsylvania, founding of, 35;
    Whitefield and, 5, 6, 85, 86, 87, 90,
    91, 98, 99
free will, 113
freedom of conscience, liberty of
    choice, and moral freedom, 110,
    111–15, 123–24, 127n9
Freedom of the Will (Edwards), 113
French and Indian War, 157
French Revolution, 8
Friedman, James, 155
Frondes, 27
Frost, Thomas, 68

Galatians 5:1, as favorite text of
    revolutionary preachers, 123
Galen, 22, 26
Galileo Galilei, 24, 26
Garden, Alexander, 92
Gaskill, Elizabeth, 65
gender. *See* women and gender
George I (king of England), 32
George III (king of England), 17, 47,
    120, 130, 158
Georgia: Bethesda (orphanage),
    Whitefield's fundraising for, 5, 85–89,
    91–100; Ephrata Plantation, 97;
    Franklin on lack of materials and
    workers in, 85, 90; slavery in, 87,
    97, 107n36
Georgia Malcontents, 107n36
Georgia Trustees and Whitefield's
    Bethesda orphanage, 87–88
German Pietism, 5, 88
al-Ghazali, 19
Gill, John, 136
Gill, Sarah Prince, 136
Glorious Revolution (1688),
    28–30, 120, 121
Golden Hill, Battle of (1770), 136
Goldstone, Jack A., 2–3, 4, 8, 17, 173
Gore, Samuel, 136–37
governing body of Dartmouth, 53

*Government Corrupted by Vice,
    and Recovered by Righteousness*
    (Langdon), 118
Gradus ad Parnassum, 160
Graffigny, Françoise de, 7
Graham, Billy, 101
Graves, Matthew, 42
Gray, Edward G., 126n3
Great Awakening, 3, 5, 6, 8, 34–35, 86,
    119, 128n24, 155
Green, Karen, 144
Grenville, George, 44, 46, 48
Griffin, Emma, 4–5, 65, 174
Griffin, Patrick, 132
Griswold, Matthew, 115, 120, 123
The Group (Mercy Otis
    Warren), 143–44
gunpowder weapons,
    development of, 21–22

Habersham, James, 93, 94
Halle orphanage, Germany, 88–89
Halley, Edmund, 29
Hampden, John (pseudonym of James
    Otis), 134
Hanby, George, 71
Hanchett, Arthur, 154
Hancock, John, 138, 143
Harmonices Mundi (Kepler), 26
harmony of the spheres, 25–26
Harvard, 33, 55, 98, 111, 118
Hastings, Selina, Countess of
    Huntingdon, 93, 119
Haudenosaunee (Iroquois), 9, 41, 157
heliocentrism, 24–25
Hemmingway, John, 71
Herodotus, 8
Hinduism, 19–20, 28
History of Dartmouth College (Baxter
    Perry Smith), 39
History of England (Macaulay), 130,
    132–34, 136, 144, 146
*History of the Rise, Progress, and
    Termination of the American*

Revolution (Mercy Otis Warren), 130–31
Hobbes, Thomas, 30, 31
Hoefnagel, Dick, 170n4
Holland. *See* Netherlands
Hood Museum of Art, Dartmouth College, 153
Hooke, Richard, 29
Hopkins, Ernest, 159
Hopkins, Samuel, 112, 113, 123
Hopkins, Stephen, 125, 127–28n20
Horler, Moses, 69
Hovey, Richard, and Hovey Murals, 159–60, *160*, 171n8
Hume, David, 10, 33, 35
Humphrey, Walter Beach, 159–60, *160*, 171n8
Huntingdon, Selina Hastings, Countess of, 93, 119
Huske, John, 44, 60n32
Hutcheson, Francis, 6, 114, 127n13
Hutchinson, Foster, 137, 140
Hutchinson, Thomas, 8, 130, 131, 137–43, 145

I Ching, 19
India: caste system in, 2; Europeans arriving in, 22; famine and civil war in, 27; Mughals in, 22, 24, 28; synchronicities connecting Middle East, China, and Europe to, in 18th century, 2; traditional authority and its challengers in, 18, 19–20
Indian Charity School. *See* Moor's Charity School
Indians. *See* Native Americans
Industrial Revolution in Britain, 4–5, 65–76; awareness of industrialization and its consequences, 68–69; concept of, 66, 68; demand for workers and steadiness of work, 72–74, 75, 83n47; factory employment and wages, 4, 69–71; living standards debate, 65–67; patents of 1769 launching, 3, 5; qualitative approach to, via working class autobiographies, 67–68; status, sense of self-worth, and power balance, 74–75; urbanization and entry into trades, 71–73, 82n34
Intolerable Acts, 123
Ireland: British control of, 28, 29; educational institutions in, 55; financial activity of British empire in, 48
Iroquois (Haudenosaunee), 9, 41, 157
Islam and Arab world, 19, 20, 22, 27–28, 112

Jacobite rebellions (1715, 1719, and 1745), 30
James II (king of England), 28–29, 31
Jefferson, Thomas, 34
jelali rebellions, Ottoman Empire, 24
Jesuits, 24, 31
Johnson, Samuel, 127n9
Johnson, Sir William, 41
Johnson, Stephen, 115, 119–10
Jones, Griffith, 89

Kamensky, Jane, 126n3
Kemeny, John, 54, 168
Kepler, Johannes, 24, 25–26
Khmelnitsky Cossack uprising, 27
Koasek Band of Abenaki Nation, 154

land dispossession and land acknowledgments, 153–54, 160–62
Langdon, Samuel, 111, 116, 118
Latin School started by Wheelock, 156, 160, 170n4
latitudinarians, 112
Lebanon, Connecticut, Wheelock's school in. *See* Moor's Charity School
Lee, Arthur, 10
Legalism, in China, 19
Legge, William, 2nd earl of Dartmouth, 17, 41, 52, 109, 123
Leibniz, Gottfried Wilhelm, 27

Lennox, Charles, 3d Duke of Richmond, 44
Leviathan (Hobbes), 30
liberty, female personification of, 145
liberty of choice, liberty of conscience, and moral freedom, 110, 111–15, 123–24, 127n9
Liberty's Dawn: A People's History of the Industrial Revolution (Griffin), 4
Lillie, Theophilus, 136
Lincoln, John, 70
Locke, John, 30–31, 35, 114, 127n9, 127n13
logarithms, development of, 27
Louis XIV (king of France), 28, 29
Lovekin, Emanuel, 73
Luther, Martin, 2, 11, 23
Lutherans, 23

Macaulay, Catharine Sawbridge, 8, 129–30, 132–34, 136, 141, 143–46
Machiavelli, Niccolo, 35
Madison, James, 35
Mallard, George, 69
Marcroft, William, 70
marriage patterns in early modern Europe, 7
Marshall, John, 34
Marx, Karl, 65
Mary II (queen of England), 29, 31
Mason, John, 161
The Massachusetts Spy, 140
Mather, Cotton, 88
Mayhew, Jonathan, 112–13, 117, 127n13
Mencius, 15n4, 19
Merton, Robert, 23
Methodists and Methodism, 6, 94
Mohegans (Mohawk/Mohicans), 9, 41, 42, 157, 159–62, 171n9
Mongol invasions, 19
Monroe, James, 34
Montagu, John, 140
Montaukett, 156
Montesquieu, 8, 33, 35

Moor's Charity School: combined with Latin School, 156, 170n4; Congregationalism promoted by, 53; fundraising for, 41–42, 98, 107n34, 157–59; Native American students at, 8, 10, 53, 156–57; as part of regional network of Native organization and resistance, 160–62; purposes of Wheelock in setting up, 156–57; relationship to Dartmouth College, 3, 10, 40–43, 54, 166–67; Sir William Johnson's concerns about, 41; women admitted to, 8, 156, 162
moral freedom, liberty of choice, and liberty of conscience, 110, 111–15, 123–24, 127n9
Moral Sense school, 6, 114, 127n13
Mountjoy, Timothy, 83n47
Mughals in India, 22, 24, 28
Muhammad (prophet), 19
Mullins, J. Patrick, 7–8, 129, 174
Mullins, Steve, toby jug commissioned by, 154–55, *155*, 159

Namier, Lewis, 60n37
Napier, John, 27
Narrative (Wheelock), 157
Native Americans, 8–10, 153–68; American Protestant interest in conversion of, 87, 112, 113, 119; break-up correspondence between Occom and Wheelock, 9, 159, 165–68; at Dartmouth, 54, 159, 168; Dartmouth standing on Abenaki lands, acknowledgment of, 153–54; escalating conflicts in Indian country, 157; evolution of Wheelock's educational plans away from, 54, 158–59; funds raised in Europe by Occom and, 41–42, 157–59, 161, 167; harsh discipline, withdrawal from Wheelock's Schools due to, 41, 159; in Hovey Murals, 159–60, *160*; land dispossession and land acknowledgments, 153–54, 160–62;

limitations on integration into British American society, 54, 158, 159; at Moor's Charity School, 8, 10, 53, 156–57; moral freedom, limitations on religious and political claims of, 124; *The Occom Circle* (digital resource), 9, 154, *162,* 162–65, *164*; perspective on founding of Dartmouth/Moor's, 160–63; poor wages paid to, as missionaries, 156, 165; racist assumptions of Wheelock regarding, 156–57, 166–67; Ralph Wheelock and, 165; regional network of Native organization and resistance, 160–62; relationship between Moor's/Dartmouth and, 41–42, 54; in Royal Charter of Dartmouth, 53, 158–59; toby jug commissioned by Steven Mullins, 154–55, *155,* 159; Wheelock's interest in education of, 9–10, 17, 39, 54. *See also* Occom, Samson; *specific Indian communities, e.g.,* Oneida

Neo-Tories, 44
Netherlands, 23, 24, 27, 29, 31
A New Astronomy (Kepler), 25
New Divinity, 113
New England Company, 156
New Hampshire: application of Patriot ideology in, 48–52; counties, creation of, 49–50; educational aims of Wentworth for, 50–52, 54; road construction in, 50, 51–52
New Hampshire Gazette, 39, 44, 45, 47–48, 56
New Lights, 127n11, 155–56
New London Gazette, 120
Newport, RI, British bombardment and occupation of, 123
Newton, Isaac, 18, 27, 29, 32
North, Benjamin, 69
North, Frederick, Lord North, 56

Occom, Samson: "alma mater" pun, 166–67, 171n15; biographical information, 156, 160–61; break-up correspondence between Wheelock and, 9, 159, 165–68; British Isles, tour of, 9, 10, 41; execution of Moses Paul, sermon at, 163; funds raised in Europe by, 41–42, 157–59, 161, 167; Montauketts, mission to, 156; perspective and intentions of, 160–63; on poor wages paid to Indian missionaries, 156, 165; on racist assumptions of Wheelock, 156–57, 166–67; Scottish Enlightenment and, 10; on separation between Moor's and Dartmouth College, 42, 166–67; toby jug featuring, 154–55, *155,* 159; Wheelock and, 9, 155–56; Whitefield and, 6, 86, 100

The Occom Circle (digital resource), 9, 154, *162,* 162–65, *164*
Old Lights, 127n11
Oliver, Andrew, 137–38, 140, 156
Oliver, Peter, 137, 140–42
Oliver, Thomas, 73
Oneida, 41, 157, 159, 163
Orientalism, 8, 140
Orozco Murals, 159
Osborn, Sarah, 122–23
Otis, James, Jr., 8, 130, 131–36, 138–39, 141–46
Ottoman Empire, 22, 24, 27, 28, 140
Oxford University, 29

Paine, Thomas, 127n4
Parker, Geoffrey, 27
Partridge, Oliver, 42
Pascal, Blaise, 24
Patriots, 3–4; confederal model of empire embraced by, 4, 48, 55–56; educational institutions, support for, 55; implementation of ideology in New Hampshire, 48–52; John Wentworth, Patriot ideological

commitments of, 43–48; naming of college for 2nd earl of Dartmouth and, 52; political program and beliefs, 44–46, 52, 55–56; radical Boston Whigs compared, 130
Paul, Moses, 163
Penn, John, 42
Pennsylvania Gazette, 99
Perkins, George, 17
Persian Letters (Montesquieu), 8
Petty, Sir William, 1
Philadelphia Academy, 98, 107n34
Philadelphia Hospital, 98, 107n34
Pietas Hallensis (Francke), 88–89
Pietism, German, 5, 88
Pincus, Steve, 3–4, 8, 39, 154, 174
Pitt, William, Earl of Chatham, 44
Plato, 18
political economy, 10–11; Britain, political ideology and party divisions in, 60n37, 62n78; confederal model of empire, 4, 48, 55, 56; conversion dynamics, political implications of idioms of, 110, 111, 115, 117, 119, 120, 122–24; divine right of kings/divine royal authority/absolute kingship, 28–30, 32, 39, 114, 117; religion affected by political unrest in 18th century, 27–33; science/technology and rise of rational design, 3, 18, 27–33, 35, 36. *See also* American Revolution; Patriots; revolution and religion in New England; Warren, Mercy Otis
Political Economy Project, Dartmouth College, 1
Popish Plot, 121
Postlethwayt, Malachy, 55–56
Powell, James, 74
Powell, Timothy, 163
Pratt, Charles, Lord Camden, 44
predestination/divine election, doctrine of, 112, 113
Presbyterians, 3, 23, 28, 34, 92, 127n4
Princeton University, 35

Prosperity Gospel, 6, 87, 101
Protestants and Protestantism, 23–24, 27, 32, 127n11. *See also specific denominations*
Providence Plantation, South Carolina, 95–97
Ptolemy, 19, 22, 24–25, 36
Puritans, 27, 33, 113, 120–21

Quakers, 28, 93
Quebec Act, 111

reason/rational design, rising belief in, 18, 21–27, 32, 33
Recollections (Frost), 68
Reformation, 2–3, 10, 23–24
religion: Connecticut, anti-revival statute in, 119; conversion dynamics, political implications of idioms of, 110, 111, 115, 117, 119, 120, 122–24; Dartmouth, founding purposes of, 3; European Marriage Pattern and, 7; Great Awakening, 3, 5, 6, 8, 34–35, 86, 119, 128n24, 155; Hume's skepticism regarding, 10; lack of religious test for Dartmouth students, 4, 53; moral freedom, liberty of choice, and liberty of conscience, 110, 111–15, 123–24, 127n9; political unrest in 18th century affecting, 27–33; Reformation, 2–3, 10, 23–24; science/technology and, 3, 18, 31–32, 34–35, 36; traditional authority and, 19–20. *See also* revolution and religion in New England; *specific religions and denominations*; Whitefield, George, commercial theology of
Renaissance, concept of, 10
revolution and religion in New England, 6, 109–24; common history, community adherence to, 120–22; conversion dynamics, political implications of idioms of, 110, 111, 115, 117, 119, 120,

122–24; evangelical humiliation/ self-scrutiny, 110, 116–18; Galatians 5:1 as favorite text of revolutionary preachers, 123; limitations of discourse of liberty, 124; moral freedom, liberty of choice, and liberty of conscience, 110, 111–15, 123–24, 127n9; separation from old associations and commitment to new community, 110, 115, 118–22; Wheelock's reportage on, 6, 109, 122, 124

Revolutionary War. *See* American Revolution

Richardson, Ebenezer, 136–38, 139–42, 145

Richmond, Charles Lennox, 3d Duke of, 44

road construction in New Hampshire and access to Dartmouth, 50, 51–52

Robinson, John, 134–35, 145

Rockingham, Charles Watson-Wentworth, 2nd Marquess of, 44, 46, 49, 50, 60n33

Rogers, Nathaniel, 138

Roman Catholics. *See* Catholics and Catholicism

Rowe, John, 138

Rowland, David, 123

Royal Charter for Dartmouth, 4, 6, 9, 17, 39–40, 42–43, 51, 52–54, 158

Royal Dominion in American colonies, 29, 30, 121

Royal Society, 18, 29

Rushton, Adam, 70

Russel, William, 98–99, 107n36

Russia, 27

Rutgers University, 35

Rymer, Edward, 83n47

Safavid Persians, 22

sanctification, 121

Sawbridge, James, 129–30, 145

Schweitzer, Ivy, 8–9, 153, 174

science, technology, and the modern world, 2–3, 17–36; American university foundations and the Great Awakening, 33–35, 36; political implications and effects, 3, 18, 27–33, 35, 36; reason/rational design, rising belief in, 18, 21–27, 32, 33; religious implications of, 3, 18, 31–32, 34–35, 36; spinning machine patent (Arkwright), 3, 18; steam engine patent (James Watt), 3, 18; traditional authority, world based on, 18–21. *See also* Industrial Revolution in Britain

Scotland: British control of, 28; educational institutions in, 33, 55; financial activity of British empire in, 48; origins of Great Awakening in, 34

Scottish Enlightenment, 3, 6, 10, 17, 33, 35

Scottish Society for the Promotion of Christian Knowledge (SSPCK), 158, 170n7

Seider, Christopher, killing of, 130, 136–37, 139–43, 146

self-scrutiny/evangelical humiliation, 110, 116–18

Seward, William, 88, 89, 91, 94, 107n36

Shaw, Benjamin, 70, 71

Sidney, Algernon, 122

Simons, Daniel, 42

Six Nations, 41–42

slavery: Adam Smith's denunciation of, 10; Christianization of the enslaved, 96, 97; in Georgia, 87, 97, 107n36; legal and customary status of, in 18th century, 2; moral freedom, limitations on religious and political claims of, 123; Walpoleian defense/Patriot critique of, 45–46, 47; Whitefield's reliance on, 6, 86–87, 95–97; Whitefield's views on, 106n32

Smith, Adam, 10, 33

Smith, Baxter Perry, 39
Smith, Charles Jeffrey, 157
Smith, John, 93
Smith, William, 71
Smylie, James, 127n4
Society for the Promotion of Christian Knowledge (SPCK), 89, 158, 170–71n7
Sons of Liberty, 52, 111, 132, 135, 136, 137, 140
South Carolina: College of Charleston, 55; Providence Plantation, 95–97
South Carolina Gazette, 95
Spain: "black legend" of Spanish colonialism, 11; revolts in Portugal, Catalonia, and Sicily against monarchy of, 27; War of Jenkins' Ear (1739) and, 48; Whitefield's Bethesda orphanage, capture of supplies intended for, 90, 94
Spanish Armada, 121
spinning machine patent (Arkwright), 3, 18, 36
Spinoza, Baruch, 23
St. George's Fields, London, Massacre of (1768), 137
St. John's University, Annapolis, MD, 34
Stamp Act: founding purposes of Dartmouth and, 44, 46, 47, 52; Mercy Otis Warren and, 131, 132, 134; revolution and religion in New England and, 109, 115, 120, 121, 122, 126n3
standards of living, 1–2, 7–8, 65–67
steam engine patent (James Watt), 3, 18, 36
Stern, Philip J., 1
Stiles, Ezra, 42, 113
Stimson, Shannon, 1
Stockbridge Mohicans, 42
Stout, Harry, 105n14
Strafford, William Wentworth, 2nd earl of, 50
Stuart, John, 3d Earl of Bute, 44, 48

Sufism, 27–28
Sugar Act, 127–28n20, 132
Susquehanna Company, 59n21
Swan, William, 74

Taylor, Alan, 41
technology. *See* Industrial Revolution in Britain; science, technology, and the modern world
Tennent, Gilbert, 92
Tennent, William, 35
Terrick, Richard, 43
thanksgiving, 120–21
Thomas Aquinas, 19
Thornton, John, 109, 124, 167–68
toby jug commissioned by Steven Mullins, 154–55, *155,* 159
Tomlinson, John, 44
Torricelli, Evangelista, 24
Tough, John, 73
Townshend Acts, 111, 132, 133, 136, 137, 144
Toynbee, Arnold, 66
trades, entry into, 71–73, 82n34
traditional authority, world based on, 18–21
Trecothick, Barlow, 43–44
Trenton, Battle of, 129
Turner, Charles, 120–21
Tuscarora, 157
Two Treatises of Government (Locke), 30–31

Uncas (Sachem of Mohegans), 160–61
universities and colleges: foundations in American colonies, 33–35, 36; meaning of university versus college, 53–54; New Hampshire, educational aims of Wentworth for, 50–52, 54; provincial government support for, 54–55; Scotland, educational institutions in, 33, 55. *See also* founding purposes of Dartmouth; *specific establishments*
University of Pennsylvania, 35

Upanishads, 19
urbanization and industrialization, 71–73

Valeri, Mark, 6, 8, 109, 174
Veda, 19, 20
Vikings, 22
Voltaire, 33

Walpole, Horace, 50
Walpole, Sir Robert, 45, 48
Wampanoag, 163
War of Jenkins' Ear (1739), 48
Warrants, General, 44
Warren, James, 129, 131, 143, 144, 146
Warren, James, Jr., 150n24
Warren, Joseph, 137
Warren, Mercy Otis, 7–8, 129–47; *The Adulateur,* 8, 130, 139–43, 145–47; critical events leading to American Revolution and, 132, 136–38, 143, 146–47; *The Defeat,* 143–44; female patriotism, development of argument for, 130, 143–44, 145–47; *The Group,* 143–44; *History of the Rise, Progress, and Termination of the American Revolution,* 130–31; ideological framework of, 130–32; Macaulay and, 8, 129–30, 132–34, 136, 141, 143–46; older brother James Otis Jr. and, 8, 130, 131–36, 138–39, 141–46; political radicalization of, 129–30, 138–39, 146–47; *rebel lady,* self-identification as, 129, 147
Washington, George, 34, 129
Watson, James, 71
Watson-Wentworth, Charles, 2nd Marquess of Rockingham, 44, 46, 49, 50, 60n33
Watt, James, steam engine patent, 3, 18, 36
Watts, Isaac, 119
Wealth of Nations (Smith), 10
Webster, Daniel, 3, 17, 40, 43, 53, 56
Welsh charity schools run by Griffith Jones, 89
Wentworth, Benning, 44, 48, 49, 52, 60n32
Wentworth, John: application of Patriot ideology in New Hampshire by, 48–52; development of Patriot ideology, 4, 43–48; educational aims of, 50–52, 54, 168; Royal Charter for Dartmouth, assistance in securing, 51, 54, 55, 158; Wheelock on revolutionary spirit in New England to, 122
Wentworth, William, 2nd earl of Strafford, 50
Wesley, Charles, 87, 105n24
Wesley, John, 105n24, 116
West, Samuel, 113–14, 117, 120
Westminster Confession, 112
Wheelock, Eleazar: African Americans and, 10; Anglo-Protestant expansionism of, 11; biographical information, 155–56; break-up correspondence between Occom and, 9, 159, 165–68; British politics, awareness of, 62n78; as justice of the peace, 51; Latin School started by, 156, 160, 170n4; master/servant balance of power in household of, 4; *Narrative,* 157; Native Americans, interest in education of, 9–10, 17, 39, 54; Occom and, 9; racist assumptions of, 156–57, 166–67; on revolutionary spirit in New England, 6, 109, 122, 124; Scottish Enlightenment and, 10; toby jug featuring, 154–55, *155,* 159; Whitefield and, 5, 6, 86, 100; women, on instruction of, 8, 10. *See also* founding purposes of Dartmouth; Moor's Charity School
Wheelock, Ralph, 165, 171n13
Whigs: founding purposes of Dartmouth and, 44–46, 52; revolution and religion in New England and, 114;

Mercy Otis Warren and, 130–33, 135–37, 141, 143, 144, 146
Whitaker, Nathaniel, 41–42, 86, 100, 109, 122, 157, 158
Whitefield, George, commercial theology of, 5–6, 85–101; advertisements and published financial accounts, 91–92, 93–94, 95, 99–100; audits of accounting practices, 95, 98–100, 107n36; Bethesda (orphanage in Georgia), fundraising for, 5, 85–89, 91–100; controversies with other ministers, use of, 92–93, 105n14; definition of commercial theology, 85–86; divine providence in, 86–87, 88–90, 92–94, 96, 97, 99–101; Elisha Williams and, 119; financial and critical setbacks experienced by (1741–1743), 94–95; Franklin and, 5, 6, 85, 86, 87, 90, 91, 98, 99; initial reliance on occasional collections (1738–1742), 86, 87–94; later reliance on "visible fund"/regular income sources (1743–1747), 86–87, 95–100; modern Prosperity Gospel and, 6, 87, 101; Moor's/Dartmouth and, 42, 51, 86, 98, 100–101, 107n34, 157, 167; private subscriptions, use of, 6, 87, 97–98; repeal of Stamp Act and, 122; sermons of, 85, 90–91, 98; slave labor, reliance on, 6, 86–87, 95–97; slave trade/slavery, views on, 106n32
Wildman's Club, 44, 52, 60n33
Wilkes, John, 44
William III of Orange (king of England), 29–30, 32

William and Mary, College of, 34, 35
William of Ockham, 21
Williams, Elisha, 118–19
Winthrop, Fitzjohn, 55
Witherspoon, John, 35
women and gender: European Marriage Pattern, 7; factory employment of women, 69–70; Hovey Murals, Native American women in, 160; James Otis on, 8, 133; liberty, female personification of, 145; life and living standards in 18th century, 1–2, 7–8; Moor's Charity School, women admitted to, 8, 156, 162; patriotism, female, Mercy Otis Warren's argument for, 130, 143–44, 145–47; Wheelock and instruction of, 8, 10; working class autobiographies, male dominance of, 67–68. *See also specific women*
Wood, Thomas, 71
Woodbridge, Timothy, 42
Woodrooffe, William, 98–99, 107n36
working class autobiographies, 67–68. *See also* Industrial Revolution in Britain
Wright, William, 73
Wyss, Hilary, 171n14

Yale, 34, 55, 113, 119, 155, 156

Zaccheus, Whitefield preaching on conversion of (Luke 19:9–10), 91, 105n14
Zagarri, Rosemarie, 139

About the Authors

Kristen Beales is a visiting scholar in the Warren Center for Studies in American History at Harvard. She received her PhD from the College of William & Mary, where she won the Distinguished Dissertation Award in the Humanities and Humanistic Social Sciences in 2019. Her book manuscript, *Spirited Exchanges: The Religion of the Marketplace in Early America,* which has been supported by the American Philosophical Society, the Fred W. Smith National Library for the Study of George Washington, and the Huntington Library among many others, examines the relationship between religion and capitalism in the long eighteenth century.

Henry C. Clark is senior lecturer and program director of the Political Economy Project at Dartmouth College. An early modern historian, he is the author or editor of six books, including *Compass of Society: Commerce and Absolutism in Old-Regime France* (Lexington 2007) and *Montesquieu: My Thoughts* (ed. and trans., Liberty Fund 2012). Present projects include *The Moral Economy We Have Lost: Obstacles to Commercial Society* (under review) and *Taking Liberty Seriously: Political Economy and the Moral Origins of Modernity* (draft mostly complete).

Jack A. Goldstone is the Virginia E. and John T. Hazel, Jr., Chair Professor of Public Policy at the Schar School of Policy and Government, George Mason University. He has won research fellowships from the J. S. Guggenheim, Mellon, Carnegie, and McArthur Foundations and many awards. Goldstone is best known for his writings on the history and theory of revolutions, including *Revolution and Rebellion in the Early Modern World* (25th anniversary edition Routledge 2016) and *Revolutions: A Very Short Introduction* (Oxford 2014).

About the Authors

Emma Griffin is professor of modern British history at the University of East Anglia. She is the editor of the *Historical Journal*, and the president of the Royal Historical Society. She is the author of five books, including *Liberty's Dawn: A People's History of the Industrial Revolution* (Yale 2013) and, most recently, *Bread Winner: An Intimate History of the Victorian Economy* (Yale 2020).

J. Patrick Mullins is assistant professor of history at Marquette University, where he also serves as public history director. He has published *Father of Liberty: Jonathan Mayhew and the Principles of the American Revolution* (Kansas 2017) and is preparing *Killing Kings: Violence, Art, and Memory in the Transatlantic American Revolution*, a study of the cultural origins of the American Revolution in light of transatlantic debates from 1750 to 1776 over the execution of King Charles I in England in the previous century.

Steve Pincus (Dartmouth '84) is the Thomas E. Donnelly Professor of British History and the College at the University of Chicago. His books include *Protestantism and Patriotism* (Cambridge 1996), *England's Glorious Revolution: A Documentary History of the First Modern Revolution* (Bedford 2005), *1688: The First Modern Revolution* (Yale 2009, winner of the Forkosch Prize of the American Historical Association), and *The Heart of the Declaration: The Founders' Case for Energetic Government* (Yale, 2016). He is presently working on a study of the global British empire.

Ivy Schweitzer is a professor of English and creative writing at Dartmouth College, where she also holds an appointment in the women's, gender, and sexuality program. She specializes in American literature, especially early American studies, women's literature and culture, and feminist studies, and works in digital and public humanities. She is the editor of the *Occom Circle Project*, and is co-producer of the film *It's Criminal: A Tale of Prison and Privilege*, based on her prison teaching.

Mark Valeri is the Reverend Priscilla Wood Neaves Distinguished Professor of Religion and Politics in the John C. Danforth Center on Religion and Politics and Professor of History (by courtesy) at Washington University in Saint Louis. His books include *Heavenly Merchandize: How Religion Shaped Commerce in Puritan America* (Princeton 2010). His current project concerns conceptions of conversion, Protestant descriptions of other religions, and politics in Anglo-America from 1653 to 1765.

www.ingramcontent.com/pod-product-compliance
Lightning Source LLC
Chambersburg PA
CBHW061715300426
44115CB00014B/2700